Aging Asia: The Economic and Social Implications of Rapid Demographic Change in China, Japan, and South Korea

Edited by
Karen Eggleston and Shripad Tuljapurkar

THE WALTER H. SHORENSTEIN
ASIA-PACIFIC RESEARCH CENTER

THE WALTER H. SHORENSTEIN ASIA-PACIFIC RESEARCH CENTER (Shorenstein APARC) is a unique Stanford University institution focused on the interdisciplinary study of contemporary Asia. Shorenstein APARC's mission is to produce and publish outstanding interdisciplinary, Asia-Pacific–focused research; to educate students, scholars, and corporate and governmental affiliates; to promote constructive interaction to influence U.S. policy toward the Asia-Pacific; and to guide Asian nations on key issues of societal transition, development, U.S.-Asia relations, and regional cooperation.

The Walter H. Shorenstein Asia-Pacific Research Center
Freeman Spogli Institute for International Studies
Stanford University
Encina Hall
Stanford, CA 94305-6055
tel. 650-723-9741
fax 650-723-6530
http://APARC.stanford.edu

Aging Asia: The Economic and Social Implications of Rapid Demographic Change in China, Japan, and South Korea may be ordered from:
The Brookings Institution
c/o DFS, P.O. Box 50370, Baltimore, MD, USA
tel. 1-800-537-5487 or 410-516-6956
fax 410-516-6998
http://www.brookings.edu/press

First printing, 2010.
13-digit ISBN 978-1-931368-20-9

Aging Asia: The Economic and Social Implications of Rapid Demographic Change in China, Japan, and South Korea

SHORENSTEIN APARC STANFORD

THE WALTER H. SHORENSTEIN ASIA-PACIFIC RESEARCH CENTER

CONTENTS

ACKNOWLEDGMENTS

This book is based on contributions of scholars from China, Japan, South Korea, Singapore, and the United States who participated in a conference on February 26, 2009, at the Bechtel Conference Center at Stanford University. Cosponsored by the Asia Health Policy Program (AHPP) and the Stanford Center on Longevity, "Aging Asia: Economic and Social Implications of Rapid Demographic Change in China, Japan, and Korea" brought together experts in demography, economics, biology, political science, medicine, health services research, social policy, and psychology to discuss a wide range of topics. Several of the key contributions to the conference developed into the chapters of this book.

The AHPP is made possible by the generous support of the Council for Better Corporate Citizenship. We thank Dr. Gi-Wook Shin, director of the Walter H. Shorenstein Asia-Pacific Research Center (Shorenstein APARC) at Stanford University, for supporting this project. We are grateful to the authors for their contributions and to Michael Armacost, distinguished fellow at Shorenstein APARC and former U.S. ambassador to Japan and the Philippines, for writing the preface and welcoming the book into the Center's series for distribution through the Brookings Institution Press.

Debbie Warren and Lisa Lee of Shorenstein APARC, and Adele Hayutin and Miranda Dietz of the Stanford Center on Longevity, were instrumental in bringing the February 2009 conference to fruition. We thank Raziel Davison, Crystal Zheng, and Qiong Zhang for excellent research assistance. Special thanks to Fayre Makeig for careful copyediting and Victoria Tomkinson for cheerfully managing the manuscript through the Shorenstein APARC and Brookings publication process.

Finally, Karen thanks Kesi, Adrian, and Alanna for their love and support.

PREFACE

This project, which Karen Eggleston defined and organized, is as timely as it is important. She collected a stunning array of knowledgeable and experienced scholars and practitioners to address a subject that is capturing the attention of a growing number of policymakers.

I am certainly not an expert on the subject. I do not know whether or not "demography is destiny." But as one who has long been interested in developments in Asia, it is obvious that many intriguing demographic trends are reshaping the prospects for prosperity and peace in the region:

- The absolute growth in Asia's population has probably peaked. Russia's population is declining. Japan's soon will. North Korea requires a robust birth rate to offset the consequences of natural disasters and official malfeasance.
- Fertility has seen a sweeping decline in Asia. In combination with the rapid aging of populations in Japan and South Korea, this decline is contributing to the "graying" of the area—a natural consequence of longer lives and smaller families.
- The distribution of population within the region is undergoing major change as well. South Korea's population was less than 30 percent of Japan's in 1975. If current trends hold, it would be about 40 percent by 2025. If the Korean peninsula is unified, it could reach 60 percent of Japan's current total. And, during that same time frame, China will probably lose its status as the world's largest population to India, while Russia continues to shrink in size relative to its neighbors.

These trends can have important psychological and political effects. To begin with, can one seriously imagine a resurgent, militaristic Japan with a declining and aging population? How will Russia protect valuable natural resources in the Far East from encroachment by China, whose population in the area vastly outnumbers local Russians?

Prospects for economic growth are most promising where the ratio between working-age cohorts and dependents (either children or retirees) is increasing; that is, where the number of workers is growing relative to those who rely on them for their livelihoods. For Japan, the worker-to-dependent ratio has already become a drag on growth. South Korea, Taiwan, and China are benefiting from the "demographic dividend," which an improving worker-to-dependent ratio produces—fewer dependents through reduced fertility, and a bulge in the number of working-age people. But this dividend will eventually come to an end, sooner for the "Asian Tigers" than for China. But even in China, the median age in 2025 is expected to be over 40, and its population will age rapidly thereafter. Some maintain that China's challenge will be whether its people get old before they get rich. This question, I suspect, is very much on the minds of China's leaders.

Russia's experience is in some respects unique and tragic. Life expectancy was lower in 2001 than it was forty years earlier. For Russian men it was five years less. Much of the decline occurred in peacetime, in the absence of any obvious political catastrophe. It was the result not of infectious diseases but of chronic behavioral problems. And there are no easy or quick fixes. North Korea's recent census suggests that it also faces a mortality crisis, but the North's problems can be attributed to official incompetence or mendacity rather than natural demographic causes. A single statistic highlights Pyongyang's situation: the height requirement for service in its army was lowered several years ago from 4'11" to 4'7".

I will not try to draw cosmic conclusions from these data. But the trends are eye-catching, and they remind us that we need to pay attention to developments that affect the composition and public health of populations in Asia. That is why there is so much in this volume worth pondering.

Michael H. Armacost
Shorenstein Distinguished Fellow
Shorenstein APARC
Stanford University

INTRODUCTION

Karen Eggleston and Shripad Tuljapurkar

How will rapid population aging impact the economies and social protection systems of Japan, South Korea, and China? This book addresses that question by showcasing cutting-edge, policy-relevant research from multiple disciplines. The first section focuses on demographic trends and their economic implications. The second section more closely examines select topics of social insurance financing, medical care, and long-term care (LTC) in a global comparative perspective. Numerous chapters also highlight the implications of these demographic and social trends for U.S. policy and business.

Rather than choose a narrow set of issues to analyze in great detail for all three countries, we have instead opted for a broad range of topics and a mixture of explicitly comparative and country-specific perspectives. Four chapters (1, 2, 9, and 10) offer multicountry comparative perspectives on demographic change and economic growth, social transitions, and how individuals and communities are coping with chronic diseases such as diabetes and dementia. Further, each of the three countries is covered in depth in chapters that focus on specific economic and social issues. Japan is considered in chapters 3 (on intergenerational transfers) and 6 (financing health care); South Korea's new LTC insurance program and pension policies are the subjects of chapters 7 and 8; and chapters 4 (gender and migration) and 5 (marriage and elderly support) focus on China. Finally, chapter 11 offers a comparative perspective by discussing Singapore's approach to support for the elderly.

The authors wrote these chapters with at least three common goals in mind. First, we seek to provide a broad-brush picture of the demographic trends in Northeast Asia and their social and economic implications. A second goal is to help policymakers, business decision-makers, and academics to think through what countries can learn from one another with respect to opportunities of population aging, including policies that could have large positive impacts on private-sector "gray tech" trade and investment. A third, interrelated goal is to identify the knowns and unknowns—the almost-certain trends and the key factors still shrouded in uncertainty. Bracketing the uncertainties can inform policymaking as well as articulate a research agenda. The book will thus be of interest to a broad audience interested in multiple aspects of population aging: policymakers and private-sector leaders as well as representatives from multiple professions and academic disciplines.

In this introduction, we first discuss the demographic shifts affecting East Asia and how they compare to the population changes taking place globally.

The second section presents an overview of the book and previews the main arguments of each chapter.

Demographic Change, Aging, and Policy

Two main factors have led to population aging over the past half century, both of which David Bloom discusses in chapter 1, "Population Aging and Economic Growth." The first is a decline in fertility to levels close to or even below replacement (see figure 1.5 of Bloom's chapter) and the second is a decline in mortality that has increased world average life expectancy (see figure 1.6) by nearly 67 percent. These factors produce the changes that constitute aging: a shift in population age structure toward fewer young and more elderly, who are themselves living longer postretirement lives. As Bloom describes in detail, these changes are occurring across the world; East Asian trends mirror what is happening elsewhere. Here we highlight aspects and consequences of aging that complement the discussion in subsequent chapters. Some issues are assessed in country-specific contexts in later chapters but others remain a subject for future research.

Aging is taking place at different speeds and different times around the world. One useful index of aging is the total dependency ratio, conventionally defined as the ratio of the number of nonworking people to working people. In practice it is common to define "working" people as those aged 15–65. We can separate this total dependency ratio into a young dependency ratio (where the numerator counts only nonworking youth) and an old dependency ratio. Trends in dependency have been and continue to be shaped by the historical fact that aging around the world has always begun with fertility decline and then progressed with subsequent mortality decline. As a result the population of nonworking young falls first and produces a decrease in total dependency, followed by an increase in the population of nonworking old that leads to an eventual increase in total dependency. Figure A shows the early stage of declining total dependency in a selection of low- and middle-income nations. Contrast this pattern with that in figure B, for a selection of high-income nations, in which the total dependency is either level or increasing. This historical pattern is mirrored in the more detailed comparison shown in figure C, where we display total dependency (the upper curve in all panels) for Japan, South Korea, and China. In each panel there are two lower curves: the falling curve is young dependency and the rising curve is old dependency. There is a clear sequence here with South Korea following Japan, and China following South Korea.

These historical sequences are reflected in the timing and pace of economic change around the world. The early phase of declining total dependency leads to what Mason and Lee (2006) call the *first demographic dividend*, in which capital is freed by saving some expenditure on the young, and the proportion of the working-age population increases. Among economies around the world today, the fastest growing, including China, are benefiting from this early phase

Figure A. Total Dependency Ratio in China, India, Malaysia, Thailand, and Vietnam, 1980–2030

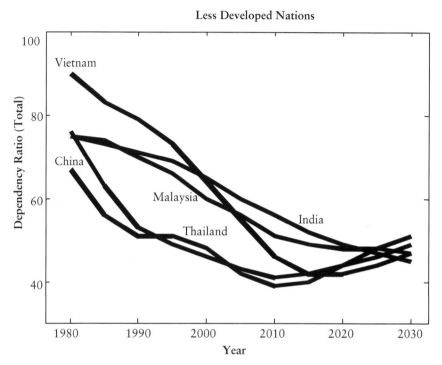

Less Developed Nations

Source: United Nations Population Division, "World Population Prospects: The 2008 Revision Population Database," http://esa.un.org/unpp/index.asp?panel=2.

of aging. Some estimate that between 1982 and 2000, about 15 percent of China's unprecedented rapid growth in output per capita stemmed from this first demographic dividend (Wang and Mason 2008, 147). The later phase of rising total dependency is the period under scrutiny in many of the chapters in this book. A major question about this second phase is whether social, economic, and policy changes will turn a period of growing old-age dependency into one of positive opportunity and growth. As Mason and Lee point out, there is a potential *second demographic dividend* to be enjoyed, if aging in the second phase leads to positive effects on economic growth that offset the potential costs of a growing fraction of old and nonworking people. The chapters that follow examine many aspects of the costs of aging and of the benefits that a large elderly population can provide.

Figure B. Total Dependency Ratio in Japan, Singapore, South Korea, the United States, and the United Kingdom, 1980–2030

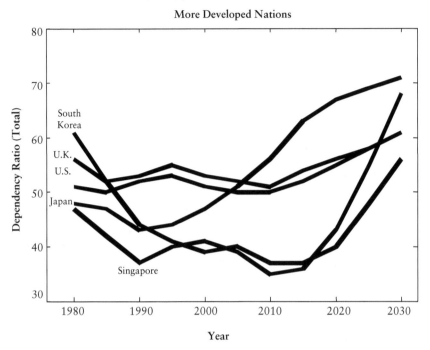

Source: United Nations Population Division, "World Population Prospects: The 2008 Revision Population Database," http://esa.un.org/unpp/index.asp?panel=2.

Broad comparisons of the kind we have made above are useful but conceal other important trends. One such trend is the emergence of a large difference between male and female life expectancy over the past fifty years of mortality decline. This difference, well recognized in the more developed nations, also characterizes recent history and near-term projections for less developed nations. Figures D and E display male and female life expectancy for a selection of low- and middle-income Asian countries using United Nations medium projections through 2030. Note the sizeable differences expected in 2030, with females living between five and eight years longer than males. Given that in more developed countries, people aged 65 will live about twenty years more, a difference of five years between the sexes is large in the context of postretirement lives. This difference is the result of sex differences in mortality starting around middle age, so that the older population in most countries has a significantly higher percentage of women than men. For perspective, it may be worth recalling here that the ratio of men to women is close to 1 at ages under 40, with a few exceptions. At age 75, in the more developed countries, the ratio of men to women falls to near 0.7 and then drops rapidly with increasing age. Over the next two decades we will see this increasing imbalance in sex ratios at older ages in most of East Asia. There are obvious social and economic consequences of this differential that deserve further study.

Figure C. Comparing Trends in Dependency Ratios in Japan, South Korea, and China, 1980–2030

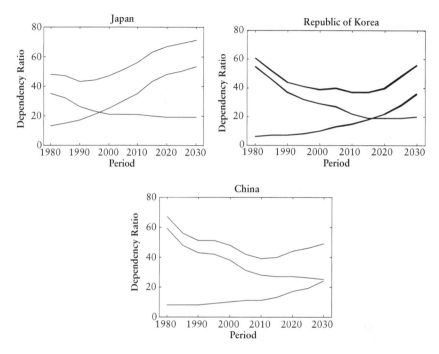

Source: United Nations Population Division, "World Population Prospects: The 2008 Revision Population Database," http://esa.un.org/unpp/index.asp?panel=2.
Note: In all panels, the upper curve represents total dependency; among the two lower curves, the falling curve is young dependency and the rising curve is old dependency.

National trends such as those shown in figure C, which indicate change in total dependency over time, produce a misleading impression that the progress of aging is smooth and monotone. In practice, it is usually uneven in both time and space. For example, consider the population pyramid for China shown in figure F for the year 2000, with females on the left and males on the right. Notice the two striking booms in the population structure centered at ages 10 and 30: these are very large cohorts that will make their way through the

Figure D. Male Life Expectancy in China, India, Malaysia, Thailand, and Vietnam, 1980–2030

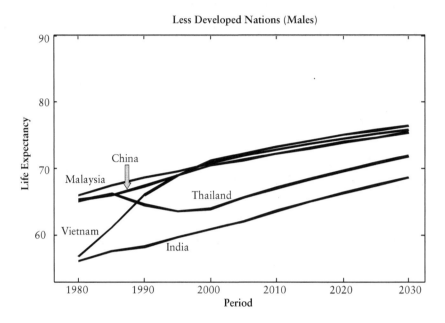

Source: United Nations Population Division, "World Population Prospects: The 2008 Revision Population Database," http://esa.un.org/unpp/index.asp?panel=2.

pyramid over time. Such baby booms generate large imbalances in the demands they make when young or old, and in the contributions they make when of working age. To appreciate these, one need only reflect on the impact of the U.S. baby boom on economic, social, and political life in the United States over the past thirty years—and the promised impact in decades to come. The economic and social consequences of the population waves in figure F are likely to be large in China, as discussed in Tuljapurkar, Pool, and Prachuabmoh (2005). In addition to these waves, both population and dependency tend to vary across space within countries. This variation, which may be between rural and urban areas or among regions with different patterns of historical development, can also strikingly affect the consequences of aging. More research on these matters is needed.

Changes in demographic structure affect a vast array of socioeconomic realities in a given society, ranging from labor-force participation, savings, and economic growth, to living arrangements, marriage markets, and social policy. Even national security policies may be directly implicated. Below-replacement fertility rates in Japan and South Korea have prompted searches for appropriate policy responses. When South Korea's health ministry announced in 2009 that the country's birth rate of 1.19 (the second lowest in the world after Hong Kong) was expected to fall to 0.96 by 2011, the leader of the Grand National Party stated that "we must deal with this problem with the sense of urgency that the country could deteriorate and face extinction" (*Choson Ilbo* editorial, August 31, 2009).

Figure E. Female Life Expectancy in China, India, Malaysia, Thailand, and Vietnam, 1980–2030

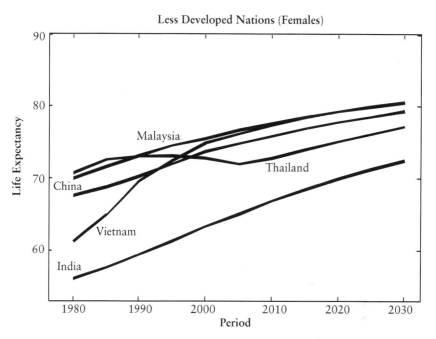

Source: United Nations Population Division, "World Population Prospects: The 2008 Revision Population Database," http://esa.un.org/unpp/index.asp?panel=2.

Perhaps foremost among the policy challenges identified in the popular press and among policymakers is the impact that aging has on the financing of social protection programs such as pensions, health insurance, and LTC. When looking at the world for insights about how other countries deal with similar challenges, Americans often look to Europe, the United Kingdom, and Canada. Rarer is the comparison to Organisation for Economic Co-operation and Development (OECD) counterparts across the Pacific, such as Japan and South Korea. Yet President Obama has clearly articulated the vision of the

United States as a Pacific nation,[1] and there are developments in East Asia that merit consideration in U.S. policy debates. Both Japan and South Korea have enacted LTC insurance, for example, to smooth the transition to an aging society.

Figure F. The Population Age Structure in China, 2000

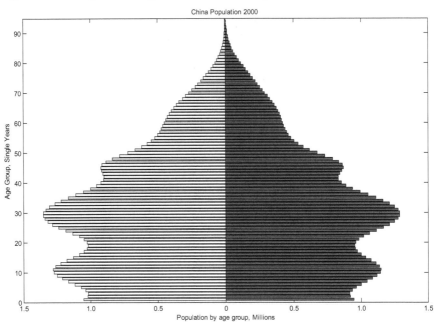

Source: United Nations Population Division, "World Population Prospects: The 2008 Revision Population Database," http://esa.un.org/unpp/index.asp?panel=2.

Or consider health-care reform. In 2009 and 2010, health reform regularly grabbed headlines in the Unites States as the political leadership in Congress and the White House struggled with how to control cost, expand access, and improve quality. Meanwhile Japan and Singapore are tackling the problem of

---

[1] President Obama said in a 2009 speech in Tokyo: "The United States of America may have started as a series of ports and cities along the Atlantic, but for generations we also have been a nation of the Pacific. . . . I am an American President who was born in Hawaii and lived in Indonesia as a boy . . . the Pacific Rim has helped shape my view of the world. . . . The fortunes of America and the Asia Pacific have become more closely linked than ever before. . . . As America's first Pacific President, I promise you that this Pacific nation will strengthen and sustain our leadership in this vitally important part of the world" (www.ft.com/cms/s/0/9e985a46-d0c2-11de-af9c-00144feabdc0.html).

providing universal coverage to populations older than the United States' with health systems that, although different in terms of public financing and the role of market forces, rank among the best in the world (and far higher than the United States) according to the World Health Organization (WHO 2000). One may quibble with the ranking, but it is indisputable that Japan spends a much smaller share of gross domestic product (GDP) on health care than the United States. This is so even though it (like the United States) maintains a fee-for-service payment system and is one of the oldest and longest-lived societies in the history of the world. Japan and South Korea are also democracies, where health policies occasionally engender heated debates. In South Korea, for example, physicians went on nationwide strike three separate times to oppose the separation of prescribing from dispensing.[2] Japan's incremental reforms rarely spur such drama, but the passions aroused by end-of-life care—embodied in the bizarre "death panels" controversy in the U.S. health reform debate of 2009—has its counterpart in the bitter nickname for Japan's separate insurance plan for the oldest of the elderly: "hurry-up-and-die" insurance. These issues notwithstanding, Japan, Singapore, and Hong Kong all offer health systems that, though far from perfect, provide reasonable risk protection and quality of care for populations much older than that of the United States, offer a diverse range of government and market roles in financing and delivery, and spend far less per capita than in the United States.

China also embarked upon major national health reform in 2009, the culmination of years of post-SARS soul-searching for a health-care financing and delivery system that fits with the nation's dynamically transforming society and economy (Chen 2009; CPC Central Committee and the State Council 2009; Eggleston 2010). It may surprise many Americans to know that public financing as a share of total health spending was lower in socialist China over the past decade than in the United States. Now, China has pledged about $124 billion over three years to expand basic health insurance, strengthen public health and primary care, reform public hospitals, and improve pharmaceutical policy. Like the fiscal stimulus to weather the 2009 financial crisis, China has moved quickly, while acknowledging that successful health reform will be "an arduous and long-term task" (CPC Central Committee and the State Council 2009). Still, if China can envision universal health coverage for 1.3 billion while "getting old before getting rich," surely the United States can find a way out of its own political conundrums about health reform and plot a path toward a more sustainable future trajectory.

This book does not cover all aspects of population aging in East Asia nor all the ways in which U.S. policy and business opportunities will intersect with demographic change in the region. It does provide an overview of key issues that illustrate the salience and complexity of population aging. After reading these chapters, no one should doubt the important role that aging plays in the Asia-Pacific's social and economic future.

---

[2] For details, see chapters on South Korea by Kwon and Yang in Eggleston (2009).

Overview of the Book

The first section of the book focuses on demographic change, intergenerational transfers, and economic growth. In chapter 1, David Bloom introduces the broad trends of population aging and economic growth. The share of the population aged 60 and over is expected to increase in every country in the world between 2000 and 2050. The 60+ population, which constituted 9 percent of the population in 1950 and 10 percent today, is projected to make up 22 percent by 2050. These changes reflect three phenomena: (1) the aging of the large baby-boom generation, (2) declines in fertility rates, and (3) an increase in life expectancy by two decades over the past half century, with substantial further increases projected. Bloom points out that these changes can have profound implications for a variety of economic issues related to health, education, pension finance, savings, labor supply, and economic growth.

Notwithstanding these potential challenges, Bloom argues that population aging may have less of a negative effect on economic growth than some have predicted. In itself, the changed age distribution would be expected to cause the labor-force participation rate to decrease. Nevertheless, the ratio of labor force to population will actually increase in most countries. A lower youth dependency rate and increased female labor-force participation (resulting from lower fertility rates) will counterbalance the shifting of adults toward older ages at which labor-force participation is lower. In addition, behavioral and policy responses to population aging—including higher savings for retirement, alternate pension funding plans, and (possibly) increased migration from labor-surplus to labor-deficit countries[3]—suggest that population aging will not necessarily significantly impede economic growth.

In chapter 2, Shripad Tuljapurkar addresses how demography shapes individual, social, and economic transitions in Asia. His analysis views aging as a part of several broad and connected transitions, including rapid economic and demographic change, the rise of socioeconomic gradients and inequalities, changes in socioeconomic networks and culture, and changing linkages between individuals, families, and the state. These transitions affect everyone—not just the elderly—and provide a wider but essential context for discussions that do focus on the elderly alone. For example, Tuljapurkar uses China's case to illustrate how demographic change can be sharp and unexpected, with annual 1 percent changes in the labor pool representing 8–10 million people and challenging the stability of programs for training young workers and providing pensions. Spatial variation will amplify this temporal variation. Next he discusses inequality of income, wealth, and human capital, and the implications of gradients of fertility and mortality across socioeconomic status. Noting that the typical kinship network has diminished considerably—in China, for example,

---

[3] To cite an Asian example, a recent South Korean report predicts that foreigners will account for one-tenth of Korea's population by the year 2050 (Kim 2009).

it is about 10 percent of what it was a few decades ago—Tuljapurkar points out that the state has emerged as a principal provider of support and care for the elderly, supplanting the role of family and kin. Although this change has been ongoing in Western countries for a long time, it is in fact relatively recent in Asia and will strongly shape the future of the region.

In chapter 3, Naohiro Ogawa, Amonthep Chawla, and Rikiya Matsukura shine a spotlight on how intergenerational transfers are changing as Japan's population rapidly ages. The authors draw upon recent work undertaken in connection with the Japanese component of the National Transfer Accounts project, as well as research on the second demographic dividend mentioned earlier. The authors empirically examine the pattern of intergenerational transfers between 1984 and 2004, in per capita and aggregate terms. The age profiles of both public and private transfers, coupled with asset reallocations, changed considerably over this period. In particular, with respect to intrafamilial transfers, the age at which an average individual shifted from a net giver to a net receiver changed dramatically between 1984 and 2004. The authors' calculations show that the crossing age increased from 64 years old in 1984 to 71 years old in 1994, and 77 in 2004. Moreover, during Japan's so-called lost decade, the elderly played a crucial role in providing financial assistance to their adult offspring and grandchildren through intrafamilial transfers. These results suggest that even though multigenerational coresidence has deteriorated over the past few decades in Japan, Japanese elderly still provide financial support for their offspring when the latter face economic difficulties. For this reason, Ogawa and colleagues conclude that the elderly should be considered latent assets rather than liabilities in contemporary Japanese society.

In chapter 4, Shuzhuo Li, Marcus Feldman, Xiaoyi Jin, and Dongmei Zuo discuss their recent research on gender, migration, and the well-being of the elderly in rural China. The mass outflow of rural labor has not only accelerated the aging process in rural China but has also had far-reaching implications for the household-dominated care of the elderly in China. To study how the outflow of rural labor affects the living conditions of the elderly in rural China, the authors analyze longitudinal data from a three-stage sample survey on the well-being of the rural elderly in Anhui Province, as well as data from a sample survey of rural-urban migrants in Shenzhen, Guangdong Province. Their analysis focuses on both the inflow and outflow regions of the rural population and emphasizes a gender perspective. Li et al. find that tradition and change coexist in elder care in rural China. The outflow of the younger generation has had dual effects on the well-being of the elderly who remain in rural areas. By working away from home, migrant children can provide their parents with better economic aid but less direct care and emotional support. The younger generation's migration also places additional burdens on their parents in terms of child care and agricultural work, which affect health and well-being. With migrant children working in cities, the traditional filial culture is ebbing, while daughters' ability to support their parents has increased. The large-scale migration of rural populations under long-term low fertility rates has altered the traditional mode of household elderly care, which relies on support from male children. The authors conclude with some suggestions for improving the well-being of China's rural elders.

Chapter 5, by Maria Porter, focuses on family dynamics and the role of marriage in determining the welfare of the elderly in China. Spouses, children, and grandchildren are often the main lines of support for China's elderly population. How do family members decide who will provide care for the elderly and where they should live? As a result of the one-child policy, many members of younger generations have no siblings with whom they can share the responsibilities of supporting elderly parents. The one-child policy, along with strong preference for sons, has also led to highly skewed sex ratios at birth. Once the generations born under the one-child policy reach old age, many men may potentially remain unmarried and childless. Who will take care of these men as they age? In this chapter, Porter reviews some of the previous research on aging-related issues in China and examines several factors regarding care provided to the elderly. These include how individuals have responded to marriage market conditions in the past, as well as differentials in elderly care according to elders' marital status. Porter argues that the current (albeit preliminary) evidence points to a particular need to address the care requirements of unmarried elderly in rural China.

The second section of the book focuses on the sustainability of social insurance programs, chronic disease, and LTC. In chapter 6, Naoki Ikegami discusses the challenge of financing health care in rapidly aging Japan. The demographic structure of Japan changed from a pyramid in 1950 to a column in 2000, and will become a reverse pyramid in 2050. Increasing longevity and lower birth rates drive similar trends throughout the developed world, but Japan is unique in that its baby boom lasted only three years (1947–49). Consequently, a large cohort of Japanese elders is now retiring. Although the proportion of those aged between 65 and 74 in the general population will increase only from 11 percent to 12 percent between 2005 and 2025, the proportion of those aged 75 and over will double from 9 percent to 18 percent. These demographic shifts will have a major impact on health-care expenditures. The 75+ cohort already constituted 29 percent of total health-care expenditure in 2005; by 2025, that figure will increase to 49 percent. From a physician's perspective (excluding obstetricians and pediatricians), this will mean that close to three-quarters of all patients will be elders. The typical hospitalization will be of a frail elderly patient admitted on a stretcher and discharged in a wheelchair, requiring seamless care between hospital and community settings. Ikegami reviews the financing of health care in Japan to draw lessons about how to mitigate the younger generation's burden, contain total health expenditures, reform health insurance for the elderly, and make LTC affordable.

The book next turns to South Korea and its reforms related to LTC and pensions. In chapter 7, Soonman Kwon discusses population aging and the July

2008 introduction of LTC insurance as South Korea's fifth social insurance system. LTC insurance aims to ease the financial burden of the elderly and to reduce the financial pressure that social admissions of the elderly put on the health insurance system. Kwon argues that experts and government bureaucrats spearheaded introduction of LTC insurance in an era of progressive administrations. Similar to health insurance, Korean LTC insurance is a contribution-based financing mechanism supplemented by government subsidies. It provides benefits-in-kind for aging-related LTC. The limited role of cash benefits and the noncoverage of LTC related to disability are still controversial. Financial concerns limit coverage to between 3 and 4 percent of the elderly, using a strict assessment process for functional dependency and eligibility. Private providers dominate service delivery. Kwon discusses how payment influences the quality of LTC services, and how the interaction between LTC and welfare services, as well as the relatively limited government role, may challenge financing and delivery of LTC in Korea.

Chapter 8, by Byungho Tchoe, describes how South Korea's public pension reforms have been spurred by widespread concern that rapid population aging and low fertility will overburden those schemes. He traces the pension system's evolution since the early 1960s. The National Pension Service (NPS) was introduced in 1988, when South Korea hosted the Olympic Games. At first its coverage was limited to workplaces with more than ten employees. But the NPS achieved universal coverage in 1999, only eleven years after its inception. During the 1998 economic crisis, public pension schemes expanded both in size and cost, raising concerns over their financial sustainability. A series of pension reforms since the mid-1990s has raised the level of contributions, reduced the income replacement rate, and increased the pensionable age. On the other hand, the level of income protection appears inadequate. Already, the poverty rate is higher and the wealth gap is wider among older South Koreans than their younger counterparts. This trend is expected to continue for a significant period. The challenge, then, is to raise the sustainability of public pension schemes while at the same time strengthening income protection for the elderly. Any meaningful pension reform will have to coordinate with health-care, labor, and social welfare policies and overcome conflicts between competing interest groups.

In chapter 9, Karen Eggleston and coauthors from six countries discuss the growth of chronic noncommunicable disease in the Asia-Pacific, focusing on diabetes. They first summarize diabetes prevalence, risk factors, and treatment patterns in Japan, South Korea, and China. They also provide descriptive "patient journeys" for several countries (including Thailand, Malaysia, Vietnam, and India) that illustrate how patients face significant barriers to using outpatient services consistently and having diabetes diagnosed early enough to prevent the onset of complications. The authors conclude that health financing and delivery systems in the region—originally designed to control infectious diseases and treat episodic, acute medical conditions—need to reorganize to emphasize primary and secondary prevention of chronic disease, patient education in self-management skills, and community-based primary care.

In chapter 10, Dolores Gallagher-Thompson and colleagues discuss an issue of growing importance that often receives limited policy attention: how communities and families cope with the challenges of caring for family members who have dementia. The authors pay particular attention to research conducted in Mainland China, Taiwan, and Hong Kong. They first describe what dementia is and discuss the way it is perceived in Chinese culture. They then review dementia caregiving practices and costs in the three regions, as well as the associated policies and program plans. Policies in the three regions feature differing degrees of collaboration between the government and community organizations to support persons with dementia and their caregivers. Evidence of the relative effectiveness of different approaches remains limited.

Finally, in chapter 11 Meng-Kin Lim presents an overview of a contrasting approach to support for the elderly: that of Singapore. Singaporeans are coerced during their productive years to save for their own future health-care needs through Medisave. They insure against major illnesses through MediShield. Those who are needy and have no family support can turn to the Medifund scheme. Supplemental schemes such as ElderShield and Medifund Silver help seniors pay for LTC, while means-tested public assistance from the government and various charitable organizations are available. The government also sets aside significant amounts annually from budgetary surpluses for the Eldercare Fund, which ensures that sufficient subsidies are available for voluntary welfare organizations that offer help to the elderly. Lim argues that Singapore's unique cost-sharing and risk-spreading formula has to some extent reduced wasteful overuse and moderated rising health-care costs, and that the government's intervention in the imperfect health-care market has encouraged demand-side responsibility while discouraging supply-side waste. Singapore's policies all place primary reliance on the family for caregiving, with institutional care as a measure of last resort. The government also invests in elder-friendly physical infrastructure and community service delivery systems.

We hope these chapters provide a rich summary of the many ways in which population aging will affect the economies and social protection systems of Japan, South Korea, and China, and by extension the Asia-Pacific region, including the United States.

References

Chen, Zhu. 2009. "Launch of the Health-care Reform Plan in China." *Lancet* 373 (April 18): 1322–23.

Chosun Ilbo (English edition). 2009. "Gov't Must Tackle Low Birth Rate as Nation's Top Agenda." Editorial, August 31. http://english.chosun.com/site/data/html_dir/2009/08/31/2009083100771.html.

CPC (Communist Party of China) Central Committee and the State Council. 2009. *Yiyaoweisheng tizhi gaige jinqi zhongdian shishi fang'an 2009-2011nian*

[Implementation plan for the recent priorities of the health-care system reform, 2009–2011], PRC official translation. http://shs.ndrc.gov.cn/ygjd/ygwj/t20090408_271137.htm.

Eggleston, Karen, ed. 2009. *Prescribing Cultures and Pharmaceutical Policy in the Asia-Pacific*. Stanford, CA: Shorenstein Asia-Pacific Research Center.

Eggleston, Karen. 2010. "'*Kan Bing Nan, Kan Bing Gui*': Challenges for China's Healthcare System Thirty Years into Reform." In *Growing Pains: Tensions and Opportunities in China's Transformation*, edited by Jean C. Oi, Scott Rozelle, and Xueguang Zhou. Stanford, CA: Shorenstein Asia-Pacific Research Center.

Kim, Yoon-mi. 2009. "Korea in 2050: One in 10 Will Be Foreign." *Korea Herald*. www.koreaherald.co.kr/NEWKHSITE/data/html_dir/2009/09/04/200909040024.asp.

Mason, A. and R. Lee. 2006. "Reform and Support Systems for the Elderly in Developing Countries: Capturing the Second Demographic Dividend." *Genus* 62: 11–35.

Tuljapurkar, S., I. Pool, and V. Prachuabmoh, eds. 2005. *Population, Resources and Development: Riding the Age Waves*, vol. 1. Dordrecht: Springer.

Wang, Feng, and Andrew Mason. 2008. "The Demographic Factor in China's Transition." In *China's Great Economic Transformation*, edited by Loren Brandt and Thomas G. Rawski, 136–66. Cambridge: Cambridge University Press.

WHO (World Health Organization). 2000. *The World Health Report 2000—Health Systems: Improving Performance*. Geneva: WHO.

Demographic Change, Intergenerational Transfers, and Economic Growth

POPULATION AGING
AND ECONOMIC GROWTH

David E. Bloom[1]

Population aging looms as a dominant demographic concern in many countries. Between 2000 and 2050 the share of global population aged 60 and above is expected to double. In 1950, the elderly accounted for 8 percent of the world's total population. Today, they make up 11 percent, and are projected to constitute 22 percent (roughly two billion people) by 2050 (see figure 1.1). Recent declines in fertility rates and increases in life expectancy, along with the trajectories of past birth and death rates, are the catalysts for this momentous shift in the global age structure. Many believe that this widespread and rapid aging of the population will have significant societal and economic implications. Much of the public discourse on this phenomenon is alarmist—one newspaper headline referred to it as the "old-age tsunami" (Eberstadt 2005). There is considerable concern that, in the near future, many countries will be inundated with elderly individuals who will consume more output than they produce, and that this shift will dramatically alter individual and national income trends.

Notwithstanding the sheer numbers shown in figure 1.1 and the potential challenges they present, population aging may have less dramatic negative effects on economic growth than some have predicted. Several factors support this view. First, the elderly are healthier than ever before. Because of the compression of morbidity (that is, the onset of chronic illness being postponed to later ages), the number of old-age years spent in good health is on the rise. A healthier elderly population is likely to be more economically productive and, on balance, less demanding of resources. Second, lower youth dependency rates and higher female labor-force participation rates—both due to decreased fertility rates—will result in an increased ratio of labor force to population in most countries. This relatively larger labor force will help boost the growth rate of income per capita. Third, the potential for behavioral and policy responses to population aging—including increased investment in human capital, higher savings for longer periods of retirement, alternate pension funding plans, and

[1] This chapter is based on a talk given at the February 2008 conference "Aging Asia: Economic and Social Implications of Rapid Demographic Change in China, Japan, and Korea." It draws on various pieces of work done jointly with David Canning, Günther Fink, Jocelyn Finlay, Michael Moore, and Younghwan Song. Helen Curry, Marija Ozolins, and Larry Rosenberg provided valuable assistance in the preparation of this chapter.

21

increased migration from labor-surplus to labor-deficit countries—means that population aging will not necessarily impede economic growth.

Population Aging: Dynamics and Drivers

World population is projected to increase by a factor of 3.5 from 1950 to 2050. By contrast, the 60+ population will increase by a factor of 10 and the 80+ population will increase by a factor of nearly 30 (see table 1.1).

Figure 1.1 Number of People Worldwide Aged 60+ and 80+, 1950–2050

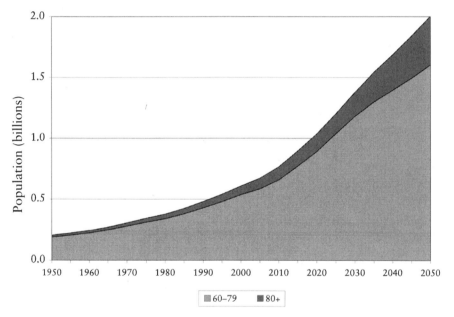

Source: United Nations, *World Population Prospects: The 2006 Revision.*

Figure 1.2 shows the age distribution, the aging of birth cohorts, and changes in the size of a given age group over time. Each colored "slice" represents the age distribution of the global population at a given point in time. The changing shape of these slices reveals the increasing share of the global population over 60. The world is still in the early stages of what will be a significant demographic shift toward an older population.

Table 1.1 United Nations Population Data and Projections

Number of elderly in world, millions			
	1950	2000	2050
60+	205	609	2,005
80+	14	70	402
Share of world population, %			
	1950	2000	2050
60+	8.1	9.9	21.8
80+	0.6	1.1	4.4
Annual average growth rate of population			
1950–2000		2000–2050	
60+	80+	60+	80+
2.20%	3.22%	2.41%	3.55%

Source: United Nations, *World Population Prospects: The 2006 Revision.*

Figure 1.2 World Population (by Five-year Age Group, 1950–2050)

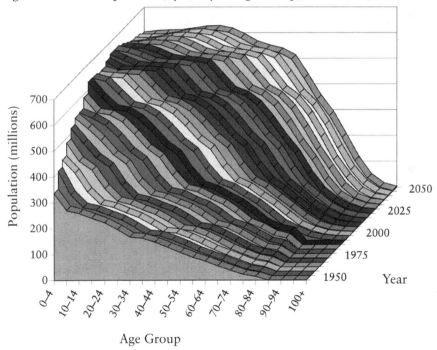

Source: United Nations, *World Population Prospects: The 2006 Revision.*

Disaggregating the data reveals considerable heterogeneity across regions (see figure 1.3). The share of the 60+ population ranges quite widely, accounting for 5 percent of the total population in Africa and 21 percent in Europe. There is much less heterogeneity across regional time trends. Rapid population aging will take place in all regions for decades to come, with the 60+ population ranging from 10 to 35 percent in 2050. There is also considerable heterogeneity within these regions.

Figure 1.3 Share of 60+ Population by Region

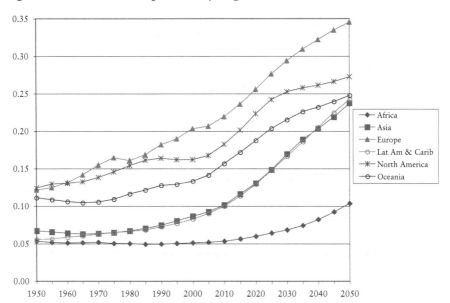

Source: United Nations, *World Population Prospects: The 2006 Revision.*

The phenomenon of population aging is not limited to wealthy industrialized countries such as Japan, South Korea, and Spain. Figure 1.4 shows United Nations projections of the 60+ population in China and India, alongside Japan. The shares of the elderly population have remained low over the past fifty years in both China and India, but are projected to increase rapidly over the next half century. By 2050 people aged 60+ will constitute 20 percent of India's population and 30 percent of China's—totaling over 0.75 billion people. This is more than the total 60+ population of the world today.

Figure 1.4 Population Aging in China, India, and Japan

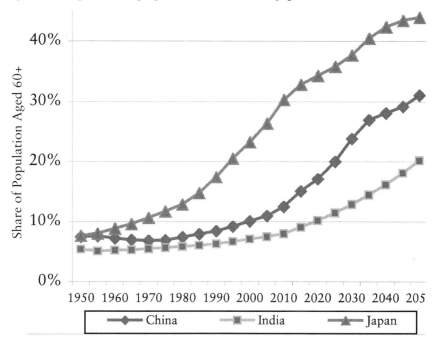

Source: United Nations, *World Population Prospects: The 2006 Revision.*

Of the forces that drive population aging, declining fertility and mortality rates play a major role. Past variations in birth and death rates also significantly shape national demographics. For example, the 1946–64 baby boom in the United States has translated into the swelling of the 60+ cohort today. In parts of the developing world, where the number of surviving children increased as health improvements reduced child mortality dramatically over the past several decades, elderly populations have been and will continue to be boosted by the aging of these large-sized cohorts.

Declining fertility rates around the world (see figure 1.5) are central to the major demographic shifts of the past fifty years, including the growing share of people aged 60 and over. The world's total fertility rate fell sharply from about 5 children per woman in 1950 to slightly over 2.5 in 2006. It is projected to drop to about 2 by 2050, which is just below the long-term population replacement rate of 2.1 children per woman. This global decrease is largely attributable to changes in fertility in the developing world, which can be ascribed to a number of factors, including declining infant mortality rates, greater levels of female education, increased labor-market opportunities for women, and increased access to modern contraception.

Figure 1.5 Declining Total Fertility Rate, by Level of Development

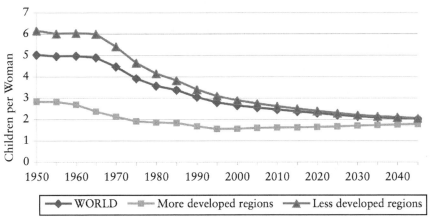

Five-year Period Beginning

Source: United Nations, *World Population Prospects: The 2006 Revision*.

Rising life expectancy is another key driver of population aging. Around the world, life expectancy increased by nearly two decades between 1950 and 2000 (from 46 years in 1950–55 to 66 years in 2000–05). Adding two decades to global life expectancy in the space of fifty years is a remarkable achievement, especially considering that life expectancy fluctuated around 30 years throughout most of human history.

Although most projections concur that life expectancy will continue to rise, there is little consensus about whether there is a limit to its increase. Some forecasts (for example, Oeppen and Vaupel 2002, and Vaupel and Gowan 1986) project that life expectancy in the wealthy industrialized countries will surpass a hundred years during the second half of this century, as technologies improve and lifestyles become healthier. Other scholars (for example, Fries 1980; and Carnes, Olshansky, and Grahn 2003) assert that life expectancy will plateau at 85 years, citing data that link past increases in life expectancy to past declines in infant and child mortality. As these declines are not repeatable, they cannot contribute to further gains. Still others expect that emerging global threats, such as influenza and climate change, will moderate the rise of life expectancy.

Figure 1.6 Increasing Life Expectancies, by Level of Development

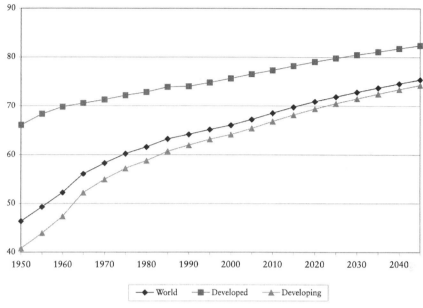

Five-year Period Beginning

Source: United Nations, *World Population Prospects: The 2006 Revision.*

Implications

From a policy perspective, population aging poses many challenges. As it is an unprecedented phenomenon, there are few insights to be gained from past experience. Even so, some information can be garnered from existing data and observations. It is evident that older individuals tend to have different behaviors and demands than younger ones. Older people typically work less and therefore save less, which translates into less labor and capital available to economies. Older people also require more health care and may rely on pensions or savings to support themselves. People aged 80 and over present different and increased needs for health services, full-time care, and financial resources outside of personal savings. As the number of those aged 60 and over increases, further demands are placed on government and family resources. In addition, this burgeoning age group could in some places emerge as a strong political bloc able to hamper governments' capacity to adopt policies that threaten (or appear to threaten) health and pension benefits.

As figure 1.1 illustrates, the most dramatic increases in aging have not yet occurred. This is fortunate, as it means that policymakers have a window of opportunity in which to anticipate and prepare for the demographic shift. And there are still other reasons to be hopeful. First, there is a historically strong positive association between life expectancy and per capita income (Preston 1975). Second, the compression of morbidity may ease the impact of population aging. If elderly people today and in the future are healthier than those of preceding generations, their demands for health care will be less, and many will be able to work, save, and contribute to their economies for longer. Many studies, most focused on the United States, suggest that the compression of morbidity does indeed occur and will reduce the burden of population aging (Fries 1980, 1989; Crimmins 2004; Crimmins et al. 1997; Costa 2002).

Third, worldwide differences in the timing of aging may also limit potential negative impacts. Because rich countries are generally aging more quickly than poor ones, migration of working-age people to rich countries has the potential to compensate for the large cohorts of elderly retirees in these countries and, in theory, lessens the negative effects of population aging on their economies. For example, Europe's need for workers (due to a high percentage of elderly people and few children) could be met, at least in part, by sub-Saharan Africa's large working-age population. However, it is uncertain whether the world will capitalize on these potential benefits. Many countries, instead of welcoming migrants, have instituted barriers to immigration, usually in an effort to protect their citizens from the competition of low-wage workers, to preserve traditions or cultural and ethnic uniformity, or in response to other anti-immigrant sentiments. Policymakers who hope to counterbalance the negative effects of population aging will have to address these issues. Initiating early action on these and other policy opportunities will better prepare countries for the social, economic, and political effects of an altered population structure in the future.

The Economic Impacts of Population Aging

Changes in the population age structure may exert a significant influence on economic growth as people's economic needs and contributions vary over their life cycles. The ratio of consumption to production tends to be high for the youth and elderly but low for working-age adults. Labor supply, productivity, and savings—all key drivers of economic growth in the aggregate—vary across workers' life cycles. Among these factors, labor supply and savings are generally higher among working-age adults than among those aged 60 and over. Assuming other factors to be equal, therefore, a country with a large elderly cohort is likely to experience slower economic growth than one with a high proportion of working-age people.

Many studies suggest that population aging will diminish the productive capacities of national economies. In 1999 Peter Peterson sounded an alarm with an article in *Foreign Affairs* (Peterson 1999) in which he described global aging as a "threat more grave and certain than those posed by chemical weapons, nuclear proliferation, or ethnic strife." In assessing the consequences of population change, this and other alarmist literature tends to assume that age-specific behavior will remain constant with respect to earnings, employment, and savings.

This approach may generate misleading predictions for two reasons. First, most existing studies fail to factor in a host of behavioral and policy adjustments that will not only occur naturally in response to population aging, but will also tend to mitigate the economic consequences of this demographic phenomenon. As people respond to changing expectations of their life cycle, including how long they will live and how healthy they will be in old age, behavioral changes are likely to alleviate the negative economic consequences of aging. For example, the expectation of living longer may induce people to remain in the workforce for longer and to draw upon their savings at a later stage. In flexible policy environments that anticipate trends of population aging (and links to economic performance), governments may have the opportunity to implement new and better retirement policies, pension plans, and health-care financing that not only buffer but encourage or take advantage of behavioral changes. In addition, one factor underlying population aging is reduced fertility rates, and fewer children allow families to invest more in education. Such investments have a high rate of return, as educated individuals earn more and effectively contribute more to the national income.

The second source of misleading predictions about the consequences of population aging is most studies' narrow focus on a single demographic indicator—the increase in the elderly dependency ratio. One would expect this increase, when considered apart from all other factors, to cause the labor-force participation rate to decrease. But in most countries, the percentage of labor-force participants will actually increase: lower youth dependency and increased female labor-force participation, both the result of lower fertility rates, will counterbalance—and more than offset—the decrease in labor-force participation that arises from overall population aging. Table 1.2 shows this phenomenon on a global scale. The labor-force participation rate (that is, the share of the population aged 15 and older that is in the labor force) is decreasing, and is expected to continue doing so in coming decades. But because of declining fertility rates, the labor force as a share of the total population has been rising and is projected to rise further—even in the face of considerable aging worldwide.

Table 1.2 Global Labor Force: 1960, 2000, and 2040

	1960 Actual	2000 Actual	2040 Projected
Labor-force participation rate (labor force/ population 15+)	67.4	66.4	62.1
Labor force/total population	42.4	46.5	48.6

Source: Bloom et al. 2008.

Population aging of this size and nature has no counterpart in past global experience, and so demographers and economists must rely on models to analyze its effects and to explore possible outcomes. One well-established empirical model of economic growth is known as the conditional convergence model. This model, which focuses on the growth rate of income per worker, has two key features. First, countries are assumed to have a steady-state level of income per worker that depends on relevant characteristics of the economy, such as its policy environment, human resources, physical capital stock, and geography. Second, the growth rate of income per worker depends on the deviation between the steady-state income per worker and actual income per worker (Barro and Sala-i-Martin 2004). While many consider income per capita to be the single best measure of living standards and economic development, this model focuses on income per worker.

This income-per-worker model of growth can be used to make inferences about the growth of income per capita, under the assumption that either (1) every member of the population is a worker, or that (2) the growth rate of the working-age population is identical to the growth rate of the overall population. The first assumption ignores one of the most significant constructs in demography and the social sciences—the life cycle. The second implies that populations are demographically stable, an assumption decisively negated by the patterns discussed. Therefore, this model should not be used to make inferences about the growth of income per capita.

A relatively simple way to introduce population dynamics into the conditional convergence model is to utilize an identity that holds that income per capita equals income per worker multiplied by workers per capita. The application of this identity to the income-per-worker growth model yields an equation describing the growth of income per capita as a function of the initial level of income per capita, a country's characteristics, the initial ratio of working-age population to total population, the growth rate of that ratio, and the growth rate of the population. By incorporating the growth rate of the working-age population and the overall population, this model more adequately addresses the changes that occur as the population ages.

The fundamental causes of economic growth are famously difficult to pin down, and efforts to develop a comprehensive model are ongoing. Nevertheless, the line of inquiry discussed here (that is, the modified conditional convergence model) has produced a number of key results that confirm the importance of age structure to economic growth. In the short run, increases in the working-age share of the population have positive effects on economic growth. With respect to long-run dynamics, higher steady-state levels of the working-age share of the population also have positive effects on economic growth. Age groups within the population affect economic growth differently. Increases in youth dependency impede the growth of income per capita in both the short and long term. By contrast, increases in the elderly dependency ratio only impede income per capita growth in the short run. In the long run, these increases do not have a statistically significant impact on income per capita growth. Such results are consistent with the view that although the potential negative effect on economic growth conveyed by high fertility cannot be offset by behavioral and institutional changes, that of increased longevity can. In addition, projections of youth and old-age dependency suggest that the impending increase in elderly dependents will be more than offset by a decline in youth dependents.

These results and arguments suggest that population aging is not an imminent economic crisis for the world, but rather a more modest challenge for particular economies, such as the developed countries of Europe. Declining fertility, for example, has contributed to women's greater labor-force participation, which may stimulate economic growth. Fewer children mean healthier, smarter, and better-educated children. As health, cognition, and education translate into higher adult productivity, lower fertility is tantamount to an increase in the effective labor force.

Increases in longevity and the number of healthy years in a lifetime may also drive economic growth. As people save more in anticipation of longer retirement periods, greater longevity may result in higher savings rates. Savings translate into investment, which fuels the accumulation of physical and human capital and technological progress, all classic drivers of economic growth. It is natural for people to respond to longer life expectancies by planning for longer working lives. Of course, these behavioral responses are not a given, especially as public policy has been extremely sluggish in adapting to the new demographic realities. For example, mean legal retirement ages worldwide have not risen in tandem with increasing life expectancies.

Summary and Discussion

For the greater part of the past century, the prevailing concern in the demographic field was the exponentially increasing world population, a trend caused by the combination of lowered mortality rates and continued high fertility rates. The literature of the time reflected this concern, with many studies predicting the dire consequences of high population densities and population growth rates. These alarmist predictions have not come to pass: income per capita on average worldwide has increased at a faster rate than global population.

The size and nature of the current demographic shift toward the elderly is unprecedented. Analysis of its effects is only beginning; demographers and economists still lack the tools and models to fully understand possible outcomes. However, new models designed to account for this change provide an opportunity to determine appropriate behavioral and policy responses to the new demographic realities.

Policymakers have the ability to lessen the potential negative effects of aging on economic growth. In many instances, the challenges presented by population aging are not inherent but are tied to rigid or outdated policies and institutions. Policies that account for natural incentives that individuals

31

face during the life cycle, which would encourage behavioral adjustments in the light of population aging, need to be further developed. As noted earlier, behavioral and policy responses such as saving for retirement and redesigning pension funds, along with the potential for increased migration from labor-surplus to labor-deficit countries and a more highly educated and hence more productive population, suggest that population aging need not significantly impede economic growth.

Several studies are already addressing the questions raised by this unprecedented global phenomenon. The U.S. Health and Retirement Study (HRS), funded by the National Institute on Aging, is an innovative study designed to better understand elderly well-being, with a focus on how individuals and households are preparing for and coping with the economic and health requirements of advancing age. In recent years, the HRS has led the effort to collect data on the elderly worldwide. There are currently twenty-four countries involved in such studies, including full-scale studies in the United States, United Kingdom (English Longitudinal Study of Ageing), Europe (Survey of Health, Ageing, and Retirement in Europe), Israel, and New Zealand. Pilot studies are being conducted in China, India, Japan, and South Korea. The science-based, longitudinal focus of the HRS and the power of international comparisons and harmonization of data collection and analysis techniques may improve the chances of fine-tuning policy to accommodate population aging.

Even with the help of data gathered through the HRS, policy decisions based on demographic predictions cannot accommodate all future scenarios. Health shocks or changes in fertility could alter the balance between the youth and the elderly in unforeseen ways. Projections of life expectancy are tenuous; changes in diet and lifestyle and advances in medical and public health technologies could raise or lower longevity. Climate change, war and conflict, and other non-health-related phenomena could also have impacts on longevity. Today's ongoing compression of morbidity is in part due to new health technology, but the pace of future technological advances is unclear.

Although these shifting circumstances serve to further complicate efforts to determine and address the effects of population aging, it is evident that the past century has seen a triumph in the world's ability to address the challenge of demographic shifts. The world economy has demonstrated the capacity to absorb and take advantage of striking increases in population numbers. As long as today's policymakers act quickly to prepare for the changes promised by population aging, this next major demographic shift is likely to cause much less collective hardship than many anticipate.

References

Barro, Robert J., and Xavier Sala-i-Martin. 2004. *Economic Growth*. Cambridge, MA: MIT Press.

Bloom, David E., David Canning, and Günther Fink. 2008. "Population Aging and Economic Growth, Program on the Global Demography of Aging." Working Paper

No. 31, Program on the Global Demography of Aging, Harvard Center for Population and Development Studies, April.

Carnes, B. A., S. J. Olshansky, and D. Grahn. 2003. "Biological Evidence for Limits to the Duration of Life." *Biogerontology* 4: 31–45.

Costa, D. L. 2002. "Changing Chronic Disease Rates and Long-term Declines in Functional Limitation Among Older Men." *Demography* 39 (1): 119–37.

Crimmins, E. M. 2004. "Trends in the Health of the Elderly." *Annual Review of Public Health* 25 (1): 79–98.

Crimmins, E., Y. Saito, and D. Ingegneri. 1997. "Trends in Disability-free Life Expectancy in the United States, 1970–90." *Population and Development Review* 23 (3): 555–72.

Eberstadt, Nicholas. "Old Age Tsunami." Wall Street Journal, November 15, 2005.

Fries, J. 1980. "Aging, Natural Death and the Compression of Morbidity." *New England Journal of Medicine* 303: 130–35.

———. 1989. "The Compression of Morbidity: Near or Far?" *Milbank Quarterly* 67: 208–32.

Oeppen, J., and J. W. Vaupel. 2002. "Broken Limits to Life Expectancy." *Science* 296: 1029–31.

Peterson, P. G. 1999. "Gray Dawn: The Global Aging Crisis." *Foreign Affairs* 78, no. 1 (January/February): 42–55.

Preston, S. 1975. "The Changing Relation Between Mortality and Level of Economic Development." *Population Studies* 29 (2): 231–48.

United Nations. 2007. *World Population Prospects: The 2006 Revision.* CD-ROM. New York: UN Population Division.

Vaupel, J. W., and A. E. Gowan. 1986. "Passage to Methuselah: Some Demographic Consequences of Continued Progress Against Mortality." *American Journal of Public Health* 76: 430.

HOW DEMOGRAPHY SHAPES INDIVIDUAL, SOCIAL, AND ECONOMIC TRANSITIONS IN ASIA

Shripad Tuljapurkar[1]

The aging of East Asia and much of the rest of the world is viewed as the major demographic trend of our times. Much of the interest in this transition derives from its fiscal consequences, especially the costs of the postretirement elderly, in terms of both their consumption and their health care. Much research on aging therefore focuses on analyzing fiscal and generational costs, trends in health status and health expenditures, the long-term future of economies, and social and fiscal policy responses. These topics are, properly, the subject of many chapters in this book. This chapter uses a different lens to view the transitions that produce and accompany aging. I view aging, instead, as part of several broad and connected transitions. These are rapid economic and demographic change, the rise of socioeconomic gradients and inequalities, changing socioeconomic networks and culture, and changing linkages among individuals, families, and the state. These transitions affect everyone, not just the elderly, and provide a broader but essential context for discussions focused on the elderly.

Age Waves and Demographic Instability

Aging is a consequence of declining fertility and declining mortality. The former results in a decline in the number of young people born into a population, and the latter results in an increase in the number of elderly people. Much demographic and economic analysis of aging takes a long view of these changes, on a time scale of many decades, so that aging appears as a smooth and apparently inexorable transition from a youth-heavy population that spends a lot on young people to an elderly-heavy population that spends too much on old people.

Yet demographic change is often disorderly in time, that is, sharp and unexpected. For example, since 1950 fertility in China has fallen from between 5 and 6 children per woman to a current range of 1.5 to 2. In fact, most of the fertility change was concentrated in time, in the late 1970s with the "Later,

---

[1] The author was supported in part by a grant from the National Institute of Aging. This work benefited from many discussions with Ryan Edwards, Ronald Lee, and Uli Steiner.

Longer, Fewer" campaign and then around 1990 with the one-child policy. Other unusual and rapid changes have also had large but rapid effects on mortality and fertility, such as the "Great Leap Forward." Demographic change is also often disorderly in space, meaning that over a given period different spatial regions in a country may undergo distinct changes in mortality, fertility, and migration. Thus, fertility and fertility policy vary by a factor of two when we compare different prefectures or counties across China (Gu et al. 2007). This spatial gradient in fertility is large between urban and rural areas, and metropolitan areas in particular have extraordinarily low fertility even relative to China's low overall fertility (Poston 2000). Mortality change in China has also been uneven over time, with major reductions in child mortality, for example, taking place in the past three decades. Mortality is also much higher in rural than in urban areas (Zimmer, Kaneda, and Spess 2007).

Why and how does this kind of variation matter? At the macro level, the fact that fertility and mortality have changed unevenly means that China's age structure today, and for many decades to come, is and will be shaped by baby busts that accompany sharp fertility reductions (Wang and Mason 2008). One important consequence is that the growth rates of economically important population segments, such as the potential labor force (aged 15–65) and the old population (aged 65+), will not be steady over the next few decades. Figure 2.1 displays annual growth rates from 2010 to 2050 for these two segments based on World Bank projections (United Nations projections yield a similar result). The dashed line marks a zero growth rate. Notice that both growth rates oscillate over time, a result of the uneven aging of the uneven population structure. The size of the potential labor force is projected to grow slowly for a decade, stabilize for the next decade, and then enter a two-decade decline in size that will eventually reverse. The over-65 population's growth is projected to be strikingly high over the next three decades but there are large year-to-year variations in the growth rate. Given that a 1 percent change in the labor pool represents 8–10 million people and a 1 percent change in the older population represents 1–2 million, these annual variations are large. There can be large effects on the size and stability of programs such as those for training and educating young workers, and on pension programs.

Temporal variation can, of course, be amplified by spatial variation. For example, the two rates of growth discussed above are certainly uneven across regions. The growth rate of the elderly can be much higher than the aggregate growth rate in rural areas that have sustained out-migration of young people, and much lower in urban areas that allow permanent in-migration of labor. Regional changes in the size of the labor pool are likely to interact with regional economic change in complex ways that deserve careful analysis (Liang and Ma 2004).

Figure 2.1 Annual Growth Rates (%) of the Potential Labor Pool (population aged 15–65) and the Elderly (aged 65+) in China

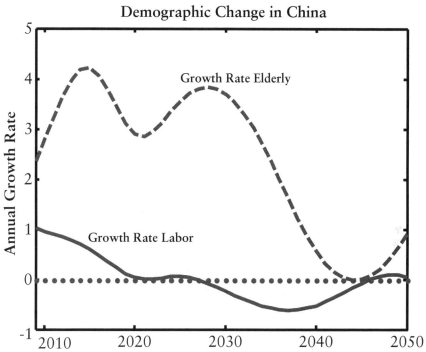

Source: Author's calculations.

Pool (2005) refers to such variability as chaotic age flows. He argues convincingly that individual and policy responses to demographic change need to take account of the speed and magnitude of changes that affect critical age groups. The latter are the ages of what Rindfuss (1991) calls high demographic density, and typically encompass periods of transition including, for example, graduation from high school, entry into college or a first job, childbearing, and retirement. These are the ages at and near which government policy plays an important role in constraining available choices, and the timing and success of individual transitions. These are also ages at which cohort effects—that is, the behavior of current and past cohorts at the same age—can play an important role in determining behavior (for a relevant discussion, see Macunovich 1996). When the structures of populations change in such a way that different critical ages are affected, research and policy must effectively integrate those different demands and needs. The literature on aging (for example, see David Bloom, chapter 1 in this book) recognizes the importance of behavioral responses to aging, but these vary by age and deserve more careful analysis.

37

Inequality

We use the term *inequality* broadly to describe unequal distributions of income, wealth, or education, and also to describe what are usually called gradients, such as a socioeconomic gradient in mortality or fertility. Inequalities of various kinds matter a great deal to aging nations.

Research, policy, and public debate on aging are broadly concerned with two goals that are, in some ways, contradictory. On the one hand, there is considerable discussion of aging as a problem, so the goal is to maintain fiscal balance over time between payments to the elderly and the economic growth needed to keep up with these payments. In the simplest terms, the options for dealing with the problem are (1) to reduce payments to the elderly so that they must pay the difference, (2) to increase wages and aggregate output by increasing productivity faster than the rate at which the size of the labor force declines, or (3) to redefine the elderly so that people who are retired under current policy continue working longer (and old age dependency is reduced by definition).

On the other hand, aging is (reasonably) seen as the successful realization of the goal of increased longevity. In this context, improving health and increasing longevity are the objectives, but these are surely at odds with the fiscal incentive to reduce the costs of the elderly. The academic literature on aging suggests ways of reconciling these goals, but that subject lies beyond the scope of the present discussion. Simply put, there is considerable scientific and social investment in improving health and lengthening lives, and inequalities matter.

We continue to use China as our primary example. Economic inequalities in China have been studied extensively, especially in the context of Kuznet's famous argument that inequalities should narrow in the later stages of economic development. The recent literature on the subject has also been concerned with the effects of globalization. Candelaria and Hale (2009) discuss trends in regional (provincial) inequality in China and the relationship of this inequality to a variety of possible drivers, such as education. Real wages have a coefficient of variation of 0.3 among provinces (corresponding to a Gini of about 31 percent). There is substantial but somewhat smaller variation in the proportion of people doing agricultural work, and in migrant flows. There is much larger variation in the fraction of people with college educations, and in education spending per capita. These inequalities have an impact on several aspects of policy.

On the growth side, inequalities in educational attainment and spending mean there are inequalities in human capital and in investments related to human capital. Both matter to the trajectory of economic growth. The growth rate of an economy in the long term is the sum of the growth rates of output per worker and the number of workers. Aging drives the latter, and as we have seen in figure 2.1, it will soon be zero or negative in China. Hence it is key to aim for an increase in productivity, and this in turn depends on the human capital of the labor force. Policy that aims to increase productivity must invest in the growth of human capital, via education and training, and these efforts have to focus on the worst-off regions. The same issue is debated for the same reasons in all aging societies.

Wage inequality usually translates into inequality in lifetime earnings and in lifetime accumulation of savings. The savings of the elderly are an important determinant of whether they can support themselves and their standard of living in old age. Inequality in China is further complicated by the rules governing migration and residence, and these may offset the usual role that migration plays in equalizing wages across regions. Thus migrants who are subject to restrictions on residence and social services may suffer in terms of both lifetime income and savings. If so, inequality in savings among the elderly may be even higher than inequality in wages. Public pension systems are often progressive in that they aim to provide a relatively high level of support to those with relatively low lifetime wages. This is sensible policy, but an increase in the inequality of savings will increase the costs of a pension system.

Inequality also matters to rich industrialized countries, such as Japan. For example, research in the United States (Butrica and Uccello 2005) shows that the retirement wealth of cohorts close to age 65 is highly unequal. The median wealth level is modest, but more surprisingly, as much as half of this median wealth is the present value of anticipated Social Security payments. Much of the discussion of the "burden" of Social Security in the United States ignores this distributional fact. It is worth recalling here that one of the signal achievements of the U.S. Social Security system was a significant reduction of poverty among the elderly population. A similar benefit should be expected from organized pension systems elsewhere, and must be weighed against the costs of these systems.

Regional inequality in China certainly also reflects urban-rural inequality. A particular aspect of the latter is that public pension coverage for the rural population has only recently begun, and thus the fiscal burden of aging costs in China must include the start-up and ongoing costs of any pensions and health care for rural populations. Given that about half of China's elderly population is rural, the incremental costs are substantial (see the discussion of possible rural pension schemes in Yang, Williamson, and Shen 2009).

Turning to other aspects of aging, let us consider health and longevity. There has been considerable work showing that socioeconomic gradients exist in health and mortality and that social policy has become increasingly concerned with disparities and their reduction (Marmot 2007). It is clear that some kinds of inequality matter to health and thus to aging; many of the same factors also affect life expectancy and thus matter to longevity. Another dimension of inequality is the actual age at death, as contrasted with the average age at death (which is in fact life expectancy). Edwards and Tuljapurkar (2005) have examined inequality in the age at death and shown that variation within socioeconomic categories or spatial regions is substantial as compared with variation among them. From a policy perspective, we care most about deaths that occur at early ages relative to a modal age at death. Therefore, a proper target for policy aimed at increasing longevity is to reduce these early deaths; inequality in age at death is a useful index for measuring progress.

Networks and Culture

We have stated that one driver of aging is a decline in fertility, conventionally measured in terms of the total fertility rate (TFR). There has been considerable research on how lower fertility and economic growth affect household size and composition. A trend toward smaller households and reduced coresidence between the young and elderly is widely documented in East Asia and elsewhere. Along with this, there is a direct relationship between the TFR and the size of kinship networks.

We can measure the size of a kinship network by asking how many living first cousins a person has. A simple calculation based on work by Goodman, Keyfitz, and Pullum (1974) shows that the size of a kinship network is proportional to the square of the total fertility rate (or TFR^2). If we consider that China's TFR has fallen from 5 to around 1.5, the size of the typical kinship network has fallen to about 10 percent of what it was a few decades ago. What does this thinning of kinship networks imply?

In traditional societies, kinship networks were a primary source of information and support in many aspects of life, including finding a spouse, providing child care, finding a job, starting or growing a business, lending financial support, learning about cultural norms and practices, and supporting migration. For the elderly, kinship networks were a traditional source of care and insurance. Increasing geographical mobility, as people move far from home to find jobs, has exacerbated the thinning of networks that results from a low TFR. The traditional roles of kinship networks have been and are rapidly being taken over by other kinds of structures. For individuals, information flow increasingly comes from social networks, religious groups, political groups, or the state. There is a greater demand for services of various kinds for all ages, including child care, care of the elderly, and many kinds of credit and insurance. A variety of service providers have stepped into this breach, ranging from insurance companies to those who offer care for children and the elderly. However, the government fills many of the gaps in all of these areas.

These trends matter to a variety of questions related to aging policy. Fertility choice is an important example. Demographers and others have long studied the factors that drive fertility down and sustain the demographic transition that leads to aging (Casterline 2001). An important component is ideational change (Cleland and Wilson 1987) and the diffusion of new ideas along social networks. Similar processes need to be studied, understood, and turned to use in policies that aim to change current fertility (as in Japan; see Ogawa, Chawla, and Matsukura, chapter 3 in this volume). But the social networks along which ideas and norms now propagate are no longer primarily kinship networks; they include a range of new social networks including those made possible by the Internet. Similar considerations apply to policies related to behavioral choices.

For example, the age of retirement has historically been set by pension policy. But in many countries a large percentage of individuals choose to retire at the official age or earlier. A shift to later retirement would fiscally benefit virtually all aging societies, but needs broad adoption and support. Information networks may be a key to shifting norms about retirement age.

These questions also relate to newer challenges that accompany projected aging trends. Elderly people increasingly live on their own, not with their adult children, and not in proximity to other kin. At the oldest ages, 75 and up, the elderly population will be increasingly female-dominated because of the male-female mortality differential noted in the introduction to this book. As a result, the integration of the elderly into the social lives of the young will require new kinds of social networks. The spousal benefits provided by pension systems, the design and structure of retirement communities, and the provision of health and care services to the elderly, must take into account the changing gender composition of the elderly.

Individuals, Family, and the State

The thinning of kinship networks has, as pointed out above, accompanied changes in family size and structure. In particular, nuclear families have become the norm in most countries, including those in East Asia. There has been a decline in coresidence as parents live by themselves after their children move away. In many parts of China and elsewhere in East Asia, many parents have no children or only one child. These changes are or will be part of a continuing reworking of the relationship among individuals, family, and the state. In modern times, the state has emerged as a principal provider of support and care for the elderly, supplanting the role of family and kin. Although this change has been ongoing in Western countries for a long time, it is in fact relatively recent in Asia.

Scholars and policymakers continue to explore ways in which the state's role can be restructured. Some proposals argue that the individual should guarantee his or her own old-age support by saving enough for old age. Other proposals argue for a continuing and even expanded role for the family, requiring transfers from children to parents to cover some part of the costs of caring for the elderly. But both children and parents, and others, must grapple with two essential issues. The first is that virtually all proposals require effective means of providing information to people and of changing their perceptions, norms, and expectations. This is especially important because people have both a stake in and the capacity to influence policy change, and will not necessarily support new policy, however well conceived it may be. This problem brings to mind the story of the soon-to-be-retired citizen who, when asked if he was worried about the demise of public pensions by the time he did retire, replied, "No. We'll vote it back in."

The other essential issue that many proposed policy changes neglect is the need for insurance, both for savings and for health care. Investment disasters may destroy the best-laid individual savings plan, and health is an intrinsically uncertain commodity. Kinship networks and traditional families were at one time the main protection against such risks. Now, even when such networks do exist, they no longer fulfill that role. Aging policy must uncover ways in which individuals can insure themselves against such risks.

References

Butrica, B., and C. Uccello. 2004. "How Will Boomers Fare at Retirement?" Working Paper 2004–2005, AARP Public Policy Institute.

Candelaria, C., M. Daly, and G. Hale. 2009. "Beyond Kuznets: Persistent Regional Inequality in China." Working Paper Series, Federal Reserve Bank of San Francisco.

Casterline, J. 2001. "Diffusion Processes and Fertility Transition: Introduction." In *Diffusion Processes and Fertility Transition: Selected Perspectives*, edited by John B. Casterline. National Academy Press, 1–38.

Cleland, J., and C. Wilson. 1987. "Demand Theories of the Fertility Transition: An Iconoclastic View." *Population Studies* 41: 5–30.

Edwards, R., and S. Tuljapurkar. 2005. "Inequality in Life Spans and a New Perspective on Mortality Convergence across Industrialized Countries." *Population and Development Review* 31: 645–74.

Goodman, Leo G., N. Keyfitz, and T. Pullum. 1974. "Family Formation and the Frequency of Various Kinship Relationships." *Theoretical Population Biology* 5: 1–27.

Gu, B., W. Feng, G. Zhigang, and Z. Erli. 2007. "China's Local And National Fertility Policies at the End of the Twentieth Century." *Population and Development Review* 33: 129.

Liang, Z., and Z. Ma. 2004. "China's Floating Population: New Evidence from the 2000 Census." *Population and Development Review* 30 (3): 467–88.

Macunovich, D. 1996. "Relative Income and Price of Time: Exploring Their Effects on U.S. Fertility and Female Labor Force Participation." *Population and Development Review* 22: 223–57.

Marmot, M. 2007. "Achieving Health Equity: From Root Causes to Fair Outcomes." *The Lancet* 370: 1153–63.

Pool, I. 2005. "Age-structural Transitions and Policy: Towards Frameworks." In *Population, Resources and Development: Riding the Age Waves*, vol. 1., edited by S. Tuljapurkar, I. Pool, and V. Prachuabmoh. Dordrecht: Springer.

Poston Jr., D. 2000. "Social and Economic Development and the Fertility Transitions in Mainland China and Taiwan." *Population and Development Review* 26: 40–60.

Wang, F., and A. Mason. 2008. "The Demographic Factor in China's Transitions." In *China's Great Economic Transformations*, edited by Loren Brant and Thomas Rawski. Cambridge University Press, 136–66.

World Bank Population Projections (HNPSTATS). http://web.worldbank.org.

Yang, Y., J. Williamson, and C. Shen. 2009. "Social Security for China's Rural Aged: A Proposal Based on a Universal Non-Contributory Pension." *International Journal of Social Welfare* 18.

Zimmer, Z., T. Kaneda, and L. Spess. 2007. "An Examination of Urban Versus Rural Mortality in China Using Community and Individual Data." *Journals of Gerontology* (Series B) 62, S349.

CHANGING INTERGENERATIONAL TRANSFERS
IN AGING JAPAN

Naohiro Ogawa, Amonthep Chawla, and Rikiya Matsukura[1]

I n this chapter we examine the extent to which rapid population aging has influenced the pattern of intergenerational transfers in Japan over the past two decades. To achieve this objective, we applied the methodology of the National Transfer Accounts (NTA) project to both micro- and macrolevel data from the period 1984–2004.[2]

We will first review some key features of Japan's demographic dynamics during the postwar period. We will then discuss (1) Japan's first demographic dividend induced by age-compositional shifts and its relationship to Japan's long-term economic growth, and (2) a rapidly changing pattern of familial transfers among various age groups in Japanese society over the past two decades.

Japan's postwar fertility decline was one of the first of its kind to occur in the non-Western world and was the greatest in magnitude among all the industrialized countries. Following a short-lived baby-boom period (1947–49), Japan's fertility dropped at a phenomenal rate (Hodge and Ogawa 1991; Ogawa and Retherford 1993; Retherford and Ogawa 2006). Between 1947 and 1957, the total fertility rate (TFR) halved, from 4.54 to 2.04 children per woman, as shown in figure 3.1. Subsequent to this rapid fertility decline, only minor fluctuations around the replacement level occurred until the first oil crisis in 1973. Thereafter, the TFR started to fall again, and by the mid-1990s it had fallen below 1.5 children per woman. In 2005 the value of the TFR plummeted to 1.26—the lowest in the postwar period—before a slight rebound to 1.37 in

[1] Research for this article was funded by two grants from the National Institutes of Health (NIA), R01–AG025488 and AG025247. This work was also supported by a grant obtained by the Nihon University Population Research Institute from the Academic Frontier Project for Private Universities, a matching-fund subsidy from the Ministry of Education, Culture, Sports, Science and Technology (MEXT) for the period 2006–10. Furthermore, the authors are grateful to the United Nations Population Fund (RAS5P203) and the Japan Medical Association for their financial assistance.

[2] A fuller explanation of the NTA's basic concept and the computational assumptions employed, along with definitions of other key variables, is available on the NTA website, www.ntaccounts.org.

2008. If fertility were to remain constant at the present level, each successive generation would shrink by approximately 35 percent. Some demographers refer to this post-1973 fertility decline as Japan's second demographic transition (Ogawa and Retherford 1993; Retherford and Ogawa 2006; Ogawa, Retherford, and Matsukura 2009).

In tandem with these changes in the TFR, the size of the birth cohorts varied considerably over the period but showed an overall decline, as illustrated in figure 3.1. During the baby-boom period there were, on average, approximately 2.7 million births per year, but by 1957 the number of births had decreased to 1.6 million. In the early 1970s, despite the decline in the TFR, the number increased to more than two million—an "echo effect" of the baby-boom cohorts having children of their own (now often called second-generation baby boomers). Since then, births have again trended downward. Fewer than 1.1 million babies were born in 2008, 60 percent less than the total annual number of births recorded during the baby-boom period in the late 1940s.

Figure 3.1 Trends in the Number of Births and TFR in Japan, 1947–2008

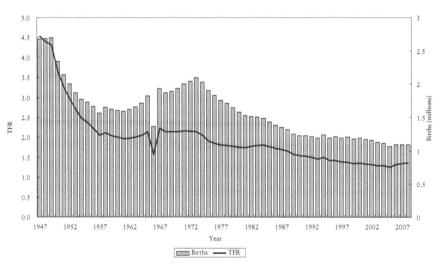

Source: Ministry of Health, Labor and Welfare, various years, a.
Note: TFR = total fertility rate.

Japan's recent low TFR has attracted a great deal of attention both domestically and internationally (Retherford and Ogawa 2006; Ogawa, Retherford, and Matsukura 2009). In contrast, a rather limited amount of attention has been paid to the unprecedented rapidity with which its mortality transition has been under way. Age-specific mortality rates have declined considerably over the past several decades. Between 1947 and 1965, Japan's life expectancy at birth rose from 50.1 to 67.7 years for men and from 54.0 to 72.9 years for women. When it joined the Organisation for Economic Co-operation and Development in April 1964, Japan's life expectancy for both men and women was the lowest among the member countries (Mason and Ogawa 2001). By the mid-1970s, however, it was among the highest. In 2007 male life expectancy at birth reached 79.2 years to become the third highest in the world, following Iceland (79.4 years) and Hong Kong (79.3 years). Female life expectancy rose to 86 years, the highest in the world, followed by Hong Kong (85.4 years) and France (84.1 years). Moreover, between the early 1950s and 2007, life expectancy at age 65 grew substantially—from 11.4 to 18.6 years for men and from 13.4 to 23.6 years for women—which implies a marked increase in the length of the average retirement period. Now husbands and wives are more likely to grow old together.

Primarily because of such long-term improvements in life expectancy, the number of centenarians has been increasing at an annual rate of 13 percent over the past four decades, making them the fastest-growing segment of the entire Japanese population. In addition, as shown in figure 3.2, the average age of the one hundred oldest deaths in a year rose at a surprising pace over the period 1950–2007. This has been particularly true since the early 1970s, when Japan's social security benefits increased markedly. Similarly, the modal age of death changed dramatically, as depicted in figure 3.3, jumping from 0 to 79 years in 1958 in the case of women, and from 0 to 75 years in 1960 in the case of men. In 2007 it was 91 years for women and 87 for men, both of which are the highest in the world. As a result of these long-term changes in the mortality pattern over the past few decades, outstanding annuity and medical insurance policies (rather than life insurance contracts) constituted more than half of the products sold by Japanese life insurance companies in 2008 for the first time in Japanese history.

Due to these transformations in fertility and mortality, the age structure of the Japanese population has also shifted markedly, as indicated in table 3.1. The proportion of those aged 65 and over increased from 4.9 percent in 1950 to 20.2 percent in 2005, making Japan's national population the oldest in the world in 2005. (In 2008 the corresponding figure was 22.1 percent.) The proportion of the so-called oldest-old persons (aged 75 and over) in the total population jumped from 1.3 percent in 1950 to more than 10.4 percent in 2008. It should be stressed that these oldest-old people are very likely to become bedridden and/or to suffer from senile dementia. The provision of medical care for this group will be a difficult social issue in the years to come.

45

Figure 3.2 Average Age of the Hundred Oldest Deaths in Japan, 1950–2007

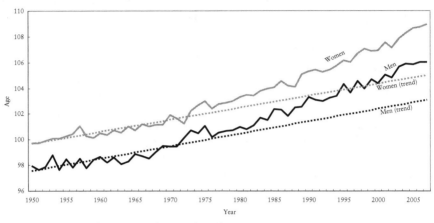

Source: Ministry of Health, Labor and Welfare, various years, a.

Figure 3.3 Modal Age of Death in Japan, 1947–2007

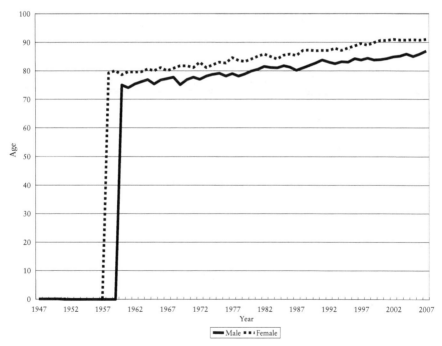

Source: Human Mortality Database.

In contrast to the rapidly growing elderly population, the under-15 population has been declining for twenty-eight consecutive years, and Japan now has fewer children than at any time since 1908. Furthermore, the overall size of Japan's population began declining at the end of 2005. More importantly, as displayed in table 3.1, these demographic trends of low fertility and population decline are expected to persist over the period 2005–2025.

Economic Growth Performance: From the "Golden 1960s" to the "Lost Decade"

At the close of World War II, the Japanese economy was in shambles. In 1950 Japan's per capita gross national product (GNP) was only $153, lower than that of Mexico ($181) and the Philippines ($172). By the end of the 1950s, however, Japan's real per capita income had recovered to its prewar level.

During the "golden 1960s," Japan's real gross domestic product (GDP) grew at a phenomenal rate of about 11 percent per year. This extraordinary economic growth was facilitated by such factors as the use of abundant labor (equivalent to the first demographic dividend, to be discussed later), the borrowing of advanced technology from developed countries, and favorable conditions in international trade markets (Ogawa, Jones, and Williamson 1993). However, the oil crisis of 1973 triggered a series of restructuring changes in the Japanese economy and lowered its growth performance significantly.

In the mid-1980s Japan entered the bubble-economy phase, an investment boom that lasted until the first half of 1990, when the bubble burst, causing a number of leading banks and other financial institutions to go into bankruptcy. Tragically, the macroeconomic policies implemented by the Japanese government to remedy the situation were inadequate and misguided. Although many of the economic problems stemmed from globalization, the Japanese government regarded them as part of the business cycle and therefore increased government spending in the hope of boosting the economy. But little came of these efforts. It took the government several years to realize that more drastic economic restructuring policies were needed to make the Japanese economy more competitive in the international markets. Government debt accumulated at an unprecedented rate, reaching $8.5 trillion—or approximately 1.5 times the country's GDP—in 2009. Japan's current debt is, in comparison, by far the worst among all the industrialized nations. Because of such delayed policy responses, some economists call the 1990s Japan's "lost decade" (Yoshikawa 2001). Indeed, since the beginning of that decade, Japan's international competitiveness has deteriorated quickly: in the early 1990s the Japanese economy was ranked first in terms of international competitiveness, but by 2009 it had dropped to seventeenth out of fifty-seven developed countries (International Institute for Management Development, IMD, various years).

Table 3.1 Population Change in Japan, 1950–2025

Year	Total population (1,000 persons)	0–14 (%)	65+ (%)	75+ (%)	Total fertility rate	Total dependency ratio	75+/ 65+ (%)	Women 40–59/ 65–84
1950	83,200	35.4	4.9	1.3	3.65	67.5	25.7	1.82
1955	89,276	33.4	5.3	1.6	2.37	63.1	29.2	1.81
1960	93,419	33.0	5.7	1.7	2.00	60.4	30.4	1.80
1965	98,275	25.6	6.3	1.9	2.14	46.8	30.3	1.77
1970	103,720	23.9	7.1	2.1	2.13	44.9	30.2	1.69
1975	111,940	24.3	7.9	2.5	1.91	47.6	32.0	1.60
1980	117,060	23.5	9.1	3.1	1.75	48.4	34.4	1.48
1985	121,049	21.5	10.3	3.9	1.76	46.7	37.8	1.40
1990	123,611	18.2	12.1	4.8	1.54	43.5	40.1	1.30
1995	125,570	16.0	14.6	5.7	1.42	50.4	39.3	1.10
2000	126,926	14.6	17.4	7.1	1.36	46.9	40.9	0.91
2005	127,449	13.8	20.2	9.1	1.25	50.6	45.1	0.77
2010	127,013	13.0	23.0	11.1	1.24	55.6	48.0	0.65
2015	125,603	12.1	26.9	13.1	1.24	63.2	48.4	0.59
2020	123,235	11.0	29.5	15.3	1.24	67.6	52.1	0.57
2025	120,094	10.2	31.0	18.5	1.28	70.0	60.0	0.56

Source: Statistics Bureau, Ministry of Internal Affairs and Communication, various years.

In spite of such major changes in the economy, Japan's mandatory retirement policies remain among the most extreme of any industrialized nation. The proportion of firms with mandatory retirement rules increased from 69 percent in 1968 to 91 percent in 1991 and has been oscillating somewhere between 90 and 95 percent since the early 1990s. One of the principal obstacles to changing the mandatory retirement age, which is presently 60 in most cases, is the seniority wage system, under which the postponement of the retirement age leads to larger wage bills (Clark and Ogawa 1992; Clark, Ogawa, and Matsukura 2007). Nonetheless, changes in national retirement policies are likely, and the Japanese government is now attempting to encourage firms to increase the mandatory retirement age to 65. In fact, a 2004 law already requires firms to increase the age of mandatory retirement to 65 years, but it does not stipulate any penalties for noncompliance, which is why, to date, only a few companies have heeded it (Clark et al. 2009).

The other deterrent to extending the retirement age beyond 60 relates to the provision of lump-sum severance benefits, which are determined by the duration of an employee's service. In 2008 an employee with a university education and more than 35 years of service received a severance payment equivalent to 44 months' worth of his or her final monthly salary. More importantly, this lump-sum severance-pay program has recently been drawing much attention from various financial institutions because the baby-boom generations are now reaching retirement age and accumulating large financial resources that could be used for investment.

Another feature of Japan's labor market is its high labor-force participation rate among the elderly (Ogawa, Lee, and Matsukura 2005). In 2007 the labor-force participation rate for elderly Japanese men was close to 30 percent. In sharp contrast, the corresponding figure for several developed countries in Europe (France, Germany, and Austria) was well below 10 percent; it is slightly higher than 20 percent for the United States. Likewise, Japanese elderly women work longer than their counterparts in Europe and the United States.

Age Structure Transformations and the First Demographic Dividend

Postwar demographic trends in Japan have been closely tied to changes in economic growth performance (Ogawa, Kondo, and Matsukura 2005; Ogawa 2005; Ogawa and Matsukura 2007), with demographic dividends playing a key role in the process of economic development (see Mason 2001, 2007; Mason and Lee 2006). Figure 3.4 shows estimates of age-specific profiles of per capita consumption, private and public sectors combined, and per capita production (labor income) in five selected years, namely 1984, 1989, 1994, 1999, and 2004. These profiles have been estimated by drawing on private-sector information derived from the five rounds of the National Survey of Family Income and Expenditure (NSFIE), conducted during the period 1984–2004 by the Statistics Bureau of Japan, and from public-sector information gleaned from a variety of government-published data sources. Both age-specific profiles have been adjusted by using data from the National Income Product Account (NIPA). These estimated results are expressed in terms of 2000 constant prices.

There are a few points worth noting in figure 3.4. First, the age at which an average individual shifts from being a net consumer to being a net producer gradually rose from 23 in 1984, to 24 in 1989, to 25 in 1994, and to 26 in 2004. Moreover, at the other end of the life cycle, the transition from net producer to net consumer was, due to Japan's mandatory retirement age of 60, postponed only marginally from the age of 58 in 1984 to 60 in 1994—a value that, after a brief drop in 1999, still held true in 2004.

Second, the estimated age-specific profiles of per capita production increased from 1984 to 1994 but remained static over the period 1994–2004. These movements seem to reflect Japan's bubble-economy phase and lost decade, respectively (Yoshikawa 2001).

Third, the age-specific profiles of per capita consumption rose almost continuously over the period, especially at the younger and older ends of the spectrum. Per capita consumption among those aged 65 and over showed a particularly sharp increase in 2004, thanks to the implementation in 2000 of long-term care insurance (LTCI), which brought in-home care for the frail elderly—previously provided by family members on an informal basis—into the market economy. As a result, Japan's per capita consumption profiles have been increasingly similar to those for the United States and Sweden among the NTA member countries.

When a country's fertility rate begins to fall, the first demographic dividend arises due to the increase in the number of working-age persons relative to those in the non-working-age groups. To help measure the effect of such changes on overall economic growth performance in Japan over the period 1984–2004, we have averaged the five sets of age-specific per capita consumption and production profiles observed over the twenty-year period, as depicted in figure 3.5. By applying the computed age-specific results displayed in this graph as statistical weights to adjust the entire population over the period 1932–2025, we have calculated the effective number of producers, the effective number of consumers, and the economic support ratio (the effective number of producers divided by the effective number of consumers). The change in the economic support ratio represents the change in output per effective consumer due solely to changes in age structure over the period 1932–2025, as indicated in figure 3.6.

As can be seen from this graph, the support ratio grew continuously from 1948 to 1983, thus generating the first demographic dividend. The plotted result in figure 3.6 also indicates that the growth of the support ratio was noticeably fast during the golden 1960s. This finding supports the view that the unprecedented fertility reduction subsequent to the baby boom (1947–1949) played a crucial role in boosting the growth of per capita income at a remarkable rate during this period of high economic growth.

As has been the case with other developed countries, Japan's first demographic dividend was inherently transitory in nature, lasting only a few decades. After reaching its peak value in 1983, the support ratio leveled off for

Figure 3.4 Age-specific Profiles of Per Capita Consumption and Production in Japan, 1984–2004

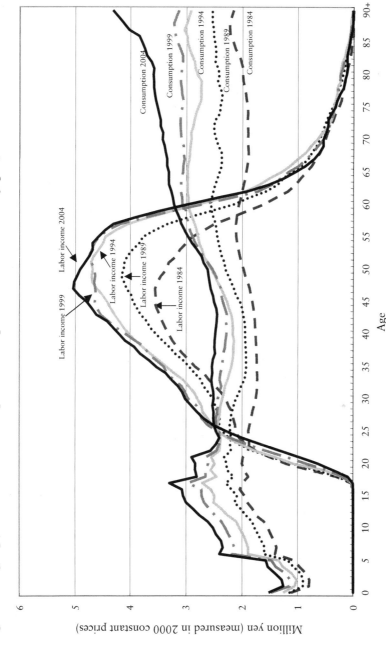

Source: Authors' review of related policy documents.

slightly more than ten years. Since 1996 the economic support ratio has been declining, and the first demographic dividend has turned decidedly negative. This change is a direct consequence of population aging.

Rapidly Growing Public Transfers and Diminishing Familial Support

Owing to the extraordinary economic recovery that started in the late 1950s, lasted throughout the 1960s, and was partly induced by the first demographic dividend, Japan managed to establish its universal pension and medical care schemes in 1961. Since then, Japan's social security system has grown remarkably. Between 1961 and 2006, social security benefits increased from 5 to 24 percent of the national income (National Institute of Population and Social Security Research, NIPSSR, 2008). Moreover, the proportion of the social security expenditure allotted to the elderly population increased from 25 percent in 1973 to 70 percent in 2006. Contributions to social security increased somewhat less than benefits, with the growing difference between benefits and contributions covered by general tax revenues.

Figure 3.5 Average Age-specific Profiles of Per Capita Consumption and Labor Income, 1984–2004

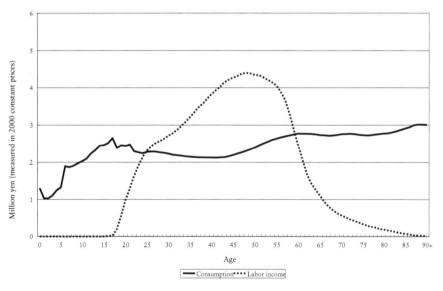

Source: Authors' review of related policy documents.

Figure 3.6 First Demographic Dividend and Population Aging in Japan, 1932–2025

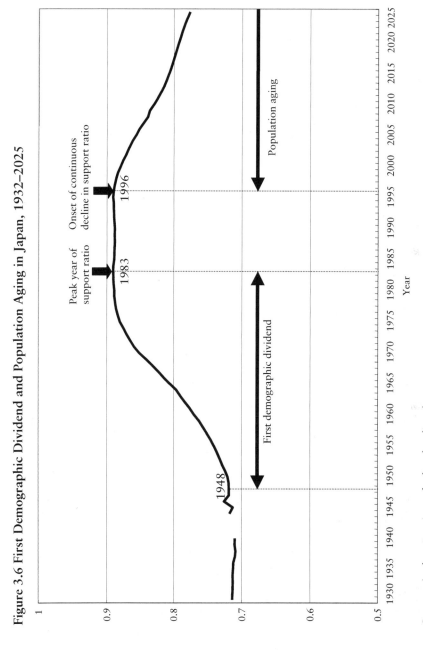

Source: Authors' review of related policy documents.

Japan's pension schemes were initially operated on the basis of a reserve-financing plan, with a large amount of reserve funds accumulated to cover the payment of old-age benefits for future retirees. The financing method was gradually shifted toward a pay-as-you-go system, however, making Japan's public pension schemes increasingly of the transfer nature. Consequently, as the proportion of the elderly population has increased over the past decade or so, the growth rate of the accumulated reserve funds has slowed down considerably.

The financial status of Japan's pension schemes has been periodically assessed, and amendments have been made accordingly. Over the twenty-year period under review, two drastic pension reforms were carried out, one in 1985 and the other in 2004. In the 1985 reform, the concept of a basic pension was introduced as a base for integrating the fragmented, occupation-specific pension schemes (Ogawa 2005). In the 2004 reform, the schedule of future contributions was fixed, with a view to restoring the younger generation's trust in government pension schemes, a move that may be regarded as a paradigm shift in Japan's social security provisions (Sakamoto 2005).

Medical insurance plans are another important component of the Japanese social security system. While the availability or lack of government finances has prompted periodic amendments to the plans over the past few decades, the absolute amount of financial resources allotted to medical care services is continuously rising. To curb the upward spiral of medical care costs, the government of Japan implemented the LTCI in 2000, with a view to reducing the length of hospitalization stays by facilitating in-home care. The LTCI is expected to reduce the caregiving burden on family members, many of whom are middle-aged women (Ogawa and Retherford 1997).

Unlike developed countries in the West, extended living arrangements are still fairly common in Japan (Ogawa and Ermisch 1996; Ogawa, Retherford, and Matsukura 2006). According to an international survey of lifestyles and attitudes of the elderly, 21 percent of Japanese people aged 65 and older lived in three generation households in 2005 (Cabinet Office, various years, a). By contrast, the corresponding figure was only 3 percent in the United States and 1 percent in Germany and France. It should be stressed, however, that due to rapid demographic shifts as well as changing lifestyles, the figure for Japan has been steadily declining over the past two decades and that the 2005 value is half of the 41 percent recorded in 1981. Similarly, data gathered by the Ministry of Health, Labor and Welfare (various years, a) show that the proportion of persons aged 65 and older who resided with their adult children declined from 69 percent in 1980 to 45 percent in 2005.

The income sources of elderly persons aged 65 and over have changed substantially in recent decades, as revealed in table 3.2 (Cabinet Office, various years, b). Not only has the proportion receiving financial support from their children decreased sharply, from 35 percent in 1981 to 11 percent in 2005, but the proportion receiving public pension benefits increased by a similar margin, from 74 to 95 percent, during the same time period. The proportion of the elderly relying on their own savings also increased, from 11 to 25 percent, between 1981 and 2005. These changes in the sources of income for the elderly are closely connected with the remarkable improvement of old-age pension benefits and considerable economic growth over the period under study.

Table 3.2 Income Sources of Those Aged 65 and Older in Japan: 1981, 1986, 1990, 1996, 2001, and 2005

	1981	1986	1990	1996	2001	2005
Work	30.3	25.9	24.4	24.0	24.1	20.6
Public pensions	73.6	84.6	89.6	92.9	92.7	95.3
Private pensions	9.0	5.3	7.3	7.2	10.6	7.2
Savings	10.8	16.7	24.7	23.0	22.0	25.2
Assets	16.2	15.4	14.6	11.3	8.6	7.5
Children	35.2	26.3	23.5	18.5	13.9	11.4
Public assistance	2.1	1.9	1.6	0.7	0.9	0.3
Other	4.3	3.3	2.6	3.0	2.6	2.4
No answer	1.0	0.3	1.7	0.2	0.1	0.0

Source: Cabinet Office, various years, a.

The time-series data of the National Survey on Family Planning (NSFP) undertaken by the Mainichi Newspapers in the late 1980s showed that Japanese women of reproductive age (younger than 50) began to reconsider taking care of their aging parents (Hodge and Ogawa 1991). The following question has been included in each round of this nationwide survey since 1966: "What is your opinion about children caring for their elderly parents?" The precoded response categories are: (1) "good custom," (2) "natural duty as children," (3) "unavoidable due to inadequacy of public support resources," and (4) "not a good custom." The proportion of those who chose one of the first two response categories ("good custom" and "natural duty as children") was stable over the period 1963–1986, but a sudden decline occurred between 1986 and 1988 when the Japanese government began to shift the costs of caring for the elderly back to families. The downward trend continued until recently, when the proportion of married women of reproductive age who chose one of the first two response categories (and thus signaled their agreement with this traditional Confucian value) rose, from 46 percent in 2004 to 52 percent in 2007.

Time-series data gathered by the government (Cabinet Office, various years, a and b) also reveal that the long-term trend of rejecting traditional family values has been reversed in recent years. For instance, when persons aged 20 and older were confronted with the question "Work outside home is for the husband, and work at home is for the wife. What do you think of this view?" 85 percent of men and 84 percent of women reacted positively in 1972, compared with 51 percent of men and 40 percent of women in 2007. But within this overall downward trend there was a small reversal: the proportion of men in their twenties who agreed to the view above declined from 78 percent in 1972 to 41 percent in 2004 but increased to 43 percent in 2007. Similarly, the proportion of women aged 20–29 who supported this view dropped from 79 percent in 1972 to 33 percent in 2002 but rose to 35 percent in 2004 and to 40 percent in 2007. Although a careful multivariate analysis is necessary to gain more insight into these data, we may speculate that the reverse trends correlate closely to rapid changes in the labor market that have not been favorable to young workers and middle-aged women of reproductive age (Clark et al. 2009).

The Changing Pattern of Public and Familial Transfers in Japan

The demographic and socioeconomic transformations in postwar Japan described above have affected the pattern and mode of intergenerational transfers. To gain further insight into these changes, we use the NTA approach. The NTA measure the intergenerational flows for a certain period of time (usually a calendar or fiscal year), and as explained in detail elsewhere (Ogawa, Retherford, and Matsukura 2009), the following expression holds in the NTA framework:

$$\underbrace{C(x) - Y^l(x)}_{\text{Lifecycle deficit}} = \underbrace{\underbrace{\tau^+(x) - \tau^-(x)}_{\text{Net transfers}} + \underbrace{Y^A(x) - S(x)}_{\text{Asset-based reallocations}}}_{\text{Age reallocations}}$$

where Y^l = labor income, Y^A = asset income, τ^+ = transfer received, C = consumption, S = saving, and τ = transfer given. This expression holds for each age (x) as well as for the whole economy. The age reallocations can be further disaggregated into public-sector and private-sector age reallocations. That is,

$$C(x) - Y^l(x) = [\tau_g^+(x) - \tau_g^-(x)] + [\tau_f^+(x) - \tau_f^-(x)] + [Y^{Ag}(x) - S_g(x)] + [Y^{Af}(x) - S_f(x)]$$

where subscripts g and f refer to "public" and "private" age reallocations, respectively.

Before we proceed to the discussion of the results, we must note three caveats about our computations. First, both "familial transfers" and "private transfers" are used interchangeably in this chapter; both terms refer to transfers coming from other family members of the same or different households. Second, although net private transfers are comprised of bequests and *inter vivos* transfers, the computation of the bequest component has not been completed at the time of this writing. For this reason, the bequests are excluded from the computational results reported here. Finally, the estimated values for the totals are adjusted on the basis of the NIPA values, thus ensuring consistency with the NIPA.

Figure 3.7 charts the reallocation of the per capita life-cycle deficits in Japan over the 1984–2004 period. The three components of reallocation include net reallocations through assets, net public transfers, and net private transfers; these are measured in 2000 constant prices on a per capita and annual basis. Panels A, B, and C illustrate the annual reallocation of the per capita life-cycle deficits observed in 1984, 1994, and 2004, respectively.

A brief comparison of the three panels reveals two points of interest. First, the composition of per capita net transfers to the elderly population changed dramatically over the twenty-year period, with the amount of per capita net public transfers to the elderly increasing significantly. Similarly, the amount of per capita net asset-based reallocations grew considerably over this time. In contrast, the relative importance of per capita net familial transfers from the young to the elderly declined to an appreciable extent. These results seem to indicate that the Japanese elderly increasingly depend on public transfers (predominantly old-age pensions and medical care services) and asset-based reallocations to support their retirement life.

Second and more important, as marked by two circles in figure 3.7 (one in panel B and the other in panel C), the amount of per capita net familial transfers to people in their 60s and early 70s was negative in both 1994 and 2004. This implies that relatively young elderly persons provide more financial assistance to their adult children and/or grandchildren than they receive from the same. It is also worth noting that the amount of such negative per capita net familial transfers from the relatively young elderly to other age groups grew during the period of Japan's lost decade.

To shed further light on the changing pattern of per capita net familial transfers over time, we computed the age at which an average individual shifted from being a net producer to being a net consumer during the 1984–2004 period. Our calculated results show that the crossing age rose from 64 in 1984 to 70 in 1994, 74 in 1999, and, finally, to 77 in 2004.

The foregoing discussions are based on the per capita life-cycle deficits in Japan during 1984–2004. Figure 3.8 illustrates the magnitude of the impact that structural changes in age had on the aggregate-level life-cycle deficits in Japan over time. The result in panel A of figure 3.8 was obtained by applying the 2004 per capita age profile of life-cycle deficits to the corresponding age groups of the population observed in 1985. In panel B, we applied the same 2004 per capita age profile of life-cycle deficits to the projected population for 2025. A cursory comparison of panels A and B clearly shows that Japan's structural shifts in age have had and will continue to have a great impact over the period 1985–2025.

Figure 3.7 Three Components of Per Capita Reallocation of Life-cycle Deficits in Japan (1984, 1994, and 2004)

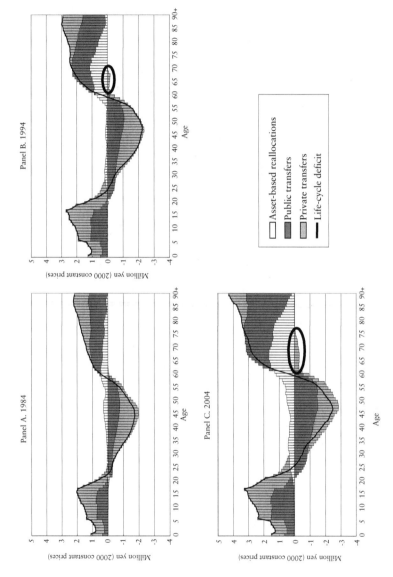

Source: Authors' review of related policy documents.

Figure 3.8 Life-cycle Deficits in Japan: 1985 and 2025 (Per Capita Age Profile for the Year 2004 Applied)

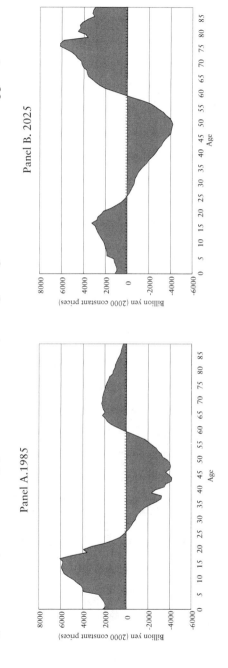

Source: Authors' review of related policy documents.

Conclusion

Drawing heavily on the NTA approach, we have reviewed select evidence of the fertility decline and age compositional shifts of the Japanese population. We have also examined the extent to which the rapid aging of Japan's population affected the pattern of intergenerational transfers over the period 1984–2004, in both per capita and aggregate terms. The age profiles of both public and private transfers, coupled with asset reallocations, changed to a considerable extent over the period in question. In particular, the age at which an average individual shifted from being a net giver of intrafamilial assistance to being a new receiver changed dramatically between 1984 and 2004, increasing from 64 years in 1984 to 70 in 1994 to 77 in 2004. In addition, during Japan's lost decade, the elderly played a crucial role in providing financial assistance to their adult offspring and grandchildren through intrafamilial transfers. These results suggest that, despite the decline in multigenerational coresidence in Japan, the Japanese elderly are still playing a vital role in providing financial support for their offspring when the latter encounter economic difficulties. Although older persons in Japan are often considered liabilities for the country, they are actually playing a key role as an economic safety net. For this reason, they should be considered latent assets in contemporary Japanese society.

References

Cabinet Office. Various years, a. *Brief Summary of the International Survey of Lifestyles and Attitudes of the Elderly*. Tokyo: Gyosei.

———. Various years, b. *Report on the National Survey on Gender-equality Society*. Tokyo: Gyosei.

Clark, R. L., and N. Ogawa. 1992. "The Effects of Mandatory Retirement on Earnings Profiles in Japan." *Industrial and Labor Relations Review* 45 (2): 258–66.

Clark, R. L., N. Ogawa, and R. Matsukura. 2007. "Population Aging, Changing Retirement Policies and Lifetime Earnings Profiles in Japan." In *Population Aging, Intergenerational Transfers and the Macroeconomy*, edited by R. Clark, N. Ogawa, and A. Mason, 17–37. Cheltenham: Edward Elgar Publishing.

Clark, R. L., N. Ogawa, M. Kondo, and R. Matsukura. 2009. "Population Decline, Labor Force Stability, and the Future of the Japanese Economy." *European Journal of Population*, special issue, 26 (2): 207–27.

Hodge, R., and N. Ogawa. 1991. *Fertility Change in Contemporary Japan*. Chicago: University of Chicago Press.

Human Mortality Database. University of California, Berkeley, and Max Plank Institute for Demographic Change. www.mortality.org and www.humanmortality.de.

IMD (International Institute for Management Development). Various years. *IMD World Competitiveness Yearbook*. Lausanne: IMD.

Mason, A., ed. 2001. *Population Change and Economic Development in East Asia: Challenges Met, and Opportunities Seized*. Stanford, CA: Stanford University Press.

———. 2007. "Demographic Transition and Demographic Dividends in Developed and Developing Countries." In *United Nations Expert Group Meeting on Social and*

Economic Implications of Changing Population Age Structure, 81–102. New York: United Nations.

Mason, A., and N. Ogawa. 2001. "Population, Labor Force, Saving and Japan's Future." In *Japan's New Economy: Continuity and Change in the Twenty-first Century*, edited by M. Blomstrom, B. Gangnes, and S. La Croix, 48–74. Oxford: Oxford University Press.

Mason, A., and R. Lee. 2006. "Reform and Support Systems for the Elderly in Developing Countries: Capturing the Second Demographic Dividend." *GENUS* 62 (2): 11–35.

Ministry of Health, Labor and Welfare. Various years, a. *Vital Statistics*. Tokyo: Health and Welfare Statistics Association.

———. Various years, b. *Comprehensive Survey of Living Condition of the People on Health and Welfare*. Tokyo: Health and Welfare Statistics Association.

National Institute of Population and Social Security Research. 2008. *Social Security Benefits for Fiscal Year 2006*. www.ipss.go.jp.

Ogawa, N. 2005. "Population Aging and Policy Options for a Sustainable Future: The Case of Japan." *GENUS* 61 (3–4): 369–410.

Ogawa, N., and J. F. Ermisch. 1996. "Family Structure, Home Time Demands, and the Employment Patterns of Japanese Married Women." *Journal of Labor Economics* 14 (4): 677–702.

Ogawa, N., and R. Matsukura. 2007. "Ageing in Japan: The Health and Wealth of Older Persons." In *United Nations Expert Group Meeting on Social and Economic Implications of Changing Population Age Structures*, 199–220. New York: United Nations.

Ogawa, N., and R. D. Retherford. 1993. "The Resumption of Fertility Decline in Japan: 1973–92." *Population and Development Review* 19 (4): 703–41.

———. 1997. "Shifting Costs of Caring for the Elderly Back to Families in Japan." *Population and Development Review* 23 (1): 59–94.

Ogawa, N., G. Jones, and J. G. Williamson, eds. 1993. *Human Resources in Development along the Asia-Pacific Rim*. Singapore: Oxford University Press.

Ogawa, N., M. Kondo, and R. Matsukura. 2005. "Japan's Transition from the Demographic Bonus to the Demographic Onus." *Asian Population Studies* 1 (2): 207–26.

Ogawa, N., S-H. Lee, and R. Matsukura. 2005. "Health and its Impact on Work and Dependency among the Elderly in Japan." *Asian Population Studies* 1 (1): 121–45.

Ogawa, N., R. D. Retherford, and R. Matsukura. 2006. "Demographics of the Japanese Family: Entering Uncharted Territory." In *The Changing Japanese Family*, edited by M. Rebick and A. Takenaka, 19–38. Abingdon, Oxon: Routledge.

———. 2009. "Japan's Declining Fertility and Policy Responses." In *Ultra-low Fertility in Pacific Asia: Trends, Causes, and Policy Issues*, edited by G. Jones, P. T. Straughan, and A. Chan, 40–72. Abingdon, Oxon: Routledge.

Ogawa, N., A. Mason, A. Chawla, and R. Matsukura. 2010. "Japan's Unprecedented Aging and Changing Intergenerational Transfers." In *The Economic Consequences of Demographic Change in East Asia*, edited by T. Ito and A. Rose, vol. 19, *National Bureau of Economic Research–East Asia Seminar of Economics*. Chicago: University of Chicago Press.

Retherford, R. D., and N. Ogawa. 2006. "Japan's Baby Bust: Causes, Implications, and Policy Responses." In *The Baby Bust: Who Will Do the Work? Who Will Pay the Taxes?* edited by F. R. Harris, 5–47. Lanham, MD: Rowman & Littlefield Publishers, Inc.

Sakamoto, Junichi. 2005. "Population Challenges and Social Security—The Case of Japan." Paper presented at the Forum on Population and Development in East Asia, Beijing, May 16–17.

Statistics Bureau, Ministry of Internal Affairs and Communications. Various years. *Population Census of Japan*. Tokyo: Japan Statistical Association.

Yoshikawa, Hiroshi. 2001. *Japan's Lost Decade*. Tokyo: International House of Japan.

GENDER, MIGRATION, AND THE WELL-BEING OF THE ELDERLY IN RURAL CHINA

Shuzhuo Li, Marcus W. Feldman, Xiaoyi Jin, and Dongmei Zuo[1]

Chinese society has been evolving from a traditional agricultural society to an industrial society since 1979, when China adopted its reform and opening-up policies. Almost simultaneously, the Chinese government implemented its family planning policy, which has resulted in a sharp decline in the country's overall fertility rate. This decline, together with a drop in the mortality rate, has exacerbated the aging of the population.

Starting in the mid-1980s, large numbers of middle-aged and younger laborers migrated from rural to urban areas. As a result, the rural population is expected to age much faster than the urban population (Zeng 2005). Currently, a reliable social security system does not exist in rural China, and the majority of the rural elderly are still almost entirely supported by their adult children (Shi 1993). Unfortunately, the outflow of labor from rural to urban areas has separated many parents from their adult children, undermining the household's function in supporting the elderly. Given the absence of general social security and community service systems in rural China, the outflow of labor may therefore have a major effect on family-based old-age support systems in the countryside.

This chapter seeks to analyze the effects of labor outflow on the well-being of the elderly, which is defined here in terms of health and the status of intergenerational support. Because there are distinct gender differences in intergenerational relationships in China's rural households, we also address the impact of gender on elderly well-being. We have selected typical inflow and outflow regions of the rural population as target survey areas. According to *China Labor Statistics 1999*, the rural population emigrating from Anhui Province accounted for 11 percent of China's total floating population, and this

[1] This study is jointly supported by a National Institutes of Health (NIH) grant (1 R03 TW01060-01A1); Programs for Changjiang Scholars; the Changjiang Scholars and Innovative Research Team (IRT0855) in Universities, through the Ministry of Education of China; the China Natural Science Foundation (70803039); a seed grant (AG017253-06) from the Center for Demography and Economics of Health and Aging (CDEHA) at Stanford University; and the Santa Fe Institute International Program.

percentage ranked third among all provinces. The rural population migrating into Guangdong Province accounted for 31 percent of the total floating population, and this percentage ranked first among all provinces (Zhang and Song 2003). As a result, we have chosen to survey, respectively, the rural area of Chaohu in Anhui Province as the outflow region, and Shenzhen—a metropolis in Guandong Province—as the inflow region.

The longitudinal survey "The Well-Being of the Elderly," supported by the National Institutes of Health (NIH) in cooperation with the University of Southern California, targeted the elderly aged 60 and above living in the rural regions of Chaohu. The survey used sampling at two levels—township and village—and consisted of a baseline survey and two longitudinal surveys conducted in 2001, 2003, and 2006, respectively. The numbers of valid samples for the three surveys are 1,715; 1,391; and 1,067, respectively. The questionnaire mainly covered basic characteristics such as social and economic status, physical and psychological health conditions of the elderly, the condition of all their living children, and intergenerational support. The "Shenzhen Rural-Urban Migrants Survey," supported by the Center for Demography and Economics of Health and Aging (CDEHA) at Stanford University and the Santa Fe Institute's International Program, targeted the inflow rural population aged 15 and above. It was conducted in April 2005 and produced 1,739 valid samples. In addition to recording the migrant workers' basic information, marital and childbearing status, and social networks, the survey collected other information related to old-age support, including age, living arrangements, source of livelihood, working ability, intergenerational support, and attitudes of migrant workers and their parents and parents-in-law.

Family Old-age Support in Rural China

Support from children has always been the primary form of assistance for the elderly in rural China. By altering children's income and family structure, the outflow of labor has disrupted the balance of supply and demand for intergenerational support among family members and has greatly affected intergenerational relationships.

Intergenerational Support Based on the Needs of the Elderly

Despite extensive labor outflow, support of the elderly is still the prime mode of intergenerational support, due to the influence of traditional filial culture. Intergenerational support is dominated by the upstream flow (from children to parents): children's support for their parents is more financial than instrumental, whereas elderly parents' support for their children is more instrumental than financial (Song, Li, and Zhang 2006). However, most of the elderly in the countryside have received both financial and instrumental support from their children or grandchildren and have provided less support to their children than they have received.

The elderly and their children also have a high level of emotional exchange (Song, Li, and Zhang 2006). In households with multiple children, the siblings often play complementary roles to meet the varied needs of their parents. In some households, for example, the elderly receive financial support from children working away from home and instrumental support from children who have stayed in the natal area. Generally speaking, the elderly with poor social, economic, and health status receive financial and instrumental support from their children (Zhang and Li 2004), whereas those with better status tend to provide their children with such support. As the elderly population ages and confronts more health problems, however, their needs will increasingly dominate intergenerational support at all social and economic levels (Song 2008).

Intergenerational Reciprocal Exchange

The elderly regard the development of their children as part of their responsibility and therefore do their best to support them. Consequently, there is some reciprocal intergenerational exchange between the elderly and their children (Cong and Silverstein 2008). Indeed, the rising incidence of children working away from home has pushed family members to engage in more intergenerational exchange to better manage family resources.

Children who migrate for work often provide financial support to their parents in exchange for instrumental support in the form of child care, a situation that promotes emotional support between generations (Zhang and Li 2004). In addition, emigration has increased exchange among siblings. Coresidence—adult children living with parents to provide the latter with old-age care—is often regarded as the cornerstone of support for the elderly. Consequently, financial support for the elderly comes from those children who do not coreside with their parents, and whose parents, in turn, provide financial support for the children or grandchildren they do live with (Zhang and Li 2004). In this way, children living with the elderly may receive compensation from children who live elsewhere. These mutually beneficial intergenerational exchanges help to improve the elder's self-rated health status and to reduce their depression (Song, Li, and Zhang 2006; Cong and Silverstein 2008).

The Impacts of Labor Outflow on the Well-being of the Elderly in Rural China

As the rural labor force moves to cities, the population of rural China is aging rapidly, adding yet more stress to areas where social and economic conditions are fragile. Labor outflow has brought changes to the different types of intergenerational support. These changes, in turn, have affected both the physical and the psychological well-being of the elderly.

Financial Support

By working away from home, children improve their economic situation, which can increase their ability to provide financial support for their parents. Figure 4.1 shows that migrant children provide the elderly with significantly higher amounts of financial support than those who never migrate; migrant children are also more likely to increase the amount of financial support to their parents (Song and Li 2008a). For the rural elderly who have no reliable income, such financial support from their children is very important for their health and psychological well-being (Song, Li, and Zhang 2006). To some extent, financial support from migrant children has offset the negative effects of the children's working away from home (Silverstein, Cong, and Li 2006); however, some studies claim that the elderly may feel a psychological burden if they receive too much financial support (Cong and Silverstein 2008).

Figure 4.1 Intergenerational Support by Children of Different Migration Status

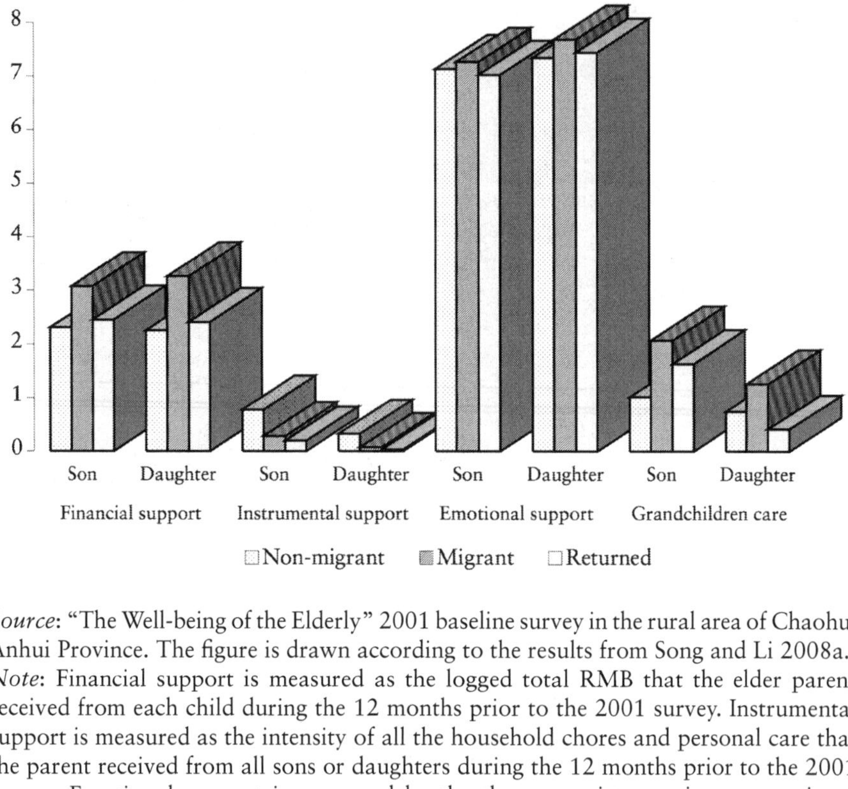

Son Daughter Son Daughter Son Daughter Son Daughter

Financial support Instrumental support Emotional support Grandchildren care

□Non-migrant ▨Migrant □Returned

Source: "The Well-being of the Elderly" 2001 baseline survey in the rural area of Chaohu, Anhui Province. The figure is drawn according to the results from Song and Li 2008a. *Note*: Financial support is measured as the logged total RMB that the elder parent received from each child during the 12 months prior to the 2001 survey. Instrumental support is measured as the intensity of all the household chores and personal care that the parent received from all sons or daughters during the 12 months prior to the 2001 survey. Emotional support is measured by the three questions on intergenerational solidarity asked in the 2001 survey. An additive scale is computed for each child, ranging from 3 to 9, with a higher score indicating a higher quality of parent-child relationship. Grandchildren care refers to the intensity of grandchildren care that the elder parents provided for each son or daughter during the 12 months prior to the 2001 survey.

Instrumental Support

Children's migration reduces the frequency of their instrumental support for the elderly. This is especially true for male children. As shown in figure 4.1, children who have never migrated provide their parents with the most instrumental support, children working away from home provide a moderate amount of support, and children who have returned home after migration provide the least instrumental support. The differences between them are statistically significant. Children's instrumental support reflects their concern for the elderly and increases the latter's psychological well-being. However, we find that only help with housework enhances the elderly's subjective quality of life, while help with their everyday life has the opposite effect, possibly because it intrudes on their privacy and makes them feel their age more acutely (Zhang and Li 2005).

Emotional Support

Migration helps children to clarify their responsibilities with respect to supporting the elderly, thereby reducing the possibility of intergenerational conflicts and conflicts among siblings. In addition, children's migration may give the elderly a sense of pride, resulting in a closer intergenerational relationship. Figure 4.1 shows that children working away from home provide the elderly with the most emotional support. This is probably because they are more willing to lend an ear to the worries and difficulties of their parents than they were prior to initial migration (Institute for Population and Development Studies 2005). Some studies, however, suggest that children's migration reduces their emotional exchange with the elderly and increases the latter's sense of loneliness because of the absence of these migrant children (Du et al. 2004).

Care for Grandchildren

Most migrant workers in cities still hold rural household registration, are subject to some restrictions on their employment, and are largely excluded from urban social security and civil services (Sun 2003). The primary aim of their working away from home is to earn money. As a result, many of them will choose to return to the countryside eventually (Liu 2004). As shown in figure 4.1, the elderly provide more care to grandchildren whose parents work away from home than to those whose parents do not migrate. Our survey of migrant workers in Shenzhen supports this pattern, indicating that most migrant workers' parents take care of children left at home (Institute for Population and Development Studies 2005). Such round-the-clock child care inevitably adds to the burden of the elderly. However, because it is regarded as a favor to their children rather than a responsibility, it results in improved status for the elderly within the family and more financial returns from the children. Consequently, the elderly in such skipped-generation households (where the elderly live with their grandchildren and the middle generation is absent) usually have a stronger sense of psychological well-being than those in other housing situations (Silverstein, Cong, and Li 2006). However, if the elderly fail to receive the economic returns

67

they expect, they are subject to more negative psychological experiences (Cong and Silverstein 2008).

How Gender-based Labor Divisions Affect the Health of the Elderly

In China's rural households, work is divided by gender. Our research shows that children's migration has defined this division even more clearly and that this division has influenced the elderly's physical and psychological well-being.

Parents' Gender Divisions and Their Effects on Elderly Well-being

Because of discrimination in education and the labor market during their prime years, female rural elderly are often worse off economically than their male counterparts (Rudkin 1993). As a result, their ability to live alone and their self-rated health are inferior (Zhang and Li 2005), and they need more family support.

Generally, elderly fathers receive more financial assistance than elderly mothers. As is shown in table 4.1, children working away from home give more financial support to their fathers than to their mothers. Elderly mothers, however, often increase the amount they receive from migrant children through strengthening intergenerational exchange, which favors mothers over fathers due to the status and function of the female in the household (Song and Li 2006). As table 4.1 shows, among elderly parents living with and taking care of grandchildren, elderly mothers receive more compensation from their children than elderly fathers.

Table 4.1 also shows that sons' migration reduces the amount of everyday care received by their elderly fathers. This is because daughters-in-law become the major providers of instrumental support after the sons' migration, and male elderly often do not want to receive everyday care from them (Huang et al. 2003). Our data show that among the elderly, more males than females are left alone when in poor health, and females are more satisfied with the help they receive (Zhang, Li, and Feldman 2005).

Generally speaking, children's migration has enabled parents to receive more economic returns, but it has also reduced the instrumental support they receive and has added to their burden with respect to the care they give grandchildren.

Children's Gender Divisions and Their Effects on Elderly Well-being

Sons provide their parents with more financial support and also receive more financial and instrumental support from their parents than do daughters (Song 2008). The outflow of labor, however, has increased the importance of daughters in old-age care.

Figure 4.1 shows that daughters working away from home give the elderly significantly more financial support than do sons. In addition, as seen in figure 4.2, daughters working away from home are more likely to increase this financial support than are sons, especially if the elderly provide care to their grandchildren (Song and Li 2008b). Sons are also less likely than daughters to increase their financial support for the elderly when they return home. According to the Chaohu

Table 4.1 Multilevel Model Estimates of the Effects on Intergenerational Support Received by the Elderly (n = 983)

	Financial Support				Instrumental Support			
	Children→ Father	Children→ Mother	Children→ Father	Children→ Mother	Father→ Children	Children→ Mother	Mother→ Children	
Migrate son: *no*								
Yes	0.277***	0.209***	−0.986*		−0.111	−0.336	−0.725*	
Migrate daughter: *no*								
Yes	0.285***	0.265***	0.322		−0.227	−0.148	−0.889**	
Grandchildren care	0.006	0.011*	0.089		0.117**	0.132*	0.208***	
Living arrangement								
• Living alone or with spouse								
• Living with children or children's spouse	0.036	0.020	1.027*		0.936**	2.418***	2.670***	
• Living with grandchildren	0.068	0.137*	−0.872+		−0.402	−0.482	−0.327	

Source: "The Well-being of the Elderly" 2001 baseline, 2003, and 2006 follow-up surveys in the rural area of Chaohu, Anhui Province. The table is based on the results from Song 2008.

Notes: (1) The measurement of financial and instrumental support is the same as in figure 4.1. The working sample is the 983 elderly parents who participated in all three-wave surveys in 2001, 2003, and 2006. The 3-level growth curve models are built in this study to explore gender, migration status, and other factors affecting the amount of intergenerational support in each survey. (2) *** p < 0.001; ** p < 0.01; * p < 0.05; + p < 0.1.

survey, then, migration has offset the effects of gender division in terms of children's financial support for their parents. However, the Shenzhen survey shows that both male and female migrant workers increase financial support for their parents to the same extent (Institute for Population and Development Studies 2005).

Figure 4.2 Random-effect Logistic Analysis of the Effects of Migration on the Division of Intergenerational Support, by Gender

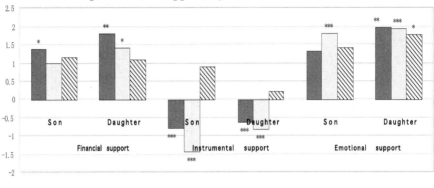

■Migrate for work ■Migrate for other reasons ▨Returned

Source: "The Well-being of the Elderly" 2001 baseline and 2003 follow-up survey in rural Chaohu, Anhui Province. The figure is drawn according to the results from Song and Li 2008.
Notes: (1) The measurement of intergenerational support is the same as in figure 4.1. In this analysis, the logistic mixed models with random effect are used to estimate the effects of the migration status of children on the likelihood of intergenerational support increase in the 2003 follow-up survey compared with the 2001 baseline survey. The random effect is introduced to eliminate the cluster effect of the children of a same elderly parent. (2) *** $p < 0.001$; ** $p < 0.01$; * $p < 0.05$; + $p < 0.1$

Figure 4.2 indicates that migration has reduced both sons' and daughters' ability to provide instrumental support to the elderly. Furthermore, sons have reduced their instrumental support by a larger amount than daughters, but the difference is shrinking (Song and Li 2008a). In addition, daughters are always more likely than sons to provide emotional support to parents, and migration tends to widen this difference (as shown in figure 4.2, migration has made daughters more likely to increase the amount of emotional support they give to their parents).

Sons' or their spouses' instrumental support has a significant positive effect on the elderly's life satisfaction (Zhang and Li 2005). Therefore, by reducing children's—especially sons'—provision of instrumental support, emigration (again, sons' emigration in particular) has a negative effect on the elderly's psychological and physical well-being.

Tradition and Change in Support of the Elderly

To mitigate the effects of labor outflow, rural households with elderly family members have made some adaptations. These demonstrate the coexistence of tradition and change in household-dominated old-age care.

The Resilience of Tradition

Earlier studies in Taiwan and Mainland China showed that sons (and daughters-in-law) play a more important role in providing financial and instrumental support to their aging parents than do daughters (and sons-in-law) (Lee et al. 1994; Yang 1996). In contrast, daughters (and sons-in-law) provide the elderly mainly with auxiliary old-age care such as emotional support and everyday care (Lee, Parish, and Willis 1994; Yang 1996; Sun 2002). Our research shows that migration does not bring fundamental changes to this traditional division of labor by gender. For instance, female migrant workers give their parents-in-law more financial support than do male migrant workers (Zhang, Jin, and Feldman 2007), and the elderly who stay at home receive more financial support from daughters-in-law than from sons-in-law (Institute for Population and Development Studies 2005). The elderly also tend to provide their sons with more help than their daughters (Zhang, Li, and Jin 2008; Institute for Population and Development Studies 2005). Caring for the grandchildren of sons is more likely to increase the elderly's psychological well-being than is caring for the grandchildren of daughters (Song, S. Li, and L. Li 2008), and financial and emotional support from sons also has greater effects on the elderly's psychological satisfaction than does the same support when provided by daughters (Zhang and Li 2005).

The traditional patriarchal concept that "men dominate outside home, women dominate at home" still forces women to be the primary caregivers in many families. This in turn reduces women's opportunities to have paid jobs in society and makes them less independent economically. Consequently, elderly women usually have lower status in households than men.

From the perspective of residential preference, the traditional stem family conforms more to the expectation of the elderly and improves their psychological well-being (Silverstein, Cong, and Li 2006). Thus, the elderly are culturally lagging behind the social changes that favor small nuclear families, which are occurring in the rest of society at the present time. Living apart from their children can lower the psychological well-being of the elderly in rural China (Silverstein, Cong, and Li 2006). A family structure called a "network family"—in which an elder lives with neither children nor grandchildren, but at least one child lives in the same village—is becoming more and more common in China. Unfortunately, the network family cannot provide the elderly with the same psychological satisfaction as it does in urban China, because it is usually considered culturally deviant.

The vast majority of the elderly who have been interviewed agree with such traditional old-age-care norms as "raising sons for old-age support" and "relying on children" (Zuo and Li 2007). Children working away from home do not seem to lose the filial concept either, and the longer they are away, the more likely they are to increase financial support to their parents (Zhang, Jin, and Feldman 2007).

Adaptation and Change

Strengthened intergenerational interdependence is a disturbing consequence of migration. The elderly and their children have tried to adapt to these substantial shifts in intergenerational exchanges.

First, the traditional filial piety culture is undergoing a transformation. In the process of modernization and urbanization, rural young people have been strongly influenced by pluralistic culture. Traditional values are gradually fading out, and elders are losing their original authority within households. As in other Asian countries, intergenerational exchange in rural China is no longer just a unidirectional contribution or sacrifice made by children for the elderly; rather, it consists of intergenerational time-money exchange (Cong and Silverstein 2008). If adult children do not reward the elderly's efforts, or the elderly cannot reciprocate, the elderly's psychological health can be damaged. The elderly pay their children's migration expenses and take care of their grandchildren, making it possible for the children to work away from home. This resembles a long-term strategic investment and improves the well-being of the elderly (Silverstein, Cong, and Li 2007). Labor outflow has forced the elderly to be more involved in such household chores as taking care of grandchildren. In skipped-generational households (which are not traditional), elderly parents receive money from children for their custodial care of grandchildren and have better psychological outcomes. In this way, family functioning is optimized (Zhang and Li 2004).

Second, with current intergenerational relations, elderly parents are in a relatively vulnerable situation compared to their children. Based on our surveys, we found that sons who leave their natal families but remain in the same village are likely to shirk the responsibility of elderly parent care. As a result, the elderly usually choose to provide more support to the children they are living with in order to affirm the old-age support agreement (Song and Li 2008a). We found that the share of financial and instrumental support duty among sons lowers the elderly's subjective quality of life (Zhang and Li 2005). Our research even reveals that some migrating children's surplus financial support for their parents may not be enough to compensate for the efforts the elderly make to take care of their grandchildren (Song and Li 2008b).

Third, the concept of elder care is changing. Our research shows that many migrant workers plan to earn enough money to support themselves when they get old or to purchase commercial old-age insurance (Ren 2007). The preference of the elderly for living with sons rather than daughters in rural China is also changing (Wang and Li 2007). Quite a few of the interviewed elderly even say that they would be willing to live in homes for the elderly if it were economically feasible (Zuo and Li 2007).

Finally, working away from home has increased rural females' income and has improved their status in the family. As a result, daughters are playing a more significant role in old-age care.

Conclusion

The outflow of rural labor has had a significant impact on China's traditional household-dominated old-age care. Although elders' beliefs and expectations remain traditional, their intergenerational support behavior has evolved to include greater reciprocity. As children's migration has increased their financial support for the elderly, it has also reduced their instrumental and emotional support and added to the burden of the elderly, who are often expected to care for grandchildren. Due to their economic dependence, the bargaining power of elderly parents in seeking help from their children is limited. With increasing age and declining health, this power will further decrease. As a countermeasure, the authorities must strengthen social security and social help for the rural elderly in financial, medical, and other dimensions, and encourage the development of community old-age care in rural areas. At the same time, the government should help to improve the elderly's economic independence by sponsoring small-scale sideline industries suitable for these older workers.

At the present time, the elderly in rural China are still deeply attached to the traditional concepts of family-based old-age support, which has some functions that cannot be fulfilled by social old-age care. Most elderly can, for example, take care of themselves most of the time and contribute to family life, especially by doing housework and caring for grandchildren. This assistance takes some of the pressure off the younger generation. The government should strengthen advocacy of the traditional culture of filial piety so as to create a social atmosphere of respect for the elderly, thereby improving elders' social and family status.

The outflow of rural labor has improved the economic capability and family status of rural women, enabling them to play a more important role in family old-age support. As the number of children declines, an increasing number of households have no male children, making the traditional mode of old-age care, which relies solely on support by sons, impractical. The traditional pattern of son-based old-age support in rural China is not only deeply rooted in the patrilineal family system but is also affected by gender-blind public policies, local village customs, and regulations regarding rights to inheritance and land use. The Chinese government has adopted nationwide practical intervention programs and policies to increase the capacity of daughters to support parents. Among these, the "Care for Girls" campaign is the most influential. One of the main components of this campaign is a capacity-building scheme for families with only daughters by means of financial assistance and media advocacy.

The female elderly are still disadvantaged in the family. They do most of the housework and are more economically dependent than the male elderly; in addition, they are in poorer physical health and in greater need of emotional comfort. Children's migration has had more negative effects on them than it has on elderly men. In sponsoring small-scale sideline industry projects, the government should therefore give priority to the female elderly to improve their ability to support themselves. The government should also emphasize grassroots social service institutions (like kindergartens and rest homes) to reduce the domestic burden on the female elderly.

In the long run, while establishing and enhancing the rural social security system, the government needs to change or eliminate the household registration system, which denies the floating rural population social security benefits enjoyed by the urban population. Measures should also be taken to improve the living conditions of migrant workers in order to increase their ability to provide the elderly with financial support. In addition, the cost of kindergartens and schools in the city should be reduced so that migrant workers may send their children there and alleviate the burden of child care on the elderly who remain in rural areas.

References

Cong, Z., and M. Silverstein, 2008. "Intergenerational Time-for-Money Exchanges in Rural China: Does Reciprocity Reduce Depressive Symptoms of Older Grandparents?" *Research in Human Development* 5 (1): 6–25.

Du, P., Z. Ding, Q. Li, and J. Gui. 2004. "The Impact of Out-migration of Adult Children to the Left-behind Elderly in Rural China" [in Chinese]. *Population Study* 6: 44–52.

Huang, H., X. Ming, H. Zhou, and S. Gong. 2003. "Gendered Caregiving in the Families with Elderly Parents: Based on the Case Study in Hong Kong" [in Chinese]. *Sociological Research* 1: 60–70.

Institute for Population and Development Studies. 2005. *Technical Report of Shenzhen Survey* [in Chinese]. Xi'an, China: Xi'an Jiaotong University.

Lee, Y. J., W. L. Parish, and R. J. Willis. 1994. "Sons, Daughters, and Intergenerational Support in Taiwan." *The American Journal of Sociology* 99 (4): 1010–41.

Liu, H. 2004. *New Theories of Rural Surplus Labor Transfer* [in Chinese]. Beijing: Chinese Economic Press.

Ren, F. 2007. "Attitudes towards Old-age Support and Its Transition among Rural Migrants in China: From Social Network Perspective" [in Chinese]. Master's thesis, Xi'an Jiaotong University, Xi'an, China.

Rudkin, L. 1993. "Gender Differences in Economic Well-being among the Elderly of Java." *Demography* 30 (2): 209–26.

Shi, L. 1993. "Family Financial and Household Support Exchange between Generations: A Survey of Chinese Rural Elderly." *The Gerontologist* 33 (4): 468–80.

Silverstein, M., Z. Cong, and S. Li. 2006. "Intergenerational Transfers and Living Arrangements of Old People in Rural China: Consequences for Psychological Wellbeing." *Journal of Gerontology: Social Sciences* 61B (5): S256–S266.

———. 2007. "Intergenerational Transfers between Older People and their Migrant Children in Rural China: Strategic Investments, Strategic Returns." Paper presented at the Annual Meeting of the Population Association of America, New York.

Song, L. 2008. "A Study on Out-migration of Young Adults and Gender Division of Intergenerational Support of Rural Elderly in China" [in Chinese]. Ph.D. dissertation, Xi'an Jiaotong University.

Song, L., and S. Li. 2006. "Intergenerational Transition and its Influence on Health of the Elderly in Rural China: A Study of Gender Differences across Generations" [in Chinese]. *Collection of Women's Studies* (4): 14–20.

———. 2008a. "Sons and Daughters: Effects of Out-migration on Division of Intergenerational Support in Rural China" [in Chinese]. *Journal of Xi'an Jiaotong University* (Social Sciences) 28 (89): 10–21.

———. 2008b. "Out-migration of Young Adults and Gender Division of Intergenerational Support in Rural China" [in Chinese]. *Population Journal* (3): 38–43.

Song, L., S. Li, and L. Li. 2008. "The Impact of Care for Grandchildren on Psychological Wellbeing of the Rural Elderly" [in Chinese]. *Population and Development* 14 (3): 10–18.

Song, L., S. Li, and W. Zhang. 2006. "Research on Impact of Intergenerational Support on Self-rated Health" [in Chinese]. *Chinese Gerontology Journal* 26 (11): 1453–55.

Sun, L. 2003. "'New Dual Structure' between Rural and Urban Areas and Rural-urban Migration" [in Chinese]. In *Rural Migrant Workers: A Socio-economic Analysis of Chinese Peasants Entering Cities*, edited by P. Li, 149–71. Beijing, China: Social Sciences Academic Press (SSAP).

Sun, R. 2002. "Old Age Support in Contemporary Urban China from Both Parents' and Children's Perspectives." *Research on Aging* 24 (3): 337–59.

Wang, P., and S. Li. 2007. "Study on Co-residence Transition of the Elderly People and Children in Rural Areas" [in Chinese]. *Population Journal* (1): 22–28.

Yang, H. 1996. "The Distributive Norm of Monetary Support to Older Parents: A Look at a Township in China." *Journal of Marriage and the Family* 58 (May): 404–15.

Zeng, Y. 2005. "China's Population Aging, Deficit of Retirement Funds, and Old Age Insurance Program in Rural Areas" [in Chinese]. *China Economic Quarterly* 4 (4):1043–66.

Zhang, Kevin H., and. S. Song. 2003. "Rural-urban Migration and Urbanization in China: Evidence from Time-series and Cross-section Analyses." *China Economic Review* 14: 386–400.

Zhang, W., and S. Li. 2004. "Research on Out-migration of Young Adults and Intergenerational Support of Rural Elderly in China" [in Chinese]. *China Soft Sciences* (8): 34–39.

———. 2005. "The Impact of Intergenerational Support to Satisfaction on Life of Rural Elderly" [in Chinese]. *Population Study* 29 (5): 73–80.

Zhang, W., S. Li, and M. W. Feldman. 2005. "Gender Differences in Activity of Daily Living of the Elderly in Rural China: Evidence from Chaohu." *Journal of Women & Aging* 17 (3): 73–89.

Zhang, Y., S. Li, and X. Jin. 2008. "Effect of Adult Children Emigration on Financial Support to Aged Parents of Three Generation Families in Rural China" [in Chinese]. *Journal of Modern Economics* (1): 8–15, 124.

Zhang, Y., X. Jin, and M. W. Feldman. 2007. "The Effects of Rural-urban Migration on Intergenerational Financial Transfer in China: A Gender-based Perspective" [in Chinese]. *China Population Science* (3): 31–40.

Zuo, D., and S. Li. 2007. "Factors Affecting Rural Elderly's Willingness to Enter the New Type Elder Homes in Rural China." Paper presented at the 8th Asia/Oceania Regional Congress of Gerontology and Geriatrics, Beijing.

MARRIAGE AND THE ELDERLY IN CHINA

Maria Porter

Longevity in China has risen dramatically since the 1960s (He et al. 2007). Given that it is the most populous country in the world, researchers and policymakers must address how such change will influence the welfare of the elderly.

Several factors make the impact of aging particularly dramatic in this context. First is China's one-child policy, instituted in 1979. As a result of this policy, members of younger generations do not have any siblings with whom to share the responsibilities of supporting elderly parents. Second, the aging population in rural areas must rely primarily on their families and their own income for support (Guo 2006). Third, China has undergone a dramatic shift from a planned economy of state-owned enterprises that offered many state guarantees (for example, pensions and health care) to a free-market system that lacks such guarantees. Finally, China has experienced unprecedented economic growth. Younger generations are acquiring significantly more wealth than their parents, making elderly dependence on children even more acute. In addition, the one-child policy and a strong preference for sons has led to widespread use of sex-selective abortion and highly skewed sex ratios at birth. Once the generations born under the one-child policy reach old age, many men may potentially remain unmarried and childless. Who will care for these men as they age?

Older adults often designate children or spouses to represent them in making decisions regarding their own long-term care or health. Yet government policies are rarely informed by the family dynamics involved in such decisions. What factors determine who provides care for disabled parents, where parents should live, and whether adult children should forgo economic opportunities that are geographically distant from ill or functionally disabled parents? If policymakers understand such family dynamics, they will be better able to formulate cost-effective plans for providing care to the disabled elderly.

In this chapter, I begin by reviewing some of the previous research on aging-related issues in China, focusing on family dynamics and the role of marriage in determining individual welfare and how household decisions are ultimately reached. I then examine several factors regarding care provided to the elderly. These include how individuals have responded to marriage-market conditions in the past, as well as differentials in elderly care according to their marital status. I will show preliminary evidence that points to a particular need to address the care requirements of future aging populations in rural China, especially those who will be unmarried.

Intergenerational Ties and Informal Care Providers in China

Economists studying intergenerational ties in China have focused on whether transfers from children to elderly parents are motivated by altruism or by an exchange motive. Secondi (1997) finds that altruism alone cannot explain transfers from children to elderly parents in China, and that child-care services may be one of the main services the elderly provide their adult children in exchange for money. In contrast, Cai, Giles, and Meng (2006) find that children provide transfers to parents whose income falls below the poverty line. This is consistent with an altruistic motive, although such transfers are not sufficient to fully compensate for negative income shocks to the elderly. Giles and Mu (2007) find that children are likely to support their parents through nonfinancial means. Young adults, for example, are less likely to be migrant workers when an elderly parent is ill.

Such issues are all the more important because long-term care in China is provided primarily by the family. This may prove particularly problematic in the coming years, since the care that family members will be able to provide will contract substantially. With the advent of the one-child policy in 1979, fertility has declined significantly, and many families will be faced with a "four-two-one" problem: four grandparents, two parents, and one child. Research in this area comes at a particularly noteworthy time, as privately supplied family care will soon dwindle, and there may be a growing need for formal institutions to play a greater role in caring for a rapidly aging population.

Public provision of long-term care is primarily available to childless elderly with insufficient income and an inability to work. Thus, family members other than spouses, and adult children in particular, are important suppliers of long-term care in China. While multigenerational households are more common in rural than in urban areas, a greater proportion of the urban oldest old live with their daughters than do the oldest old living in rural areas (Zeng and George 2000). Rural elderly are also more likely to live alone than urban elderly because those living in rural areas without a spouse or children have fewer alternatives, such as nursing homes. Out of all childless elderly, 42 percent of the urban oldest old (80 and older) are institutionalized and 18 percent live alone, whereas only 11 percent of the rural oldest old reside in institutions and 28 percent live alone. Of those with surviving children, 11 percent of the urban oldest old live in institutions, as compared with only 2 percent of the rural oldest old (Guo 2006).

While it is common for the elderly to live with their adult children, children are also likely to support their aging parents through nonfinancial means. For example, as we have seen, children are less likely to be migrant workers when an elder parent is ill (Giles and Mu 2007). This is particularly true of older women, since men are more likely to be married and less likely to be widowed, while women are more likely to live with their children. Twice as many women around age 65 reported that when they were ill their primary caregivers were their children (Zeng, Liu, and George 2003, 2005; Zimmer 2005). Widowed mothers are more likely to receive financial transfers from their adult children than are widowed fathers (Logan and Bian 2002).

These differences may reflect lower mortality selection among older males than older females. This would also explain women's persistent advantage in remaining life expectancy at ages approaching 100 (Zeng and Vaupel 2003). While female death rates at ages 80 to 84 are 26 percent lower than male rates, for centenarians the death rates are only 16 percent lower for women (Zeng and Vaupel 2003). Nonetheless, this persistence in female advantage in mortality at the oldest ages is striking; in Sweden and Japan, by comparison, remaining life expectancies of men and women converge as they get closer to age 100. This difference is also all the more striking in light of the fact that elderly women have been found to be considerably more disadvantaged than their male counterparts in a number of respects. Illiteracy rates are about 40 percentage points higher among women than men. At ages 80 to 85, the active life expectancy of men is considerably higher than for women (Zeng, Liu, and George 2003, 2005).

Such differences between men and women may lead one to believe that the well-being of elderly women should be the primary concern going forward. Yet there are a number of important demographic changes in China that will significantly affect future elderly generations, changes that point to a high likelihood of considerable challenges for aging men. Specifically, high sex ratios and declining fertility are predicted to leave many men unmarried (Ebenstein and Sharygin 2009). An increasing scarcity of women available for marriage may also improve their welfare position relative to men. But the story is not so simple. One key question is: What does economic theory tell us about how we might expect people to respond to these changes?

In the remainder of this chapter I will examine how demographic changes in fertility over the past several decades may potentially influence the well-being of future generations of elderly men and women, by impacting their decisions about marriage, household formation, and intra-household resource allocation. I will then discuss observed differences in the extent to which families provide care for the married versus unmarried elderly.

Sex Ratios and Marriage Markets

Since 1979, when families were restricted to having only one child, stories about the neglect and mistreatment of young girls have flourished in the popular press. Indeed, recent sex ratios at birth have risen considerably. In 2000 there were 118 boys born in China for every 100 girls. In the southern provinces of Guangdong and Hainan, the sex ratio has risen to 130 boys for every 100 girls. By contrast, the average sex ratio in industrialized countries ranges from 104 to 107 boys per 100 girls (Riley 2004). More recent estimates indicate the nationwide sex ratio at birth has risen to 120 (United Nations Population Division 2008). Das

Gupta, Chung, and Shuzhuo (2009) find that sex ratios in China are approaching their peak. The UN Population Division also projects that sex ratios at birth will decline over the next 50 years, but will remain above international averages and will not reach 110 until 2050 (see figure 5.1).

Figure 5.1 China's Sex Ratio at Birth, 1995–2050

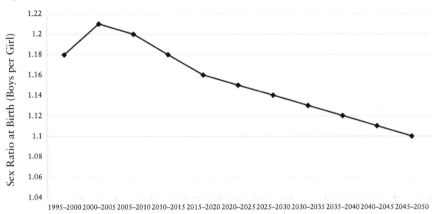

Source: United Nations Population Division, *World Population Prospects: The 2008 Revision*.

This extreme imbalance in the sex ratio points to the prevalence of sex-selective abortion, as well as severe neglect and infanticide of girls, and reflects the persistence of patriarchal values in China. At the same time this imbalance may, ironically, have a positive impact on women's status: Chinese men will find it more difficult to marry, and women may have more power in the marriage market. Such changes could potentially redefine the role of Chinese women in making household decisions. Later in this chapter, I describe some emerging research that has explored such possibilities.

While we will see that women may benefit from such demographic changes, an increasing number of unmarried men may potentially have greater difficulty once they reach old age because they will not have family members such as spouses or children to provide care. Ebenstein and Sharygin (2009) analyze future marriage-market conditions that may result from highly skewed sex ratios forecasted for the coming decades. They consider various assumptions about possible future sex ratios, fertility rates, and other related trends, including no improvement in life expectancy. Under these assumptions, their simulations postulate several negative consequences of high sex ratios, including an increased prevalence of unmarried men and negative economic and health outcomes for these men, particularly when they reach old age. Many elderly rely on families for support in old age; unmarried men will be childless, and so will face particular difficulties in old age. These would be exacerbated by other factors, as Ebenstein and Sharygin find that unmarried men have lower literacy rates, lower income, less financial wealth, poorer self-reported health, and higher mortality rates.

On the other hand, the research findings in the forecast study by Ebenstein and Sharygin (2009) are based on the assumption that men and women will not adjust to the declining scarcity of women. For example, divorce may become more prevalent. Unmarried men may then have an opportunity to marry divorced women. In addition, Porter (2009a) finds that as women become more scarcely available in the marriage market, men may wait longer to marry, perhaps in order to make themselves seem more attractive to women in an increasingly competitive marriage market. Porter also finds that high sex ratios are associated with a significant reduction in daily tobacco consumption. Such findings could be explained by the fact that tobacco is consumed almost exclusively by men, and women in China may find the habit to be a relatively unattractive one. Thus, men are likely to adjust their behavior in order to make themselves more attractive candidates in an increasingly competitive marriage market. In addition, by marrying younger women than they might otherwise, they open themselves to a larger pool of potential spouses, reducing the degree of scarcity of available women.

Adjusting to Highly Skewed Sex Ratios in the Chinese Marriage Market

Nonetheless, given the scarcity of women as a result of the one-child policy, some Chinese men remain unmarried and women have a larger set of potential husbands to choose from. Under these conditions, not only are Chinese women able to attain a better match for themselves (with a man who is, for example, better educated or wealthier than they are), but they are also able to negotiate a greater share of what economists term "the marriage surplus." This notion of a surplus is essential to the marriage-market model. Becker (1973, 1991) uses the term to refer to the additional benefit both spouses receive by being married instead of remaining single. For example, sharing responsibilities at home gives both husband and wife more time to earn income than they would have if they remained single and had to do domestic chores themselves. According to the marriage-market model, individuals marry because they benefit from doing so, whether it is by earning a higher income or simply becoming happier.

The marriage-market model also helps explain how such a surplus will be shared by husbands and wives in China. This surplus can take many forms. When two people are deciding whether to marry, they often discuss such issues as how their combined income will be allocated, how many children they want, whether they will save enough money to send all their children to college, whether they would prefer an expensive sports car to an elaborate wedding or vice versa, and whether they will both work and share equally in household chores or have one spouse work, allowing the other to remain at home to take care of the children.

Most directly, reallocation of the marital surplus could mean a higher *cai li*, the bride price given to the bride's family by the groom's family. Indeed, Wei and Zhang (2009) show that recently increasing sex ratios can explain up to half of the increase in the household savings rate between 1990 and 2007. In addition, Brown (2009) finds that provinces with higher sex ratios experience larger increases in dowry and bride prices. In fact, news media have reported a rise in the number of "runaway brides" who abandon their husbands as soon as they receive their bride price (Fong 2009).

But there are less directly measurable ways for couples to divide up the marital surplus. For example, a couple may offer more resources to their children, particularly since women generally provide more care for their children (Duflo 2000, 2003; Thomas 1990, 1994). Porter (2009a) finds that China's imbalanced sex ratio of 120 relative to an average ratio of 107 raises measures of the short-term health of sons by roughly 25 percent.

Yet some women may also benefit from changes in marriage-market conditions, possibly at the expense of older women. As we have seen, extended families have often been the norm in China, with multiple generations sharing one household and making decisions together. The elderly often live with their adult sons and daughters-in-law. Such living arrangements are especially common among older women who have outlived their husbands. To understand family dynamics in China, we would therefore have to examine not only the relationship between husband and wife, but also the ties between son and mother and between daughter-in-law and mother-in-law. In doing so, Porter (2009b) finds that since women care more about their own parents than their parents-in-law, they provide more care to their own elderly parents than to their husband's aging parents. Thus, empirical tests of the marriage-market model predict that the current imbalanced sex ratios in China will improve the situation of Chinese women within their families and give them greater say in making household decisions.

While informative, this analysis is based on a different population from the one that has been affected by the one-child policy. There are a number of possible responses to the highly skewed sex ratios. Migration across provinces has become prevalent, and women from neighboring countries may also migrate to China to take advantage of the chance to attain a high marital surplus. On the other hand, divorce is also becoming more common. Trafficking of women, prostitution, and crime may increase with rising sex ratios (Ebenstein and Sharygin 2009; Edlund et al. 2007).

Of course, with projections of 30 to 50 million surplus men, it is likely that many men may remain unmarried. In addition, because men tend to marry younger women, marriage-market conditions would reflect not only high sex ratios by birth cohort, but would also be exacerbated by declining fertility. This is commonly referred to as a "marriage squeeze" (Schoen 1983). Migration of women from neighboring countries may be necessary to alleviate such constraints on the marriage market. Yet another possibility for alleviating the situation for men as they get older relates to the fact that since women tend to outlive men, widowed women may eventually marry men who had never married.

To consider the possible consequences of these demographic changes for future aging populations in China, I next examine survey data on today's elderly population in China. In the remainder of this chapter, I consider the prevalence of remarriage and divorce among today's aging population in China, focusing on differences between married and widowed elderly in terms of the care they receive when facing disabilities.

Observed Differences among Chinese Elderly with Varying Marital Status

To begin, I briefly describe the data used here. The Chinese Longitudinal Healthy Longevity Survey (CLHLS) is a panel survey; the baseline was conducted in 1998, with follow-up surveys with replacements for deceased elders conducted in 2000, 2002, and 2005 in a randomly selected half of the total number of counties and cities in 22 provinces. These provinces were chosen because the majority of the populations in each were Han Chinese, whose age reporting at older ages has been found to be quite reliable (Zeng and Vaupel 2003; Coale 1984). The 2002 and 2005 surveys include younger elders aged 65–79, as well as the elders originally surveyed. Assessments of the quality of the survey data have found it to be generally reliable, with relatively low nonresponse rates and reasonable attrition (Gu 2007, 2008; Gu and Zeng 2004; Zeng et al. 2001).

Among the elderly aged 65 and above who were surveyed in the CLHLS, remarriage has been fairly uncommon. Table 5.1 shows the distribution of the number of times respondents had been married, comparing rural and urban men and women. While around 92 percent of urban and rural women had been married only once, remarriage among men is more common. While only 7.9 percent of women had been married twice, 14 percent of urban men had been married twice, and over 10 percent of rural men had been married twice. Thus, remarriage has been more prevalent among men in general, and urban men in particular. In order for these differences to be possible, it is likely that men who remarried married increasingly younger women.

Table 5.1 Number of Times Respondent Was Married

	Male		Female		
	Number of observations	%	Number of observations	%	Total
Urban					
1	2,571	83.96	3,740	91.73	6,311
2	432	14.11	320	7.85	752
3	46	1.50	14	0.34	60
4	11	0.36	3	0.07	14
5	2	0.07	0	0.00	2
Total	3,062	100.00	4,077	100.00	7,139
Rural					
1	3,114	87.72	4,425	91.22	7,539
2	366	10.31	383	7.90	749
3	56	1.58	36	0.74	92
4	10	0.28	6	0.12	16
5	4	0.11	0	0.00	4
6	0	0.00	1	0.02	1
Total	3,550	100.00	4,851	100.00	8,401

Source: Chinese Longitudinal Healthy Longevity Survey.

Table 5.2 shows the marital status of respondents who were married twice. Here we see that widowhood has been much more common than divorce. Of the men who remarried, 80 percent were widowers of their first marriages. Nearly 83 percent of the women who remarried were widows of their first marriages. Divorce was more common among men. Interestingly, while divorce was equally prevalent for urban and rural men, among women, divorce was more common among rural women. While 15.4 percent of urban women who remarried had divorced their first husbands, nearly 19 percent of rural women who had remarried had divorced. In this subsample, widowhood is much more common among women. Two-thirds of both urban and rural women were left widowed by their second husbands. In contrast, less than 37 percent of men were widowed by their second wives. Rural men were more commonly widowed by their second wives than were urban men. Less than 40 percent of rural men who had been married twice remained married to their second wives. But over 43 percent of urban men remained married to their second wives. These differences reflect higher life expectancies among women, particularly urban women. From this sample, we can see that while remarriage has been relatively uncommon, it has been more common among widowed men, who may marry increasingly younger women who have never married.

Table 5.2 Marital Status of Respondents Who Were Married Twice

1st marriage	2nd Marriage							
	Married		Divorced		Widowed		Total	
	No. of obs.	%	No. of obs.	%	No. of obs.	%	No. of obs.	%
Men								
Divorced	96	12.12	5	0.63	61	7.70	162	20.45
Widowed	328	*41.41*	11	1.39	291	*36.74*	630	*79.55*
Total	424	53.54	16	2.02	352	44.44	792	100.00
Women								
Divorced	25	3.58	2	0.29	93	13.32	120	17.19
Widowed	105	15.04	3	0.43	470	*67.34*	578	*82.81*
Total	130	18.62	5	0.72	563	80.66	698	100.00
Urban men								
Divorced	52	12.09	2	0.47	33	7.67	87	20.23
Widowed	186	*43.26*	7	1.63	150	*34.88*	343	*79.77*
Total	238	55.35	9	2.09	183	42.56	430	100.00
Rural men								
Divorced	44	12.15	3	0.83	28	7.73	75	20.72
Widowed	142	*39.23*	4	1.10	141	*38.95*	287	*79.28*
Total	186	51.38	7	1.93	169	46.69	362	100.00
Urban women								
Divorced	11	3.46	1	0.31	37	11.64	49	15.41
Widowed	54	16.98	2	0.63	213	*66.98*	269	*84.59*
Total	65	20.44	3	0.94	250	78.62	318	100.00
Rural women								
Divorced	14	3.68	1	0.26	56	14.74	71	18.68
Widowed	51	13.42	1	0.26	257	*67.63*	309	*81.32*
Total	65	17.11	2	0.53	313	82.37	380	100.00

Source: Chinese Longitudinal Healthy Longevity Survey.

How might marital status influence one's well-being? A number of sociological studies have found that married men in particular are generally better off than their single counterparts. For example, Waite and Gallagher (2000) show evidence of married individuals being happier and healthier, particularly men. But this question has been a difficult one for social scientists to address, because marital status often correlates with unobserved individual characteristics. For example, widowed women may marry less healthy husbands who are more likely to die earlier in part because they are themselves less healthy. While identifying the causal impact of marriage on individual well-being would be difficult with these data, we can examine how marital status correlates with a number of observed characteristics pertaining to elderly health and well-being.

Table 5.3 shows the place of death of married and widowed respondents in the CLHLS. For respondents who died in the previous survey year, a close family member was asked about the respondent's death. It is interesting that married individuals were more likely to have died in a hospital. While 16 percent of those married at the time of death died in a hospital, only 6.3 percent of those who had been widowed died in a hospital. Dying at home or in a nursing home was much more common among the widowed. Nearly 88 percent of widowed individuals died at home and 80 percent of married individuals did so. Widowed individuals are much more likely to have died in a nursing home; 4.6 percent of those widowed died in a nursing home and around 2 percent of those married died in such long-term care facilities. These statistics point out that having a spouse around raises the likelihood of entering a hospital when facing serious illness.

Table 5.3 Place of Death according to Marital Status

	Widowed		Married	
Place of death	Number of observations	% of widowed	Number of observations	% of married
Family home	4,068	87.6	701	80.3
Hospital	292	6.3	140	16.0
Nursing home	214	4.6	19	2.2
Other	33	0.7	9	1.0
Missing	35	0.8	4	0.5
Total	4,642		873	

Source: Chinese Longitudinal Healthy Longevity Survey.

When we examine caregiving costs, we see that for the most part, widowed men and women spend more on caregiving. While 3,107 widowed men and women have caregiving costs, only 533 married individuals have such costs (see table 5.4). Of those who spend on caregiving, it is the married individuals who tend to spend a greater percentage of average per capita household income. Thus, married individuals who require additional caregiving beyond the informal caregiving provided by family members are likely to be those who have disabilities and illnesses that require additional attention. Alternatively, they could be from wealthier families, and hire caregivers because their family members earn higher wages and have higher opportunity costs of time in providing care. In addition, in both rural and urban areas, approximately three to four times as many women as men incur caregiving costs. This may also have to do with the fact that women tend to live longer and also have more disabilities as they get older. Urban widows incur greater costs than rural widows, both in absolute terms and as a percentage of per capita household income. While care-provider costs are on average 27 percent of household income for rural widows, for urban widows, costs are 35 percent of average per capita household income. Widowed urban men also incur twice as much in costs as do widowed rural men when considered as a percentage of per capita household income.

Hiring caregivers or entering a formal long-term care facility are two possibilities for receiving help with disabilities, but the most common form of support in China is that provided by family members. Spouses, children, and grandchildren are often the main lines of support for China's elderly population. In table 5.5, summary statistics are provided for the number of family members who have supported the elderly respondent with any or up to all of the following six tasks: bathing, dressing, toileting, transferring in and out of a bed or chair, eating, and supervising movement. These six activities are known as activities of daily living (ADLs).

While the average number of family members helping married individuals is 1.43, for the widowed, the average number is slightly higher at 2.05. Married men in both urban and rural areas received help from more family members than their female counterparts. While urban married men relied on 1.43 family members for assistance, urban married women relied on 1.28 members. Similarly, rural married men relied on 1.66 family members, while women relied on 1.28 relatives. This may indicate that men are more likely to receive support from their wives than women are from their husbands. Widowed women generally count on slightly more than two family members for support. But there are significant differences between urban and rural widowers. While widowed urban men rely on 2.39 family members for support, widowed rural men rely on only 1.77 family members. These differences may be partly due to the relatively smaller sample sizes here. But it is also interesting to note that while rural couples tend to have had more children than urban couples, they have fewer family members who will help them when they become disabled. Migration of younger generations to urban areas may partly explain some of these differences. While urban widowers have family living close by, those who remain in rural areas may have fewer family members remaining nearby to provide support. Such differences imply that in the future there may be a greater need for providing alternative means of support to the elderly living in rural China.

Table 5.4 Cost of Caregiving and Household Income by Martial Status

	Total direct cost of caregiving (2004 RMB)				Care cost (% of income)
	Mean	Linearized std. err.	95% Confidence interval	No. of obs.	
All	4,682	906	2,906	6,458	3,704	43
Urban	4,670	1,224	2,269	7,071	1,985	37
Rural	4,697	1,346	2,056	7,337	1,719	49
Urban men	3,341	1,578	242	6,440	679	28
Urban women	5,678	1,785	2,175	9,180	1,306	42
Rural men	5,158	2,295	649	9,667	482	59
Rural women	4,305	1,549	1,267	7,344	1,237	42
All married	5,986	1,712	2,624	9,348	533	60
Urban married	5,083	2,039	1,072	9,095	330	43
Rural married	7,426	3,024	1,463	13,389	203	89
Married urban men	3,814	2,098	(319)	7,948	243	34
Married urban women	6,899	3,930	(913)	14,711	87	53
Married rural men	8,162	3,713	826	15,499	153	98
Married rural women	5,737	5,223	(4,759)	16,234	50	68
All widowed	3,374	705	1,992	4,756	3,107	27
Urban widowed	4,246	1,165	1,961	6,532	1,625	30
Rural widowed	2,532	807	948	4,116	1,482	22
Widowed urban men	2,031	1,077	(86)	4,148	421	14
Widowed urban women	4,923	1,483	2,013	7,833	1,204	35
Widowed rural Men	616	272	81	1,151	309	6
Widowed rural women	3,203	1,083	1,078	5,328	1,173	27

Source: Chinese Longitudinal Healthy Longevity Survey.

While there are interesting differences in the number of family members providing support, there are also interesting differences in the number of hours family members provide assistance on a weekly basis. Elderly respondents were asked about the number of hours their spouses, children, and grandchildren provided support in the past week. Perhaps somewhat surprisingly, widowed respondents claimed to have received more hours of support than married respondents. While both widowed urban men and women received approximately 42 hours of support in the past week, married urban men received only 27 hours of support. Married urban women received slightly more than 34 hours of support. Similarly, in rural areas, widowed women received nearly 42 hours of support, while married women received only 27 hours of support. One possible explanation for this may be positive assortative matching in health. More specifically, widowed respondents may have been married to less healthy individuals who had lower life expectancies, and may themselves be similarly less healthy than average. But one exception to this is that rural men who were widowed actually received significantly fewer hours of support than did rural men who were married. While the latter received only 23 hours of support, the former received 42 hours of support. Once again, these statistics point to a possible unmet need for care provided to rural unmarried men.

Differences in expenditure on medical care also point to a possible unmet need for unmarried rural men. According to table 5.6, among rural men, both married respondents and their families spend roughly 25 percent of per capita incomes on medical expenses. But widowed respondents and their families spend roughly 20 percent of household income on medical expenses. In contrast, both married and widowed urban men spend 35 percent of per capita household income on medical services. Their families spend roughly 28 percent of average per capita household income on medical services for them. While medical expenditures are likely higher in urban areas, this cannot explain the difference in expenditures across married and widowed respondents in rural areas, and suggests that rural widowers may be receiving less medical care.

Similarly, married rural women and their families spend considerably more on medical expenses, around 34 percent and 40 percent respectively, while widowed rural women and their families spend less, 21 percent and 24 percent respectively. But among urban women, widowed women and their families spend more on medical expenses—29 percent and 31 percent, respectively— whereas married urban women spend 24 percent, and their families spend 27 percent. These urban-rural differences once again point to the impact of the migration of younger generations to urban areas on the provision of support to the elderly who remain behind. Unmarried rural elderly may be particularly vulnerable because they do not have a spouse or many family members living nearby to provide support.

Table 5.5 Amount of Assistance Family Members Provided to Disabled Elderly Respondents

	No. of family members who assist elderly respondent with ADLs					No. of hours family members assisted elderly respondent in the past week				
	Mean	Linearized std. err.	95% Confidence interval		No. of obs.	Mean	Linearized std. err.	95% Confidence interval		No. of obs.
All	1.73	0.08	1.57	1.88	3,769	36.75	2.32	32.20	41.30	3,174
Urban	1.70	0.12	1.46	1.94	2,012	36.81	3.14	30.64	42.98	1,649
Rural	1.76	0.10	1.57	1.95	1,757	36.68	3.44	29.93	43.43	1,525
Urban men	1.67	0.24	1.20	2.15	687	32.43	4.23	24.12	40.75	531
Urban women	1.72	0.12	1.49	1.95	1,325	39.71	4.39	31.10	48.33	1,118
Rural men	1.64	0.14	1.37	1.91	498	34.02	5.79	22.63	45.40	406
Rural women	1.86	0.13	1.60	2.12	1,259	38.67	4.18	30.46	46.87	1,119
All married	1.43	0.13	1.17	1.69	545	32.91	3.90	25.26	40.57	401
Urban married	1.36	0.19	0.98	1.74	335	30.09	4.58	21.07	39.10	244
Rural married	1.53	0.16	1.22	1.85	210	36.93	6.83	23.45	50.41	157
Married urban men	1.43	0.31	0.83	2.04	248	26.88	3.94	19.10	34.66	180
Married urban women	1.26	0.16	0.93	1.58	87	34.31	9.17	15.98	52.64	64
Married rural men	1.66	0.21	1.25	2.07	156	42.21	9.58	23.23	61.20	114
Married rural women	1.28	0.24	0.79	1.76	54	26.79	6.81	13.04	40.53	43
All widowed	2.05	0.09	1.87	2.23	3,154	39.37	2.90	33.69	45.04	2,731
Urban widowed	2.10	0.14	1.84	2.37	1,647	42.31	4.30	33.87	50.76	1,387
Rural widowed	2.01	0.12	1.76	2.25	1,507	36.59	3.87	29.00	44.17	1,344
Widowed urban men	2.39	0.26	1.87	2.91	424	41.46	10.06	21.67	61.25	342
Widowed urban women	2.02	0.15	1.72	2.32	1,223	42.57	4.72	33.31	51.83	1,045
Widowed rural men	1.77	0.13	1.51	2.03	317	23.12	3.30	16.62	29.61	278
Widowed rural women	2.09	0.16	1.77	2.40	1,190	41.70	5.03	31.83	51.57	1,066

Source: Chinese Longitudinal Healthy Longevity Survey.

Note: ADLs = activities of daily living.

Table 5.6 Medical Care Expenses of Elderly Respondents

	Amount respondent spent on medical care services in past year (2004 RMB)						Amount respondent's family spent on medical care services in past year (2004 RMB)					
	Mean	% Income	Linearized std. err.	95% Confidence interval		No. of obs.	Mean	% Income	Linearized std. err.	95% Confidence interval		No. of obs.
All	2,964	27	152	2,665	3,262	15,355	3,042	28	173	2,702	3,381	15,354
Urban	3,846	30	265	3,326	4,366	6,856	3,629	29	297	3,047	4,211	6,856
Rural	2,304	24	176	1,959	2,650	8,499	2,603	27	206	2,200	3,006	8,498
Urban men	4,025	34	401	3,240	4,811	3,028	3,262	27	402	2,474	4,049	3,028
Urban women	3,684	27	352	2,993	4,374	3,828	3,961	29	433	3,113	4,810	3,828
Rural men	1,983	23	198	1,595	2,372	3,616	2,150	24	247	1,666	2,633	3,615
Rural women	2,603	25	286	2,044	3,163	4,883	3,025	30	324	2,390	3,660	4,883
All married	2,870	29	198	2,481	3,259	4,762	2,894	29	227	2,450	3,339	4,761
Urban married	3,569	30	320	2,942	4,196	2,208	3,211	27	359	2,508	3,914	2,208
Rural married	2,315	28	249	1,828	2,803	2,554	2,643	32	290	2,075	3,211	2,553
Married urban men	3,833	35	429	2,991	4,675	1,517	3,019	27	429	2,177	3,860	1,517
Married urban women	3,183	24	476	2,249	4,117	691	3,492	27	622	2,272	4,713	691
Married rural men	1,953	24	238	1,485	2,420	1,676	2,152	26	294	1,574	2,730	1,675
Married rural women	2,831	34	497	1,856	3,807	878	3,342	40	562	2,239	4,445	878
All widowed	3,139	25	246	2,656	3,622	10,101	3,359	26	286	2,799	3,919	10,101
Urban widowed	4,267	30	471	3,344	5,191	4,432	4,374	31	540	3,315	5,434	4,432
Rural widowed	2,354	20	257	1,851	2,858	5,669	2,653	23	304	2,058	3,248	5,669
Widowed urban men	4,683	32	1,078	2,568	6,799	1,373	4,208	28	1,138	1,976	6,440	1,373
Widowed urban women	4,127	29	514	3,119	5,136	3,059	4,430	31	613	3,229	5,632	3,059
Widowed rural men	1,967	19	335	1,310	2,623	1,741	2,104	20	473	1,176	3,032	1,741
Widowed rural women	2,515	21	336	1,857	3,173	3,928	2,881	24	382	2,132	3,629	3,928

Source: Chinese Longitudinal Healthy Longevity Survey.

Conclusion

In this chapter, we have seen that unmarried elderly living in rural China may be particularly vulnerable to receiving insufficient support as they get older and develop disabilities. Such vulnerability can be mitigated by the fact that rural elderly tend to have fewer disabilities than those living in urban areas, perhaps because they engage in more physical activity throughout their working lives. However, unmarried rural elderly receive considerably less support than their married counterparts, while in urban areas, married and unmarried elderly tend to receive similar levels of support from family members in particular. A potentially important factor is the out-migration of younger generations from rural areas to seek better economic opportunities in cities.

Thus, policymakers may need to focus on providing support to aging rural populations in particular. As we see greater numbers of men remaining unmarried because of the one-child policy and resulting imbalanced sex ratios, the needs of such men will need to be addressed, since they will have few, if any, family members to provide support. In addition, women may see their situations improve as highly skewed sex ratios change their marriage options and allow them to negotiate for a greater share of the marital surplus. As we have not seen such highly skewed sex ratios before, it remains to be seen how individuals will adjust their behavior to such unique circumstances. But decisions regarding household formation and the allocation of resources among family members will be affected in significant ways, and will have an important impact on individuals as they age. Understanding such family dynamics is an important line of research to inform policy decisions addressing the needs of China's aging population.

References

Becker, G. 1973. "A Theory of Marriage: Part I." *Journal of Political Economy* (81): 813–46.

———. 1991. *A Treatise on the Family*. Cambridge, MA: Harvard University Press.

Brown, P. 2009. "Dowry and Intrahousehold Bargaining: Evidence from China." *Journal of Human Resources* 44 (1): 25–46.

Cai, F., J. Giles, and X. Meng. 2006. "How Well Do Children Insure Parents against Low Retirement Income? An Analysis Using Survey Data from Urban China." *Journal of Public Economics* 90 (12): 2229–55.

Chinese Longitudinal Healthy Longevity Survey. www.geri.duke.edu/china-study.

Coale, A. 1984. *Rapid Population Change in China, 1952–1982*. Committee on Population and Demography Report No. 27, National Academy Press, Washington, DC.

Das Gupta, M., W. Chung, and L. Shuzhuo. 2009. "Is There an Incipient Turnaround in Asia's 'Missing Girls' Phenomenon?" Policy Research Working Paper 4846, World Bank, Washington, DC.

Duflo, E. 2000. "Child Health and Household Resources in South Africa: Evidence from the Old Age Pension Program." *American Economic Review* 90 (2): 393–98.

———. 2003. "Grandmothers and Granddaughters: Old-age Pensions and Intrahousehold Allocation in South Africa." *World Bank Economic Review* 17 (1): 1–25.

Ebenstein, A. Y., and E. J. Sharygin. 2009. "The Consequences of the 'Missing Girls' of China." *World Bank Economic Review* 23 (3): 399–425.

Edlund, L., H. Li, J. Yi, and J. Zhang. 2007. "More Men, More Crime: Evidence from China's One Child Policy." IZA Discussion Paper No. 1324.

Fong, M. 2009. "It's Cold Cash, not Cold Feet, Motivating Runaway Brides in China." *Wall Street Journal*, June 5.

Giles, J., and R. Mu. 2007. "Elder Parent Health and the Migration Decisions of Adult Children: Evidence from Rural China." *Demography* 44 (2): 265–88.

Gu, D. 2007. "General Data Quality Assessment for the 2005 CLHLS Wave." CLHLS Technical Report No. 2007-1. www.geri.duke.edu/china_study/CLHLS4-3.htm.

———. 2008. "General Data Assessment of the CLHLS." In *Healthy Longevity in China: Demographic, Socioeconomic, and Psychological Dimensions*, edited by Y. Zeng, D. L. Poston, D. A. Vlosky, and D. Gu, 39–59. Dordrecht, the Netherlands: Springer Publisher. www.geri.duke.edu/china_study/CLHLS4-3.htm.

Gu, D., and Y. Zeng. 2004. "Sociodemographic Effects on the Onset and Recovery of ADL Disability among Chinese Oldest-old." *Demographic Research* 11 (1): 1–42.

Guo, Z. 2006. "Living Arrangement of the Oldest Old in China." In *Longer Life and Healthy Aging*, edited by Y. Zeng, E. M. Crimmins, Y. Carrière, and J. M. Robine, chapter 15, 261–72. Springer: Netherlands.

He, W., M. Sengupta, K. Zhang, and P. Guo. 2007. *P95/07-2 Health and Health Care of the Older Population in Urban and Rural China: 2000*. U.S. Census Bureau, International population reports, U.S. Government Printing Office, Washington, DC.

Logan, J. R., and F. Bian. 2002. "Parents' Needs, Family Structure and Regular Intergenerational Financial Exchange in Chinese Cities." *Sociological Forum* 18 (March): 85–101.

Porter, M. 2009a. "The Effects of Sex Ratio Imbalance in China on Marriage and Household Bargaining." Mimeo, Unpublished Manuscript, University of Oxford.

———. 2009b. "How Marriage Market Conditions in China Influence Intergenerational Transfers." Mimeo, Unpublished Manuscript, University of Oxford.

Riley, N. E. 2004. "China's Population: New Trends and Challenges." *Population Bulletin* 59 (2): 1–40.

Secondi, G. 1997. "Private Monetary Transfers in Rural China: Are Families Altruistic?" *Journal of Development Studies* 33 (4): 487–511.

Thomas, D. 1990. "Intra-household Resource Allocation: An Inferential Approach." *Journal of Human Resources* 25 (4): 635–64.

———. 1994. "Like Father, Like Son; Like Mother, Like Daughter: Parental Resources and Child Height." Journal of Human Resources 29 (4): 950–88.

United Nations Population Division. 2008. *World Population Prospects: The 2008 Revision Population Database*. http://esa.un.org/UNPP.

Waite, L., and M. Gallagher. 2000. *The Case for Marriage: Why Married People are Happier, Healthier, and Better Off Financially*. Doubleday: New York.

Wei, S. J., and X. Zhang. 2009. "The Competitive Saving Motive: Evidence from Rising Sex Ratios and Savings Rates in China." NBER Working Paper No. 15093.

Zeng, Y., and J. W. Vaupel. 2003. "Oldest Old Mortality in China." *Demographic Research* 8 (7): 215–44.

Zeng, Y., and L. George. 2000. "Family Dynamics of 63 Million (in 1990) to More than 330 Million (in 2050) Elders in China." *Demographic Research* 2 (5).

Zeng, Y., Y. Liu, and L. George. 2003. "Gender Differentials of the Oldest Old in China." *Research on Aging* 25: 65–80.

———. 2005. "Female Disadvantages among the Elderly in China." In *Longer Life and Healthy Aging*, edited by Zeng Yi, Eileen Crimmins, Yves Carrière, and Jean-Marie Robine. Dordrecht: Springer Publisher.

Zeng, Y., J. W. Vaupel, Z. Xiao, C. Zhang, and Y. Liu. 2001. "The Healthy Longevity Survey and the Active Life Expectancy of the Oldest Old in China. Population: An English Selection." *Biodemographic Perspectives on Human Longevity* 13 (1): 95–116.

Zimmer, Z. 2005. "Health and Living Arrangement Transitions among China's Oldest-old." *Research on Aging* 27 (5): 526–55.

SOCIAL INSURANCE PROGRAM SUSTAINABILITY, CHRONIC DISEASE, AND LONG-TERM CARE

FINANCING HEALTH CARE
IN A RAPIDLY AGING JAPAN

Naoki Ikegami

B etween 1950 and 2000, the demographic structure of Japan changed from
a pyramid to a column. By 2050 it will have become a reverse pyramid
(figure 6.1) (MHLW 2008). Barring catastrophe, the projections for 2050
should prove accurate, especially for those in the 40 and over range (all of whom
have already been born). The aging of the population is a result of increasing
life spans and a decreasing birth rate. Though these trends can be observed in all
developed countries, Japan had a markedly shorter baby boom after World War
II, lasting only three years, from 1947 to 1949. This large cohort of elders—the
baby boomers—is reaching retirement age now and by 2025 will be 75+ (the
"old old"). Consequently, the proportion of the population 75 and older will
double from 9 percent now to 18 percent by 2025, while the proportion aged
65–74 (the "young old") will increase from 11 percent to only 12 percent.

These changes will have a major impact on health-care expenditures. The
75+ age group was already responsible for 29 percent of the nation's health-care
spending in 2005. By 2025, this figure is projected to be 49 percent. Overall, the
proportion of health-care spending devoted to the elderly (65+) will increase from
51 to 65 percent (figure 6.2).[1] Physicians (excluding obstetricians and pediatricians)
will find that close to three-quarters of their patients will be over 65. The nation's
health-care system will have to focus more and more on the elderly. For example,
a typical hospitalization will be that of a frail elderly patient admitted on a
stretcher and discharged on a wheelchair, requiring a seamless transition between
hospital and community caregiving. Programs that focus on the management of
a single disease will become less useful, supplanted by general care of the many
and complicated conditions typical of an elderly patient.

To meet the challenges of a rapidly aging society, it is essential to review the
health-care finance system and to address the following issues.

---

[1] Figures come from data presented at the Fifteenth Meeting of the Health Insurance
Subcommittee of the Social Security Council on May 25, 2005 (MHLW). Future
expenditures were projected using the average per capita growth rates from 1995 to
1999 of the population 75 and older and of the population younger than 75. Increases
due to aging and effects of revisions in the fee schedule were deducted from the growth
rates. Increases for the population aged 65–74 were not taken into consideration because
its percentage of the population younger than 75 will remain the same.

- Can the younger generation's burden be mitigated?
- Can total health expenditure be contained?
- Can health insurance for the elderly be reformed?
- Can the costs of end-of-life care be contained?
- Is long-term care (LTC) affordable?

Can the Younger Generation's Burden Be Mitigated?

As Japan's society ages, the younger generation must pay an increasingly large share of the older generation's health-care costs. To mitigate this burden, over the past twenty-five years, the government has been requiring elders to contribute progressively more through copayments and premiums. In 1973 copayments for people aged 70+ were waived. They were reintroduced in 1983 as small flat payments that have been raised several times since. In 2003 the copayment became a set rate: 10 percent for most elderly and 20 percent for those whose income exceeds that of the average worker.[2] In 2006 the rate for the high-income elderly was increased to 30 percent, the same rate as that for the rest of the population. There has been a de facto increase in elders' contribution to the cost of insurance premiums (which are calculated as a fixed percentage of after-tax income) as a result of a gradual reduction in tax-exempt income from public pensions. Second, strenuous efforts have been made to contain total health expenditure, as described in the next section.

Further measures have been advocated. One proposal calls for each generation to put aside some premiums into a societal savings fund (Ogura and Morishita 2006). However, people need health-care coverage (unlike pensions) at every age. The younger generation would have to pay premiums for both their current and future health care, and also subsidize the cost of their elders' care. Moreover, it is much more difficult to predict future health-care costs than pension costs, so the amount saved may turn out to be insufficient. For the same reason, individual health savings accounts (HSAs) would be even more problematic. In order to protect individuals against catastrophic costs, HSAs must be complemented by high-deductible catastrophic insurance. However, medical expenditures follow the 80/20 rule: 80 percent of the spending is for 20 percent of the patients. Data from Japan confirm this. An analysis of claims for plans covering two-thirds of the population showed that the 1 percent of claims at the most expensive end accounted for 26 percent of spending, while

---

[2] This copayment rate is applicable only up to the amount covered by the catastrophic program. After that, the rate becomes 1 percent. The threshold amount is about $350 per month for most people 65 and over and about twice that for people under 65.

Figure 6.1 Population of Japan by Age and Sex: 1950, 2000, and 2050

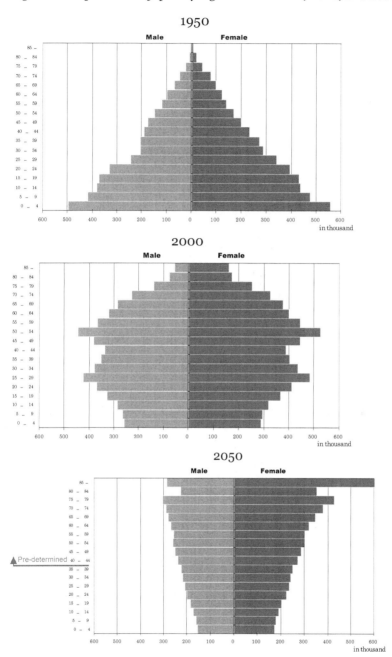

Source: MHLW 2008; www.ipss.go.jp.

Figure 6.2 Percentage of Population Aged 65–74 and 75+ versus Percentage of
Total Health Expenditures

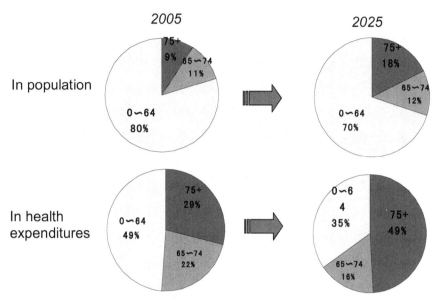

Source: Figures come from data presented at the Fifteenth Meeting of the Health Insurance
Subcommittee of the Social Security Council on May 25, 2005 (MHLW).

the bottom 75 percent accounted for only 22 percent (figure 6.3).[3] Theoretically
attractive as HSAs may be, in practice the bulk of the expenditures would end up
being met by pay-as-you-go catastrophic insurance. In the end, individual HSAs
would require just what they were designed to avoid: a transfer of payments
from the younger generation to the older generation—unless society is willing
to explicitly limit access to most elders.

Can Total Health Expenditure Be Contained?

Japan's health indices for life expectancy at birth and infant mortality are
among the best in the world, while the percentage of its gross domestic product
(GDP) consumed by health expenditures, at 8 percent, is about half that of the
United States (OECD 2008). This impressive record could be due partly to the
lower demand placed on the system by crime, illicit drug use, traffic accidents,

---

[3] Claims are filed at the beginning of every calendar month for all services provided the
previous month. The data came from the June 1993 claims of the national government-
managed plan for employees in middle to small enterprises (Seikan) and the local government-
managed plan for the self-employed and for pensioners (Kokuho) (IHEP 1996).

and the prevalence of HIV faced in other developed countries (Campbell and Ikegami 1998; Ikegami and Campbell 2004). The health-care system deserves some credit for providing universal coverage and egalitarian access without long waiting lists, which have plagued countries with socialized medicine. Japan also has the world's highest number of CT scans and MRI systems per capita. The nationwide fee schedule (tariff) has played a key role in containing costs. It serves as the one valve that controls the money flowing from insurance plans to virtually all providers, including spending on physicians, hospitals, drugs, and devices. Japan's single payment system maintains equity: the benefit package is essentially the same for all plans. It also has reduced administrative costs by eliminating individual negotiations between insurance plans and providers. Balance billing (charging more than the fees listed) and extra billing (providing services not listed in the fee schedule or prescribing for off-label use) are, in principle, prohibited.

Figure 6.3 Percentage of Insured Health-care Expenditures Billed (in descending order of claim amount), 1993

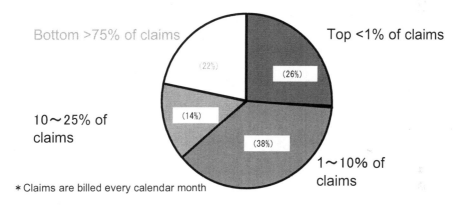

Source: National Claims Survey, 1993, MHLW, Japan. The data came from the June 1993 claims of the national government-managed plan for employees in middle to small enterprises (Seikan) and the local government-managed plan for the self-employed and for pensioners (Kokuho) (IHEP 1996).

Figure 6.4 shows the annual percentage increases in the GDP, the national medical expenditure (NME), and the average medical prices as established by the national fee schedule. The NME comprises spending on all medical services, including payments from the public health insurance system and general revenues and copayments by patients.[4] Since health and fiscal policy focuses on the

---

[4] Several total health expenditure (THE) items, in particular capital investment by the public sector, over-the-counter (OTC) drugs, health screening, private room charges,

nominal NME, rather than the per capita or deflated amount, the following analysis will use these figures.

Figure 6.4 Annual Changes in the Gross Domestic Product, National Medical Expenditures, and Fee-schedule Revision Rate in Japan, 1980–2002

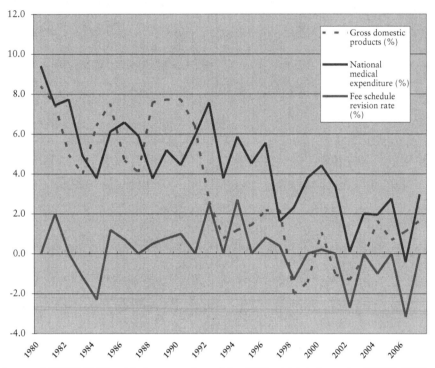

Source: MHLW 2008, with the exception of the GDP which is from the OECD 2008.

On average, from 1980 to 2002, the NME increased at an annual rate of 5 percent, compared with 4 percent for the GDP.[5] However, there are two distinct periods within that span: in the 1980s the economy expanded at a rate of 6.4 percent, but only by 2.0 percent after 1990. During the 1980s, the NME grew at about the same rate as the GDP, so medical expenditure remained constant at around 5 percent of GDP. After 1990, however, the economy declined sharply. In the latter half of the decade, the GDP did not grow at all and even contracted. During this deflationary period, the growth rate of the NME also declined, but less so than the GDP, increasing health care's share of the economy from

---

and some smaller categories are not included in the NME. As a result, the NME was equivalent to about four-fifths of the nominal THE during this period.

[5] See note 4.

4.6 percent in 1990 to 6.0 percent in 1999. This hike provoked widespread concern that health-care costs were out of control. The trend continued: in 2001, the NME increased to 6.5 percent of GDP. It has remained stable since, with increases in health-care expenditures more or less matching the nominal increase in GDP.[6]

Fee schedule revisions have, of course, affected NME growth. Revisions are negotiated between the government and providers, usually on a biennial basis. Figure 6.4 also shows the revision rate change for all procedures and drugs, adjusted for volume. Prices rose less for medical care than they did in the overall economy, averaging only 0.46 percent per year between 1980 and 2002, 1 percent lower than the 1.46 percent annual average rise in the consumer price index (CPI). The fee schedule is the most substantial factor contributing to changes in the NME; the correlation between changes in the two indices was 0.78 for the years 1980 to 2002.

Factors contributing to increases in the NME include the following: (1) demographic changes, primarily population growth and aging;[7] (2) fee schedule revisions; and (3) residual factors. Even as the nation has grown increasingly older, the birth rate has declined, so the combined effect of population growth and aging has been constant. In 1980 the increase in the NME due to population growth was 0.8 percent, while the increase due to aging was 1.0 percent, for a cumulative effect of 1.8 percent. In 2002 the population effect decreased to 0.1 percent, while the aging effect increased to 1.7 percent, for a cumulative effect of 1.8 percent. The cumulative effect has remained in the range of 1.7 to 2.1 percent (with a mean of 1.8 percent) throughout these years. It has been pointed out that aging is a negligible factor in health-care spending increases in the United States (Reinhardt 2003; Cutler and Sheiner 1999). In Japan its effect is greater because the population is becoming proportionally older faster. Also, factors that play an important role in cost increases in the United States have much less impact in Japan, so the relative *share* of aging is far greater.[8]

---

[6] The subsequent increases in the NME were about the same as the increases in the GDP. In 2004 the global rate decreased by 1.0 percent and the NME increased by 1.8 percent. In 2006 it was reduced by 3.16 percent, which led to no increase in the NME. The NME increased by 1.9 percent in 2003 and 3.2 percent in 2005, years when fee schedule revisions were not made.

[7] Effects of demographic changes are calculated in the following way: Let (Ai) be the per capita health expenditures of each age group of the year studied. If the number in each age group of the year studied is (Xi), and the number in each age group of the previous year is (Yi), then the increase due to population growth and aging is $\sum Ai*Xi/\sum Ai*Yi-1$. The residual after accounting for population growth will be due to aging. Since the same health expenditure figures are used, the effects of fee schedule revisions, advances in technology, and so on do not have to be taken into account. However, it is assumed that per capita health expenditures in each age group remain constant.

[8] The Japanese data show that the magnitude of the difference in per capita expenditures

The most problematic item is the residual factors, which include both changes in volume (the number of patient visits and hospital admissions)[9] and additional issues that are ascribed, in Japan as elsewhere, to technology. The average annual increase in this category between 1980 and 2002 was 2.8 percent (compared with 0.46 percent for fee schedule revisions). That accounts for 56 percent of the total increase in the NME. It accounted for a greater proportion of the total increase in the 1980s (67 percent) than in the 1990s (44 percent). Technology is widely believed to be the main driver of health-care cost increases (Mehrotra, Dudley, and Luft 2003). However, for nearly every year in this period, spending due to technology grew at a rate lower than the GDP growth. In contrast to the United States, where providers seem able to exploit technological advances to increase revenues, the Japanese system works to keep that impact low even though many types of high-tech medical practices, particularly in the diagnostic area, have come to be widely available. All in all, the main explanation for why expenditures are so enormous in the United States is simply higher prices (Anderson et al. 2003).

At the heart of Japan's success in containing health expenditures is its two-step method for setting prices. The prime minister takes the first step, determining the global revision based on his assessment of the political and economic situation. For example, in times of fiscal austerity the prime minister can even revise fee schedules downward, containing total health expenditure. The health ministry's Central Social Insurance Council takes the second step—making targeted revisions in individual procedures to meet the global limits imposed by the first step. The global revision rate is not applied across the board. Instead, fees are revised individually for each procedure and drug.[10] For example, the fee for a head MRI was reduced by 30 percent, from 16,600 yen ($160) to 11,400 yen ($110) in the 2002 revision, while the global rate was reduced by only 2.7 percent. There are many such examples. Through this practice, the cost impact of introducing high-tech equipment can be negated or at least blunted. This approach has not been explored in the United States. Even in sectors of the U.S. system for which prices are regulated by the government, they inevitably remain the same or increase (Ableson 2003).

---

between age groups has actually increased despite increases in longevity, possibly because a sizable amount of LTC is covered by health insurance and because the proportion spent the year before death is less in Japan. See Fukawa (1998).

[9] Since billing is made on a calendar-month basis, changes in the number of patient visits and hospital admissions are recorded as changes in the number of claims filed per enrollee during the fiscal year.

[10] The volume of each service is estimated by a national sample of claims data, providing a basis for calculating the impact of fee revisions on total expenditures.

Can Health Insurance for the Elderly Be Reformed?

To deal with the increasing proportion of health-care expenditures spent on the elderly, and in particular for those aged 75+, the Japanese government implemented a new insurance plan in April 2008. The plan turned out to be a fiasco for the governing party and was one reason for the resignation of the prime minister, Yasuo Fukuda, that September. The new plan was unpopular for a number of reasons: (1) elders were offended by its designation as "latter period" coverage, implying the next period would be death (the media caught on and started to refer to the plan as the "hurry-up-and-die" insurance); (2) there were glitches in implementation (for example, new insurance cards were not delivered on time, temporarily leaving some elders without any coverage); (3) low-income elders, who as dependents (usually on one of their children) had been waived from paying premiums, now had to pay; (4) the premiums went up for a significant minority (those living in municipalities with low health expenditures and/or high average income) as a result of the expansion of the insurance pool from the municipal to the state level; and (5) changes to the fee schedule included a small number of items applicable only to those aged 75 and over.

A new consultation fee for discussing end-of-life-care issues particularly caught the public's attention. The media criticized it, predicting that the consultations would be used to persuade elders to end their lives more quickly in order to contain costs. In the face of public uproar, the government froze implementation of the new end-of-life consultation fee just two months after its introduction, an unprecedented event in the history of the fee schedule. This indicates the difficulty of introducing different benefits for the elderly. Intergenerational equity, it seems, will remain the norm.

Can the Costs of End-of-life Care Be Contained?

Despite the uproar over the end-of-life consultation fee, many see heroic, but futile, efforts to prolong life as problematic. An effective and fair way to discourage such practices might attract widespread support. The success of any individual medical effort, however, can only be determined after the fact. A patient in critical condition—and the patient's family—may well wish to receive aggressive treatment, especially if the patient is young and the onset of the condition is sudden. It would be very difficult to deny this wish, even if the chances of recovery are slight. However, some might prefer not to receive aggressive treatment that is likely to only prolong suffering, especially if the patient is old and the onset of the condition is gradual, with no possibility of cure, as in the case of Alzheimer's disease. Physicians could facilitate that choice by explaining the prognosis and providing information about advanced directives. As people in Japan face death later and later in life—in 1968, one-third of all deaths occurred at age 75 or later, and by 2008 this was two-thirds—we might expect more of them to refuse aggressive treatment.

Still, containing end-of-life-care costs may not be easy. As we have seen, public opinion is against any explicit discrimination by age. More fundamentally, the savings from containing end-of-life-care costs may not be as substantial as some predict. Konno, for example, has estimated that, in Japan, end-of-life care constitutes 22.4 percent (2005) of an individual's lifetime health expenditures. Health-care expenditures for the last month of life (1.12 million yen per patient) constituted only 3 percent of total health expenditure in 2003, according to MHLW estimates (2008). Even as the number of deaths increases each year, from 1.1 million in 2006 to a projected 1.7 million in 2040 (MHLW 2008), the proportion of total health expenditure spent on the last month of life would still be in the range of 5 percent.

Is Long-term Care Affordable?

The expected U.S. reaction to a public LTC program would be that it is too expensive. Yet, Germany implemented public LTC insurance in 1995, and Japan did so in 2000. Both countries have found the program to be affordable and manageable. Moreover, their governments spend *less* money on LTC than the United States does through Medicaid and Medicare (Campbell, Ikegami, and Gibson 2008). The state of LTC in the United States is similar to that of its health care: expensive, uncontrollable, and inequitable.

LTC services include assistance in activities of daily living (ADLs), such as dressing and eating; assistance in instrumental ADLs, such as meal preparation, cleaning, shopping, and management of medication; home modifications, such as installing ramps, handrails, and emergency alert systems; and transportation to and from adult day-care centers and health-care facilities. Services provided by physicians are generally not included, except when the physician is employed by the LTC institution. For people under 65 with physical, learning, and mental disabilities, occupational training represents a major component of LTC. From a policy perspective, introducing LTC focused on the elderly proved to be more feasible in Japan.

Compared with health-care expenditures, those for LTC are easier to estimate and budget, since the government sets the eligibility criteria—and thus has control over the number of people eligible—and the benefits for each level of eligibility. The criteria may be strict, limiting eligibility to those who need a great deal of care (as is the case in Germany, where 11 percent of people over the age of 65 are eligible), or may extend coverage to those who require only light care (as is the case in Japan, where 16 percent of the elderly are covered) (Campbell, Ikegami, and Gibson 2009). The benefits may be kept low, covering only part of the cost of services, or generous, covering the bed-and-board costs of nursing home care. Moreover, individuals have more say in their LTC choices. In the realm of health care, in contrast, physicians determine treatment, and there is public pressure to always provide the best treatment available. Limiting resources tends to be presented as a life-or-death issue. But with LTC, different standards can be set because the public responsibility is limited to providing a "decent" quality of life. Thus, shifting services from the health-care system to the LTC system could be a way to increase efficiency and contain overall spending on care in both Japan and the United States.

Conclusion

Where Japan is now, the United States will be thirty years from now. Planning for the future should be based on proven possibilities, *not* on beliefs or wishes. Based on the experience in Japan, the following conclusions can be made:

- *The younger generation's burden can be mitigated.* Elders who have the ability to pay should do so in the form of higher copayment and premium contributions.
- *Total health expenditures can be contained.* Health-care expenditures can be set by government policy. Targeted reductions on procedure fees and drug prices would contain increases in health expenditures due to advances in technology.
- *Reforming health insurance for the elderly is difficult.* It can be expected that the public will oppose the introduction of benefit packages that discriminate against the elderly.
- *End-of-life-care costs may not significantly increase.* Although the number of deaths will increase, a growing proportion will occur after age 75, when people are less likely to choose aggressive treatment.
- *Long-term care is affordable.* A publicly funded LTC program can help to contain health expenditures by transferring services to the LTC system, where budget constraints are easier to impose.

References

Ableson, R. 2003. "Generous Medicare Payments Spur Specialty Hospital Boom." *New York Times*, October 26, p. 1.

Anderson, G., U. Reinhardt, P. Hussey, and V. Petrosyan. 2003. "Why is U.S. Spending So Much Higher?" *Health Affairs* (May–June): 89–105.

Campbell, J. C., and N. Ikegami. 1998. *The Art of Balance in Health Policy—Maintaining Japan's Low-cost, Egalitarian System.* Cambridge: Cambridge University Press, 53–86.

———. 2009. "Comprehensive Long-term Care in Japan and Germany: Policy Learning and Cross-national Comparison." In *Comparative Studies and the Politics of Modern Medical Care*, edited by T. Marmor, R. Freeman, and K. Okma. New Haven: Yale University Press.

Campbell, J. C., N. Ikegami, and M. J. Gibson. 2008. "Comparing Long-term Care Spending in Germany, Japan, and the United States." Poster presented at the Annual Meeting of the Gerontological Society of America, Washington, DC.

Cutler, D. M., and L. Sheiner. 1999. "Demographics and Medical Care Spending: Standard and Non-standard Effects." NBER Working Paper 6866, National Bureau of Economic Research, Cambridge, MA.

Fukawa, T. 1998. "Aging and Health Expenditure of the Elderly" [in Japanese]. *Byouinkanri* 35 (2): 25–34

Ikegami, N., and J. C. Campbell. 2004. "Japan's Health Care System: Containing Costs and Attempting Reform." *Health Affairs* 23 (3): 26–36.

Konno, H. 2005. "The Estimation of Lifetime Medical Expenditure—Adjusting 'Pre-death Medical Expenditure.'" *Health Economics and Policy* 16: 5–22.

Mehrotra, A., R. A. Dudley, and H. S. Luft. 2003. "What's Behind the Health Expenditure Trends?" *Annual Review of Public Health* 24: 385–412.

MHLW (Ministry of Health, Labor and Welfare). 2008. *Population Statistics of Japan 2008*. Tokyo: Ministry of Health, Labor and Welfare.

OECD (Organisation for Economic Co-operation and Development). 2008. *OECD Health Data*. Paris: OECD.

Ogura, M., and A. Morishita. 2006. "A Model Plan to Reduce the Inter-generational Disparity in Health Insurance and its Probability." In *Research in Economic Disparity*, edited by K. Kaizuka and Ministry of Finance Research Institute, 329–39. Tokyo: Chuou Keizaisha.

Reinhardt, U. E. 2003. "Does the Aging of the Population Really Drive the Demand for Health Care?" *Health Affairs* (Nov/Dec): 27–39.

Population Aging and the Introduction of Long-term Care Insurance in South Korea

Soonman Kwon[1]

In July 2008, South Korea introduced social insurance for long-term care (LTC). Such insurance was deemed necessary due to several important social and demographic changes. Chief among these is the rapid aging of the population brought about by an increase in life expectancy, combined with a sharp decline in fertility. The total fertility rate (births per woman) dropped below 1.1 in 2005, from 2.83 in 1980 (NSO 2007). At the same time, while the proportion of the elderly (persons over 65) in South Korea was only 9 percent in 2005, it is forecast to increase at an unprecedented rate, reaching 20 percent by 2026 and 38 percent by 2050, when the old-age dependency ratio (persons 65+ divided by those aged 15–64) will be 70 percent (NSO 2007).

Exacerbating these trends, the family structure in South Korea has also changed. The proportion of the elderly living with their adult children has been decreasing. Further, given their increasing participation in the labor force, women (daughters and daughters-in-law) have been less able and willing to assume their traditional role of providing informal care to family elders. Inefficiency due to social admissions has become serious as the elderly stay in acute-care hospitals longer than medically needed because public health insurance covers hospital services, but not the services provided in LTC facilities.

Economic Capacity of Elderly People

The elderly's ability to pay for LTC is limited. While a high proportion of the elderly work, their household income tends to be relatively low because many are informal sector workers. Indeed, more than half of the elderly surveyed by the Ministry of Health and Welfare (MOHW) and the Korea Institute for Health and Social Affairs (KIHASA) in 2001[2] had a monthly household income below

---

[1] This chapter is a substantially revised version of Kwon (2009a).

[2] The nationwide survey included 5,058 elderly people (average age of 72.5 years, 38 percent male, 60 percent in urban areas) who did not stay in residential facilities or institutions. It was administered from May 28 to July 10, 2001.

700,000 Korean won, or about $700. Households consisting of a single elderly person are among the poorest in Korean society: 72 percent have a monthly income below 300,000 won, and only 4.5 percent have a monthly income over 700,000 won.

The wage income of the household head was the main source of income (in terms of the percentage of total income) for approximately half of the elderly surveyed, while 20 percent depended on financial assistance from family members. Although government aid is a major source of income for 21 percent of the single elderly (the most financially disadvantaged group), it is a major income source for only 7.2 percent of the elderly overall. Family-based welfare continues to play an important role in the economic well-being of the elderly, but as cohabitation with adult children becomes less common, more public programs and private saving will be needed.

In South Korea, the problem of inequity is more serious in the elderly population than among younger people. In 2007 the Gini coefficient (a measure of income inequality) was 0.37 for those over 60 years old, while it was 0.3 for all other age groups (NSO 2007). The annual spending level of the better-off elderly was greater than that of the worse off, in the range of $6,000 for the poorest quintile and $29,000 for the richest quintile (see table 7.1).[3] Food and housing were households' two largest expenses, accounting for 36 to 53 percent of total household expenditure. Health care was the third-largest expense for the elderly in all income strata except the richest quintile, suggesting that health-care costs can still be a financial burden for the elderly and present a barrier to access to health care.

Policy Process Associated with LTC Insurance

The rapid aging of the population, changes in the family structure, women's increased participation in the labor market, the elderly's limited ability to pay for LTC, and the financial burden of elderly care on the health insurance system (e.g., social admissions in acute-care hospitals) all contributed to the decision to introduce a fifth social insurance scheme in South Korea—LTC insurance for the elderly. This new program represents a major new development in social policy and the welfare state of South Korea.

LTC insurance was proposed and implemented by progressive governments that had greatly expanded the welfare state in the years leading up to its passage (Kwon and Holliday 2007). Unemployment insurance was extended to all firms with fewer than thirty workers in 1998. The National Pension Program, which had started in 1988 for workers in large firms before being extended to the rural self-employed in 1995, was expanded in 1999 to cover

---

[3] These figures are drawn from a survey of 5,133 elderly households that was conducted from October 2005 to January 2006 by the National Pension Research Institute (National Pension Service 2006).

the urban self-employed. In 2000 a major reform of the National Health Insurance (NHI) system merged more than 350 health insurance societies, which had been centered either on workplaces (employees) or on geographical regions (self-employed), into a single-payer national organization. A minimum living standard guarantee (MLSG) was enacted in 1999 to establish a minimum income as a social right, regardless of age or ability to work.

Table 7.1 Spending of the Elderly (65+) by Household Income Level (units: 1,000 Korean won; percent)

	1st Quintile	2nd Quintile	3rd Quintile	4th Quintile	5th Quintile
Food	1,917 (31.8)	2,664 (31.0)	3,742 (26.0)	4,474 (22.7)	6,920 (23.8)
Housing	1,267 (21.0)	1,575 (18.3)	2,323 (16.1)	2,557 (13.0)	4,187 (14.4)
Clothing	186 (3.1)	258 (3.0)	472 (3.3)	651 (3.3)	1,517 (5.2)
Transportation/ Communication	564 (9.4)	910 (10.6)	1,633 (11.3)	2,466 (12.5)	4,314 (14.9)
Culture	137 (2.3)	227 (2.6)	354 (2.5)	756 (3.8)	2,300 (7.9)
Health care	867 (14.4)	1,028 (11.9)	1,980 (13.7)	2,436 (12.4)	2,008 (6.9)
Others	645 (10.7)	1,182 (13.7)	2,242 (15.6)	3,420 (17.4)	3,630 (12.5)
Total (annual)	6,025 (100)	8,604 (100)	14,404 (100)	19,705 (100)	29,045 (100)

Source: National Pension Service 2006.
Note: $1 was equal to about 950 Korean won at the time of the survey.

Care for frail, elderly people made sense as the next goal of the welfare state expansion for several reasons (Campbell, Ikegami, and Kwon 2009). First, experts agreed that the problems of the elderly were likely to worsen in the future. Second, the public supported the formation of a publicly financed program to care for the elderly, and it would have been politically risky for the government to oppose it. Third, officials of the MOHW supported the program as a means not only to expand their own jurisdiction but also to relieve the burden that the elderly were increasingly placing on the health insurance system. In 2007 the elderly accounted for 28 percent of the inpatient cases in the health insurance system (36.4 percent of inpatient expenditures), up from 17.4 percent (24.3 percent of expenditures) in 2001 (see table 7.2). The government's reluctance to extend the (tax-based) public assistance program for LTC to the poor elderly also contributed to the rather early adoption of a universal financing scheme based on a premium contribution when the elderly comprise less than 10 percent of the population.

Table 7.2 Health Insurance and the Elderly: Statistics (%)

Year	2001	2002	2003	2004	2005	2006	2007
Health insurance (HI) expenditure on the elderly as a percentage of total HI expenditure	17.7	19.3	21.2	22.8	24.4	25.9	28.2
Elderly patients as a percentage of total patients				8.8	9.2	9.4	10.0
Elderly inpatients as a percentage of total inpatients	17.4	19.3	21.3	22.8	24.5	25.0	28.0
Inpatient HI expenditure on the elderly as a percentage of total inpatient HI expenditure	24.3	26.1	28.2	29.8	31.8	33.6	36.4

Source: 2001–2007 National Health Insurance Statistical Yearbook, National Health Insurance Corporation.

The government (under President Kim Dae Jung) established a Planning Committee for Elderly Long-term Care in 2000. In 2003 President Roh Moo-hyun, who was from the same political party as Kim and who had supported LTC insurance in his election campaign, decided to launch LTC insurance by 2007. The legislation was passed in April 2007, but its implementation was delayed until July 2008. The National Health Insurance Corporation (NHIC), the single payer of the health insurance program, supported LTC insurance because it was an opportunity for the corporation to expand its operations.

LTC insurance has multiple, sometimes unclear, goals. From a social welfare perspective, it aims to ease the financial burden of the elderly to pay for LTC. It appeals to public health insurance by reducing social admissions, which in turn reduces the financial burden on taxpayers. The MOHW has tried to persuade the Ministry of Finance and Economy that LTC insurance can potentially create jobs by extending social services such as LTC. Whether LTC insurance can achieve all of these goals is uncertain now, and will depend on the system's performance in the coming years.

LTC Insurance in Germany and Japan

The social health insurance schemes of Germany and Japan have much in common with that of South Korea and thus provide useful points of comparison (Kwon 2008). The LTC insurance systems of the two countries differ, however. In Germany, sickness funds provide LTC insurance, while in Japan, local governments do. Local governments in Japan also provide health insurance for the self-employed and welfare services for the elderly. German LTC insurance is funded solely through the contributions of the insured, while in Japan it is funded through taxes (45 percent), contributions (45 percent), and copayments (10 percent). In terms of population coverage, German LTC insurance provides coverage to all who need LTC due to disability, regardless of age, whereas Japan's system covers only aging-related LTC.

In Germany, LTC insurance covers only basic needs; therefore, benefits are fixed at a certain rate and are based on the level of eligibility (dependence) rather than the actual cost of the care provided (Schneider 1999). As a result, the German LTC financing system seems more financially sustainable in the long run than that of Japan. However, the insufficient benefits of the LTC insurance system in Germany may lead many poor, old people to seek additional support from welfare programs offered by the local governments (Naegele and Reichert 2002).

In the German system, beneficiaries can choose between cash benefits and service benefits. Although the cash benefits are worth only half of the estimated value of the service benefits, the majority of people have chosen them, contributing to the system's fiscal health (Rothgang 2002). In contrast, cash benefits are not available in Japan; many Japanese women oppose them because they believe that such cash payments will increase pressure on informal caregivers (who are mostly women) to provide LTC (Campbell and Ikegami 2003).

Social Insurance for LTC in South Korea

South Korean lawmakers have not seriously considered tax-based financing for LTC. Instead, they adopted contribution-based social insurance financing because the South Korean welfare state was already based on a social insurance system, including health insurance, pension funds, unemployment insurance, and workplace injury compensation. LTC insurance, separated from health insurance, has the potential benefit of demedicalizing LTC because physicians may play a dominating role when health insurance provides LTC coverage. Such a separation can also make it easier for the government to persuade the public to pay a contribution (instead of a general tax) exclusively for LTC. However, the separation of LTC financing from health insurance financing could be a barrier to effective coordination between health care and LTC, since both systems might try to pin responsibility for payment on the other.

LTC insurance also saves administrative costs by using the existing administrative structure of the health insurer, the NHIC. The uniform contribution rate and benefit packages of LTC insurance are a vestige of the centralized, single-payer health insurance system, which administers the LTC insurance. Path dependency or similarity among social insurance systems also affects the financing mix, and LTC insurance in South Korea is not pure social insurance. Rather, it has mixed financing, with the contribution playing a bigger role than the tax subsidy. As in the case of health insurance, the MOHW plays a key role in setting policy for LTC insurance.

Population Coverage of LTC Insurance

LTC insurance covers LTC for the elderly (aged 65+), but it only provides age-related LTC for those under 65. This represents a political compromise. Everyone should contribute, thereby making everyone eligible for the benefits, but it is understandably difficult for younger people to get benefits because LTC is determinedly *age-related*. South Korean LTC insurance does *not* provide coverage for disability-related LTC. In other words, in its LTC insurance scheme, the government seeks to address only population aging and age-related problems, not problems related to LTC more generally.

Before a person receives LTC insurance benefits, he or she is tested for eligibility. The same is not true for general health insurance, which is granted without such an assessment. A visiting team from the branch offices of the insurer (the NHIC) assesses the patient's functional status for eligibility using fifty-six evaluation items based on, for example, activities of daily living (ADLs). There are three levels of functional status/limitations with corresponding benefit levels. The assessment committee in the regional offices of the NHIC—which consists of fewer than fifteen members, including a social worker and a medical doctor (or traditional medical doctor)—uses this assessment along with a doctor's report to decide whether the person is eligible to receive benefits.

The assessment process is crucial to determining the size of the population covered. Currently the assessment scheme deems that only 3 to 4 percent of the total elderly population may receive LTC insurance benefits, a proportion that likely falls short of demand. The low level of population coverage has opened the scheme up to criticism that it is not actually universal and may undermine its ability to ease the financial burden on health insurance (caused by social admissions), one of the program's goals. If the government extends the target of population coverage, the contribution of LTC insurance should increase.

The government started LTC insurance pilot programs in 2005. Under the second-year pilot programs, conducted in eight sites (three big urban cities, two small urban cities, and three rural towns) between April 2006 and April 2007, 17.2 percent of people aged 65+ applied for LTC benefits. Of the total elderly population in the pilot sites, 3.3 percent were approved, with 1.07 percent in level 1 (most serious), 0.78 percent in level 2, and 1.48 percent in level 3. Sixty-six percent of the people approved for LTC benefits used them: 46 percent of those who used LTC benefits received institutional care, 39 percent received home-based care, and 15 percent received cash benefits (offered in exceptional cases, such as when no LTC service providers were available in the region). The 34 percent of those approved for benefits who did not use them reported reasons such as getting family care instead (43.3 percent), hospitalization (17.1 percent), and financial barriers (7.1 percent).

Level and Type of Benefits of LTC Insurance

Contribution to LTC insurance is determined as a fixed percentage (currently 4.05 percent) of the health insurance contribution, and the two contributions are collected together (monthly). Overall financing consists of a government subsidy of 20 percent, copayment of 20 percent for institutional care or 15 percent for home-based care, and a personal contribution of 60 to 65 percent. The poor are exempted from copayment. LTC insurance does not cover meals or private rooms. LTC delivery in South Korea is predominantly private, and private providers can have perverse financial incentives to induce demand for the uncovered areas of service, resulting in a financial burden on the elderly. To limit this burden, an income-based ceiling should be placed on cumulative out-of-pocket payments.

LTC insurance provides service benefits in principle, and cash benefits are provided only in exceptional cases. Benefits depend on the level of functional limitations determined in the assessment process. There are ceilings on the benefits for noninstitutional care, ranging from 1,097,000 Korean won (about $1,000) per month for level 1 to 760,000 Korean won per month for level 3. The type of payment to providers varies—it may be calculated per hour for part-time home care, per visit for nursing services or help with bathing, or per day for institutional care and full-time home care.

The limited role of cash benefits in South Korea needs to be reconsidered (Kwon 2008). Although women in South Korea did not oppose them the way Japanese women did, South Korean policymakers determined that the potential for abusing such payments, combined with the potentially low quality of care that many informal caregivers provide, made them undesirable. However, cash benefits can have positive effects on consumer choice and competition among formal and informal caregivers. Setting the cash benefit level lower than the comparable service (in-kind) benefits can also result in savings, as is the case in Germany. The potential (negative) impact of cash benefits on women's participation in the labor force depends on labor-market conditions and the availability of social security programs such as paid family leave. Women in socioeconomically vulnerable groups are less likely to get jobs than wealthier women, and the jobs they do get tend to be low-paid; for this group, cash LTC benefits can be an income support.

Challenges

The number of (private) providers in the LTC sector has increased rapidly, but there are still too few LTC providers in some rural areas. But there seems to be an oversupply of home-care (visiting) providers in many urban areas, resulting in demand inducement.

The quality of care offered at LTC institutions varies widely. Accordingly, the government should monitor and evaluate the quality of care at LTC institutions and then disseminate its findings so that consumers can make informed decisions about who will provide their care. Payment to providers needs to be differentiated based on the structural measures (facility, personnel) of LTC institutions or service evaluation, and on long-term outcome measures. The training and working conditions of the LTC workers will likewise affect LTC quality. Accreditation of LTC providers, institutions, and training programs is important.

LTC should be more closely coordinated with welfare services. Currently, local governments play a very small role in LTC delivery: they provide financing for LTC for the poor (through public assistance programs) and regulate and certify LTC institutions, but have little to do with the vast majority of cases. Empowering local governments to coordinate services with the NHIC—which administers LTC insurance through its branch offices—would help to improve the efficiency of the LTC system.

Coordination between health insurance and LTC insurance is key to the continuum of care and to preventing the need for LTC in the first place. Good medical care and better health of the elderly can reduce the need for LTC. Benefit coverage of LTC insurance must be coordinated with that of health insurance, where out-of-pocket payments amount to more than 35 percent of the total health expenditure (Kwon 2009b). The relative generosity of the payments to LTC hospitals (paid by health insurance) and to LTC institutions (paid by LTC insurance) will also affect the incentives and behavior of consumers and providers. On the one hand, if the benefit coverage of LTC insurance is too stringent, the elderly will prefer acute-care hospitals—and the problems of social admissions into those hospitals will remain. On the other hand, if the benefit coverage of public health insurance is too stringent, it can place a heavy financial burden on the general population who use health care.

Conclusion

The introduction of LTC insurance marks a major change in the South Korean LTC system. The new public financing mechanism for LTC was made possible by progressive governments (under presidents Kim and Roh) that also expanded other social welfare programs. When a conservative government took power in early 2008, some were concerned that LTC insurance would not be implemented, but such a reversal would have been politically risky, as the program had already been planned and had enthusiastic supporters among the elderly and their families.

LTC insurance can potentially have a big impact on the health-care system and local welfare services, and coordination among LTC insurance, health insurance, and local governments will be important. The South Korean LTC insurance system is in its infancy and still faces many challenges, such as finding the right balance between institutional care and home-based care, achieving regional equity in the distribution of LTC providers, and ensuring, through certification and training, that all personnel and facilities offer high-quality services.

References

Campbell, J., and N. Ikegami. 2003. "Japan's Radical Reform of Long-term Care." *Social Policy and Administration* 37 (1): 21–34.

Campbell, J., N. Ikegami, and S. Kwon. 2009. "Policy Learning and Cross-national Diffusion in Social Long-term Care Insurance: Germany, Japan and Korea." *International Social Security Review* 62 (4): 63–80.

Kwon, Soonman. 2003. "Health Care Financing Reform and the New Single Payer System in Korea: Social Solidarity or Efficiency?" *International Social Security Review* 56 (1): 75–94.

———. 2008. "Future of Long-term Care Financing for the Elderly in Korea." *Journal of Aging and Social Policy* 20 (1): 119–36.

———. 2009a. "The Introduction of Long-term Care Insurance in South Korea." *Eurohealth* 15 (1): 28–29.

———. 2009b. "Thirty Years of National Health Insurance in Korea: Lessons for Universal Health Care Coverage." *Health Policy and Planning* 24 (1): 63–71.

Kwon, Soonman, and Ian Holliday. 2007. "The Korean Welfare State: A Paradox of Expansion in an Era of Globalization and Economic Crisis?" *International Journal of Social Welfare* 16 (3): 242–48.

MOHW (Ministry of Health and Welfare) and KIHASA (Ministry of Health and Welfare and Korea Institute for Health and Social Affairs). 2001. *Survey of Long-term Care Needs of Older Persons* [in Korean]. Seoul: MOHW and KIHASA.

Naegele, G., and M. Reichert. 2002. "Six Years of Long-term Care Insurance in Germany: An Overview." In *Aging and Social Policy: A German-Japanese Comparison*, edited by H. Conrad and R. Luetzeler, 123–38. München: iudicium Verlag.

National Health Insurance Corporation. 2001–2007. *National Health Insurance Statistical Yearbook* [in Korean]. Seoul.

National Pension Service. 2006. *Results of the Analysis of the Panel on Security for the Elderly in 2005* [in Korean]. Seoul: National Pension Research Institute.

NSO (National Statistics Office). *Population Statistics 2007* [in Korean]. Seoul: NSO.

Rothgang, H. 2002. "Long-term Care in Germany: Projections on Public Long-term Care Insurance Financing." In *Aging and Social Policy: A German-Japanese Comparison*, edited by H. Conrad and R. Luetzeler, 251–73. München: iudicium Verlag.

Schneider, U. 1999. "Germany's Social Long-term Care Insurance: Design, Implementation, and Evaluation." *International Social Security Review* 52 (2): 31–74.

OLD-AGE PENSION REFORM
IN SOUTH KOREA

Byongho Tchoe

In traditional South Korean society, families bear the responsibility of supporting the elderly. Though this practice has become weaker in recent years as the country has modernized, there is an implicit social contract, handed down through generations, that children—especially first-born sons—should support their aging parents. Parents, after all, spend a lifetime raising and educating their children and then distribute their property among them as inheritance after retirement.

As South Korea has industrialized, many have believed that this tradition will be supplemented by the type of modern pension system prevalent in most industrialized Western countries. But South Korea's modernization started very late: the country was not liberated from Japan's colonial rule until 1945. Though a modern and democratic South Korean government was established in 1948, it was subject to the Korean War (1950–53), during which poverty and political chaos were rampant and the economy was too unstable for the government to consider establishing any social security system. The first public pension, for civil servants and the military, was introduced in 1960, and then a private school teachers' pension was implemented in 1975. The National Pension Service (NPSS) for corporate workers, the self-employed, and farmers, was initiated in 1988; the NPSS achieved statutory universal coverage in 1999. As coverage has rapidly explanded, public pensions have experienced deficits and faced many a potential crisis. In response to such troubles, public pension programs have been under incessant pressure to reform.

In this chapter, I present the history of South Korea's public pension schemes. I review the effects of pension reforms from the perspective of sustainability, income protection, and politics; I also discuss the need for further pension reform.

The Evolution of Old-age Pensions

Introduction of Public Occupational Pensions

The administration of Rhee Syngman, the first South Korean president following liberation from Japanese colonial rule, established the foundation of a modern nation but lacked political leadership. Consequently, Rhee's administration was toppled by a mass student demonstration on April 1960. The new government introduced both a civil servants' pension and a military pension, but their actual implementation was not carried out until after General Park Jung-hee's coup d'état in May 1961. The military government's top objective was to eradicate poverty by undertaking ambitious development plans, to be carried out by a strong and stable bureaucracy. In particular, the government wanted an institutional system to safeguard the stability and livelihood of the civil service and military personnel and to provide some financial incentive to prevent their corruption. Since civil service salaries were very low, a generous old-age pension appeared to be a good way to ensure long and loyal service. Likewise, a pension was viewed as a strong incentive to keep and attract strong military personnel, who were key to deterring any threat from North Korea.

South Korea's first public pension system was thus introduced in 1960, covering just these two groups, who were considered essential for the nation's development and security. While teachers in public schools were covered under the civil servants' pension, teachers in private schools were not. This discrepancy became a serious social issue in a country where education is considered a top priority. In response to private school teachers' continued demand for coverage, the government finally introduced a private school teachers' pension in 1975.

Thanks to the rapid economic growth in South Korea during the early days of public pensions, the government thought that the economic success would continue in the future and that the budget could support more generous retirement benefits. Thus, the benefit levels of all three pension funds rose steadily. In the case of private school teachers, benefits rose automatically as the civil servants' pensions were revised. Although the government was unable to raise the salaries of civil service workers and military personnel as quickly, it increased the pension benefits and retirement allowances of these workers.

Introduction of the National Pension

Once the public pensions for civil servants and military personnel were enacted, general workers began clamoring for pensions as well. Though a voluntary retirement allowance system had been introduced in 1953, this was so meager that it was considered just a severance payment. In 1961 the government began requiring employers with thirty workers or more to provide lump-sum allowances to retiring workers, and in 1989 the government expanded the policy to all workplaces with five workers or more. Unlike the public occupational workers' pension system, this system was fully funded by employers and received no government subsidy.

As economic growth continued, the system was amended to encourage long-term service to a company, with the amount of the retirement allowance increasing progressively, according to duration of service. The minimum amount of the retirement allowance guaranteed by the law was equal to the last monthly salary multiplied by the number of years served. This change turned the system into a strong policy instrument to retain good workers. Considering that most South Korean workers retire in their mid-fifties, the lump-sum retirement allowance proved very useful: it could be used as a fund for old-age income maintenance, for starting a new business, or for children's education and weddings. Some people retired early to use this lump sum to purchase a house; in the absence of a housing mortgage system such as those found in other advanced countries, South Koreans need a fairly large amount of money to buy property. But compared with the benefits of the public occupational pensions, the retirement allowance was still quite low, and it failed to be a source of stable income protection for the elderly because it was a lump sum and, even worse,

Table 8.1 Key Features of Public Retirement Plans before Reform in 1999

	Public occupations	General workers
Coverage	Civil servants (1960), military personnel (1960), private school teachers (1975)	Corporate workers (1988), rural residents (1995), urban residents (1999)
Benefits	Pension plus lump-sum allowance; the amount of pension is 50–76 percent of final salary at retirement for 20–33 years of service, and adjusted annually by the increasing rate of wages. The other option is to take a lump sum, amounting to the final salary multiplied by years of service. The amount of lump-sum allowance is 60 percent of the final salary multiplied by years of service. Benefits begin at the time of retirement.	Pension plus lump-sum allowance; the amount of pension is 70 percent of lifetime average wage for 40 years of contributions, and adjusted annually by the consumer price index. The amount of lump sum is at least the final wage multiplied by years of employment. Pension begins at 60 years old, and lump-sum allowance is paid at retirement.
Financing	*Pension*: 4.6 percent of salary (1960), 7 percent (1970), 11 percent (1979), 13 percent (1996), 15 percent (1999), which were paid by government (half) and employees (half). *Lump sum*: government budget.	*Pension*: 9 percent of wages or incomes, paid by both employers (half) and employees (half). *Lump sum*: 8.3 percent of wages paid by employers only.

Source: Ministry of Health and Welfare, Ministy of Defense, Ministry of Public Administration, and Ministry of Labor.

it was nontransferable when workers switched jobs.[1] This is why the need for a pension system for private-sector workers was repeatedly raised.

Even though there were several attempts to initiate an NP for private-sector workers, these efforts met with strong objections from business leaders, who had difficulty even financing the retirement allowance. The business leaders wanted to convert the retirement allowance into a pension scheme if the NPSS was introduced despite their objections. But workers persisted in their demand for the NPSS, in addition to the retirement allowance.

The first National Pension Act was legislated in 1973, but implementation was postponed due to the oil shock. The Act stipulated that the benefit level of old-age pension be proportional to the income and contribution period, and the benefit be redistributive across income groups. To be eligible for pension, one must be 60 years old and have a contribution history of at least 15 years. The NPS was to be financed by contributions from both employers and employees. The base income to assess pension benefits was calculated as the average wage of a whole working period, and the replacement rates of pension to the base income were 40 percent to 80 percent for 20 to 40 years of contributions.

Another effort to introduce the NPS was thwarted by a second oil shock in the 1980s. When it was finally implemented in 1988 with a revision of the 1973 Act, the NPS provided coverage only to businesses with ten or more employees, and reduced the income replacement rate from 80 percent to 70 percent for a participant with a 40-year contribution history. The contribution rate was raised from 3 percent in 1988 to 6 percent in 2003 and 9 percent in 2008.[2] Coverage was expanded in 1992 to workplaces with a minimum of five employees. But farmers and self-employed persons were still completely left out of the public pension system, raising a serious social equity issue. In 1995, NPS coverage was extended to rural residents. Finally, in 1999, the NPS was extended to urban residents and became universal, a remarkable accomplishment given that it had been initiated only eleven years earlier.

Since the NPS benefits can be paid only to those who have contributed to the fund for at least 15 years (though some exceptions have been made for older workers), it did not help retirees receive a proper pension during its initial period of operation. For this reason, the retirement allowance has carried out an important role as a good resource for the living after retirement.

---

[1] The retirement allowance has an attractive advantage in its lump-sum cash payment, and some pensioners under the civil servants' and teachers' pensions wanted this lump-sum payment feature. Therefore, both the civil servants' and the teachers' pensions were changed to allow for benefits to be received in a lump sum, as an annuity, or in a combination of the two.

[2] Providing coverage to small enterprises with ten or more workers was possible since the retirement allowance system and the national health insurance system were already serving these workplaces, and the administrative infrastructure for collecting contributions was already in place.

The Pension Crisis and Pension Reform

Economic Downturn, Aging, and the Pension Crisis

The pension crisis was predictable, mainly because the system delivered higher benefits relative to low contributions. External factors exacerbated the problem. The first was the downturn of the South Korean economy, in particular the financial crisis of 1998, which actually accelerated public pension reform. As economic growth has slowed since the 1998 crisis, South Korea lacked confidence to finance the future huge pension commitments.

The second factor was the change in South Korea's demographic makeup: longer life expectancy achieved by better health care, combined with extremely low birth rates, meant that the aging population as a proportion of the overall population was increasing rapidly. Urgent pension reforms had to be carried out to avoid a serious crisis in pension finance (see figure 8.1). Yet more reforms are necessary: public pensions in their current state place a huge financial burden on future generations and threaten to damage the economy irreparably by reducing work incentives and thereby depleting national savings.

Figure 8.1 Rapid Aging and a Slowing Birth Rate (%)

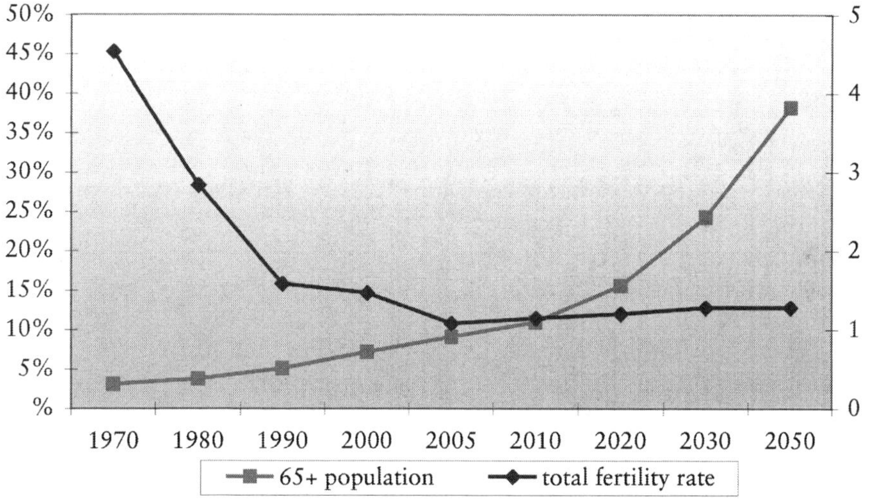

Source: National Bureau of Statistics.

Public Occupational Pension Crisis and Reforms

Causes

The public pension system was developed under the illusion that the rapid economic growth would last. As a consequence, benefit levels across all occupational pensions were repeatedly increased. For example, when the civil servants' pension was introduced in 1960, the income replacement ratio stood at 30 percent of a worker's salary at the time of retirement for retirees with twenty years' contribution and 50 percent of the final salary for those who had contributed for thirty years. The ratios were adjusted upward in 1967 to 50 percent for retirees with twenty years' contribution and 70 percent for retirees with thirty years' contribution. This was extended in 1981 to 76 percent for those who had contributed for thirty-three years. The military and private school teachers' pensions followed suit, increasing their benefits in lockstep with the civil servants' pension. At the same time, as the demand for the lump-sum retirement allowance (besides pension payment) increased, this allowance increased, reaching up to 60 percent of the last monthly salary multiplied by the years of service. As civil servants, military personnel, and private school teachers were considered to be elite groups, their pension benefits were very generous, always taking up their full budget allotment. Not surprisingly, the budget officers themselves were also eligible for these pensions.

Compared with the high level of pension benefits, the contribution rate, which was shared equally by the government and civil servants, was low. In 1960 the contribution rate was 4.6 percent of the monthly salary; this was raised to 7 percent in 1970 as pension benefits rose rapidly and to 11 percent in 1979. As the pension fund seemed available for the benefits increase, pension benefits consistently expanded.[3] This trend continued until 1993, when the civil servants' pension recorded a deficit for the first time and alarm bells began to ring. The military pension was already running deficits in 1973, and the teachers' pension, which was introduced in 1975, was expected to follow the civil servants' pension in the future.

Another factor that contributed to the crisis was the pension eligibility age—it was 60 when the occupational pensions were introduced in 1960, but in just two years the restriction on the pensionable age was lifted in 1962, and retirees who had contributed for at least twenty years were allowed lifetime pension benefits.

Moreover, when retirees were given the option to choose between a monthly pension and a lump-sum payment, many chose a lump-sum payment in the 1960s and 1970s. Recently, the preference has shifted to a monthly pension.[4] Retirees have recognized the importance of a stable old-age income, and the attraction of a lump-sum payment based on the last monthly pay has lost its merit as wage-increase rates have tapered off. Also, in response to the growing need for a lump-sum allowance besides a pension, the government has set aside a significant amount of lump-sum allowance for retirees, which amounts to 60 percent of the final wage multiplied by the years of service. Fulfilling the need

---

[3] Expansion of pension benefits included the expansion of the salary scope (which was the basis of the benefit calculation), the retirement lump-sum allowance, and the survivor's pension benefit.

[4] Sixty-seven percent of retirees chose a pension in 1996 and 94 percent in 2008.

for a lump-sum benefit has led almost all retirees to choose the pension option instead of the lump-sum option. This, along with all the other factors, has placed a great burden on pension finance.

Reforms

Unlike the NPS, which faced formidable pressure to reform from its inception and which anticipated a financial deficit in the future, the pensions for civil servants, military personnel, and private school teachers resisted and delayed reform. Strong interest groups wanted to hold on to their privileges despite the obviously imminent crisis.

Despite the objections of these groups, the first round of pension reforms was carried out in 1996. The level of contribution was raised from 11 to 13 percent, having remained in the region of 11 percent since 1979, and the pension-eligible age of 60 years was applied to new civil servants joining the service. The contribution rate was further increased to 15 percent in 1999. The second round of pension reforms, initiated in 2001, raised the contribution rate to 17 percent, called for the gradual application of the pension-eligible age to all current civil servants, changed the pension calculation basis from the last monthly drawn salary to the last three years' average salary, and indexed the annual adjustment of pension benefits to the mix of the wage increasing rate and the consumer price index (CPI). As the second round of reforms was carried out, the government decided to cover any deficits in the civil servants' pension. These reforms were applied to the military and teachers' pensions too.

Conclusion

Despite the two rounds of reform, the deficit in the civil servants' pension grew rapidly, rising from 13 percent of the total pension expenditure in 2005 to 26.5 percent in 2009. It is now projected that the government support for the civil servants' pension will increase to 60.7 percent of total pension expenditure by 2020 and to around 75 percent after 2030. Contributions as a percentage of the entire salary of civil servants are projected to be 4.4 percent in 2010, 16.7 percent in 2020, and 30–37 percent after 2030 (Moon 2009a, 9).[5]

---

[5] The ratio of government support to gross domestic product (GDP) would be 0.17 percent in 2009, 1.26 percent in 2030, and 2.57 percent in 2070.

Figure 8.2 Government Subsidy to Compensate Deficits of Civil Servant Pension (%)

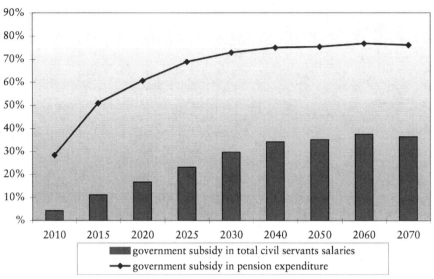

Source: Moon 2009a.

In 2007 a task force convened to reform the civil servants' pension. In November 2008 the administration submitted a reform bill to the National Assembly. The key elements of the bill include a reduction of pension benefits and an increase in the contribution rate. The income base for contributions and benefits was changed from salary to taxable income, which is broader than salary. The contribution rates were scheduled to increase from 11 percent of taxable income in 2009 to 17 percent in 2012, which are equivalent to 17 percent and 21.6 percent of salary, respectively.[6] The bill also called for changing the pension calculation basis from the last three years' average earnings to the average working-life earnings; indexing the benefits increase to the CPI; further extending the pension-eligible age to 65; and reducing the survivor's pension from 70 percent of the deceased worker's pension to 60 percent for new entrants. Fundamentally, such structural reform was intended to level the playing field for public servants and private workers, so that each group received equivalent retirement benefits. However, pension reform remains parametric in nature, in that it deals with adjustments to the coefficients of the pension benefit formula and contribution rates. Indeed, the structural reform that most members of the task force proposed was blocked by the strong objections of the civil servants' labor union.

---

[6] If calculated by using the previous basis, it is equivalent to an increase from 17 percent to 21.6 percent.

National Pension Crisis and Reforms

Causes

In 1988, the NPS instituted universal coverage. In 1999, it achieved it. Between these years, most advanced countries were experiencing serious pension crises, with reform efforts facing strong objections from participants who were about to retire. The South Korean government wanted to institute an advanced social security system and did not take such warnings seriously. From 1988 to 1999, the NPS fund reserve grew: revenues from contributions increased, while pension benefit payments were fewer, due to the strict requirement that all recipients contribute to the fund for at least fifteen years. Unlike the public occupational pensions, whose benefits are determined by last salaries, the pension benefits under the NPS are determined by the average income during the whole contribution period. This was another factor that the government did not take seriously.

The contribution rate, however, was set at 3 percent in the beginning—half paid by employers and half by employees—and raised to 6 percent in 1993, and then raised again to 9 percent in 1998. Despite these increases in contribution rates, the overall level of contribution was so low that the NPS could not meet the commitment of future pension benefits.

Reforms

Reflecting experts' warnings of an impending crisis, the government was forced to carry out pension reform in 1999 as well as to institute universal coverage. This included a downward adjustment of pension benefits from 70 percent of the average income of a participant with a forty-year contribution history to 60 percent, and a gradual increase of the pensionable age from 60 to 65 years by 2033. In fact, the National Pension Act was legislated first in 1973 with an income replacement rate of 80 percent for forty-year contributions, but when the Act was actually implemented in 1988, the rate was lowered to 70 percent in anticipation of future financial difficulty.

Despite the 1999 reform, the NPS financial crisis did not abate. The progressive government that came to power in 2003 (and which had taken power in 1998 for the first time in history) submitted a reform bill to the National Assembly in October of that year, though the reform plan did not match its political principles. The bill cut the then–replacement rate of pension benefits down to 50 percent and gradually ratcheted up the contribution rate to 15.85 percent. But the conservative opposition party demanded that the replacement rate be cut even further, to the 40 percent level. It proposed that the 40 percent pension be split between a basic pension and an income-related pension, and that the basic pension be applied for all the current elderly without contributions (and therefore be made attractive to the elderly voters), and the income-related pension be made proportional to both the income and contribution years.

Ironically, the super-progressive Labor Party supported this proposal, because the universal basic pension would improve the living of workers retiring with few contributions.

Figure 8.3 Unfunded Liability of Public Pensions as a Percentge of GDP

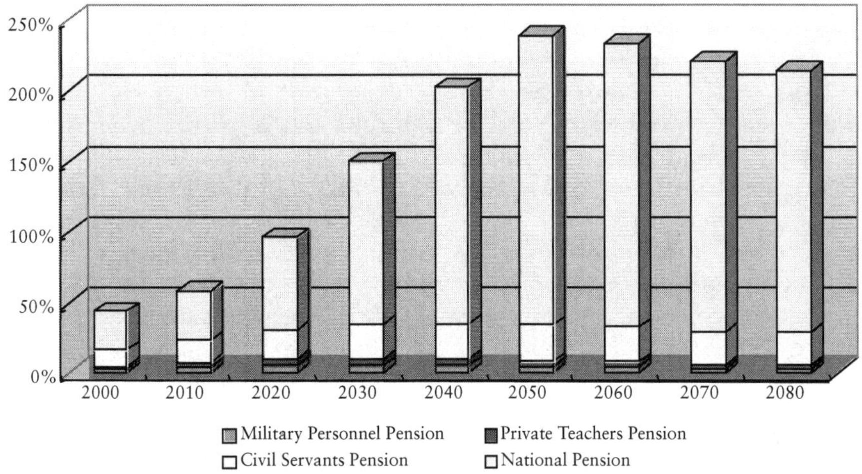

Source: Tchoe 2000.

In April 2006, both the ministry and the governing party submitted a pension reform bill under which the income replacement rate would be gradually reduced from 50 percent in 2008 to the 40 percent level by 2028. They also presented another bill of the Basic Elderly Pension Act to provide income support to the elderly through means testing, which is financed by tax revenue and thereby more like social allowances for the elderly than pension as social insurance.[7] In fact, all three parties—the government, the governing party, and the opposition party—agreed on both pieces of legislation, after a series of negotiations and compromises, as no one wanted to antagonize the general public prior to the 2007 presidential election.

Accordingly, the Basic Elderly Pension Act was passed by the National Assembly, with the support of the opposition party, in April 2007. Under the law, about 60 percent of the elderly population in 2008 and 70 percent in 2009 would be paid a monthly pension of 85,000 South Korean won (about $70, or 5 percent of the national average income), an amount that is scheduled to increase gradually, to 180,000 South Korean won (about $150, or 10 percent of the national average income) by 2028. The revised National Pension Act, passed by the National Assembly in July 2007, reduced the income replacement rate to 50

---

[7] The basic pension proposed by the opposition party aimed to provide a higher pension for the elderly as well as for survivors and disabled persons.

percent in 2008 and to 40 percent by 2028, which the opposition party demanded. But the proposal to raise the contribution rate was withdrawn—the 9 percent contribution rate was unchanged—leaving pension reform incomplete.[8]

Conclusion

Before the 2007 reform, the NPS was projected to record a deficit in 2034 and pension reserves were expected to be completely depleted by 2049. The 2007 reform merely deferred the crisis; it is now projected that the NPS fund reserve will be depleted in 2060.

Furthermore, there was a gloomy projection that the ratio of the unfunded liability of the NPS to GDP would increase drastically from 28 percent in 2000 to over 100 percent in 2030 and to 200 percent in 2050. The gross pension liability, including those of civil servants, military personnel, and teachers, was forecast to increase from 47 percent of GDP in 2000 to 240 percent in 2050 (Tchoe 2000, 76). In short, maintaining the current NPS will put an unbearable burden on future generations and adversely affect the economy, causing work disincentives and a decrease in savings.

Discussion

Sustainability

The structure of the public occupational pensions—that is, low contribution rates coupled with increasingly high benefits—led to financial crisis. The military pension incurred a deficit after only ten years of operation, but since the government had full responsibility to ensure the comfortable retirement life of the military personnel, it financed the deficit from the government budget. In the case of the civil servants' pension, however, the reform effort was reluctantly started as late as 1996, with no guarantee of financial sustainability being restored any time in the future. Even with the passing of the 2008 reform bill, the deficit in the civil servants' pension was projected to amount to 17.6 percent of the pension expenditure in 2010, 45.9 percent in 2020, and 57.0 percent in 2030, which will be met by government budgetary support (Moon 2009b, 9).

Because South Korea is the only country in the world in conflict with a Communist country, North Korea, it may be difficult to reform the military pension; the military will likely put up strong resistance. In the case of the teachers' pension, it would be possible to convince the public of the need for reform, and then the government could ask the teachers' pension to have its own financing system, on the grounds that government financial support is reaching to limit.

---

[8] The ratio of the unfunded liability of the NPS to GDP was estimated to be 16.6 percent in 2010, 16.4 percent in 2030, 55.2 percent in 2050, and 97.1 percent in 2070 (Moon 2009b, 8).

Table 8.2 Process of National Pension Reform

	1973	1988	1995	1999	2008
Replacement rate	80%	70%	70%	60%	50% (40% in 2028)
Population coverage	— (defer)	Employees	Farmers	Universal coverage, extend pension age to 65 by 2033	Means-tested basic pension for the elderly

Source: Ministry of Health and Welfare.
Note: The replacement rate refers to the proportion of pension benefits in weighted average income to 40 years of contributions.

Most experts have recommended a structural reform under which public occupational pension benefits would be equivalent to those provided by the NPS, and the retirement lump-sum allowance would be converted into a retirement pension. They also proposed that an additional defined-contribution plan (DC plan) be introduced to safeguard the old-age livelihood of civil servants if necessary. But when the civil servants' labor union resisted strongly, the reform bill became closer to a parametric adjustment, through a moderate increase in the contribution rates and reduced pension benefits. Unlike the NPS, substantial reform of public occupational pensions has not been carried out.

Figure 8.4 Projection of Reserve Fund of National Pension as a Percentage of GDP before and after 2007 Reform (%)

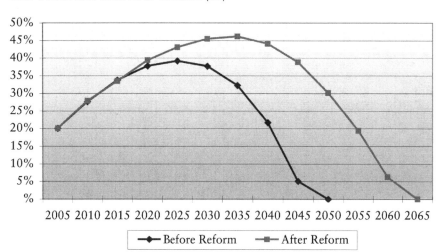

Source: Moon 2009b.

Experts have worried about the NPS's financial sustainability since its inception, and despite the two rounds of reforms, in 1999 and 2007. These reforms deferred the timing of the fund depletion from 2049 to 2060, but failed to remove the system's financial burden from ensuing generations. Further, the introduction of the basic elderly pension, which is based on tax financing, will increase the tax burden in the future as the elderly population grows. There will also be pressure to increase the benefit level of the basic elderly pension so that it guarantees the minimum cost of living. Taken together, these issues suggest that another round of pension reform is unavoidable.

The most feasible plan is to reform the NPS into a two-tier scheme that includes basic pensions and earnings-related pensions. Supporters of this plan contend that the basic universal pension will ensure a minimum standard of living for the elderly, and the earnings-related pension plus a DC plan will be sustainable. This plan has received broad support from experts.[9] The plan also proposes that the retirement lump-sum allowance should in fact be converted into a DC plan to ensure its sustainability. However, this plan has been put off course by the recent global financial crisis, which seriously damaged the credibility of financial institutions. Now it is considered too risky to leave pension funds in the financial market.

Income Maintenance

When we pay attention to sustainability, we often neglect the problem of income protection for the elderly, which is the primary purpose of a pension system. As it stands now, the income protection of both South Korea's current and future elderly is in jeopardy.

Most workers in South Korea retire in their mid-fifties, but very few retire with pension benefits. Even for most NPS recipients, the benefit amount does not cover the minimum cost of living. Consequently, a majority of retired workers continue to work to subsist, either as part-time or self-employed workers. In reality, most workers effectively retire in their mid-sixties after spending about ten years in unstable employment (Bang et al. 2008, 201). According to a 2005 survey, only 36 percent of fully retired persons and 19 percent of partial retirees receive pension benefits, and most recipients get them from the public occupational pensions. A fully retired pensioner receiving benefits from the

---

[9] The Bush administration in the United States tried to convert part of Social Security into an individual account plan but did not have the support to carry out the plan. The individual account plan was to resolve the problems of excessive administrative and marketing costs by allowing collection by the Internal Revenue Service (IRS), management of funds by the Social Security Administration (SSA), supervision by an independent board of trustees, and actual handling by a private manager (report on December 21, 2001, by the President's Commission to Strengthen Social Security). This idea influenced the Korean pension reform process.

NPS would receive the equivalent of $325 monthly, far less than the average amount—$1,358—received by retirees getting a public occupational pension (Korea Labor Institute 2005).[10]

Table 8.3 Public Pensioners, Retired Persons, and Their Pension Amounts

	Partially retired	Absolutely retired
Share of national pensioners	12% ($203)	20% ($325)
Share of public occupational pensioners	7% ($1,256)	16% ($1,358)

Source: Korea Labor Institute, KLoSA 2005.
Note: ( ) refers to monthly pension amount in U.S. dollars (at an exchange rate of 1,200 Korean won per dollar).

As seen in figure 8.5, asset-poverty incidence increases with age, rising from 24.5 percent for a person in his fifties to 57.7 percent for a person in his eighties (Nam and Kwon 2008, 18). In particular, the elderly in the low- and middle-income brackets have a very unstable old age. Since most of the elderly have no disposable assets, they depend on financial help from their children. Indeed, even those fortunate enough to have assets usually need help because they hold 90 percent of their assets in the form of property, usually a house. The Gini coefficient for income distribution among those who are aged 50+ is estimated at 0.59, and the Gini coefficient for asset distribution in this same group is 0.71 (Nam and Kwon 2008, 11), which implies a worsening disparity between income and assets after retirement. To solve the liquidity problem for elderly homeowners, the housing pension was launched in July 2007. The housing pension is a reverse mortgage under which banks provide pensions to the elderly, keeping a house as security. Most elderly people are, however, reluctant to use this system because they have a strong desire to leave their homes to their children. Likewise, the children prefer to support their parents in the hopes that they will inherit a house someday. So in 2008, only 695 persons received housing pensions.

Retirement income risks, as cited by Bodie (1990, 28–49), can be placed in the following categories: replacement rate inadequacy, social security cuts, longevity, investment risk, and inflation risk. All these risks, with the possible exception of the inflation risk, apply to the NPS in South Korea. Though the asset-management performance of the NPS has been satisfactory—with the NPS

---

[10] Considering that the average pension of retirees in the United States is $1,000 to $1,500 per month (Bailey and Kirkegaard 2009, 5), the Korean occupational pension benefits are considered quite high.

yield exceeding the market yield average—these are high-risk investments, as demonstrated by the recent financial crisis. The conversion of the retirement allowance into a retirement pension may help to stabilize income protection for the elderly, but the retirement pension would still be exposed to other risks such as longevity, investment risk, and inflation risk.

Thirty-three percent of NPS participants have failed to contribute to the system, and are ineligible for pension benefits by law. This group, most of whom are residence-based participants such as farmers, peddlers, and self-employed workers, may remain excluded from the old-age pension provision (Park, Kim, and Kim 2007, 42). About half of these residence-based participants will not be eligible for pension benefits. The lower a person's income, the more likely it is that she will fail to contribute to the NPS: contribution is less than 10 percent among those in the lowest 10 percent income bracket, and less than 30 percent among those in the bottom 20 percent (Bureau of Statistics 2000). According to the National Pension Development Committee (2003), the share of pensioners among the elderly aged 60+ would be 35 percent in 2020 and only 50 percent in 2040. Consequently, if the current NPS is continued, both the elderly of our generation and the elderly of ensuing generations would face a serious problem.

Figure 8.5 Asset Poverty Rate by Age Group

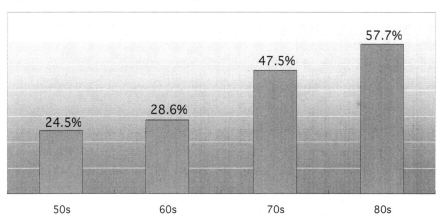

Source: Nam and Kwon 2008.
Note: The asset poverty rate refers to the proportion of households that have less than 50 percent of the median assets of 50+ households.

The NPS has failed in its mission to redistribute income and has in fact exacerbated the income gap between rich and poor. Most of the pension benefits go to the high-income groups, while the quality of life of the low-income elderly has further deteriorated. A study has found that the national health insurance system has a bigger impact on income redistribution than does the NPS (Tchoe and Kim 2005, 226–27). The findings mentioned earlier support the need to introduce a universal basic old-age pension that ensures an appropriate cost of living for the elderly. Meanwhile, the current basic elderly pension provides a modest subsidy for the elderly through means testing. Discussions about the level of basic pension benefits and their target population, however, always raise questions about both the financial sustainability and the income security of the NPS. Inevitably, such debates get bogged down in party politics.

The NPS reform of 2007 put pressure on the civil servants' pension to undertake similar reform. Prior to the 2007 reform, the benefits of the civil servants' pension were 1.4 times as high as the total benefits (pension plus retirement allowance) of the NPS workers. The 2007 reform reduced the benefit levels of the NPS, widening the gap between the civil servants' pension and the NPS. When the bill for the civil servants' pension reform was to be approved by the National Assembly in 2009, the benefits of the civil servants' pension were still projected to be 1.5 to 1.9 times as high as those of the NPS workers (Moon 2009a, 12).

Politics

As reforms to the civil servants' pension directly affect the military and teachers' pensions, these three groups, along with the occupational pension recipients, have staged joint campaigns against the reform pressure. Since several of these elite groups are involved in the policymaking and drafting process, the president and the governing party know that it is difficult to institute reform without their cooperation. Though the deficit of the civil servants' and military personnel pensions fund has been a big problem for the officials responsible for the budget, these officials themselves hope to receive high pension benefits. It is therefore unlikely that they will undertake bold and aggressive reform actions. The most vocal groups advocating for reform of the occupational pensions are academics, civic groups, and the mass media—but even some professors advocate the existing pension institutions since they too may receive generous pension benefits.

The difficulty of pension reform is reflected in the composition of the task force for the civil servants' pension reform. Of the twenty-nine task force members, comprised of public servants, experts, and members of civic groups, ten opposed the reforms. Of these, six were civil servants, two were experts recommended by the civil servants' labor union, and two came from the pensioners' association. While the National Assembly has the power to pass the legislation, the president and the governing party strongly influence its decision. It is notable that the officials working in the National Assembly and the members of the judiciary also have vested interests in the civil servants' pension. Reform plans have therefore been drafted in a manner to decrease the impact of the benefit reduction on current officials, and to transfer the brunt of the cuts and the burden of the continued deficit to newly recruited officials.[11]

The NPS reform process of 1999 and 2007 was carried out under very different political circumstances. One group—comprised of labor unions, social welfare scholars, progressive nongovernmental organizations, progressive political groups, and the Ministry of Health and Welfare—stressed income protection over financial sustainability. The other group—made up of employers' groups, economists, conservative political groups, and the ministries in charge of finance and the economy—emphasized sustainability over income protection. The conflicts between the groups continued throughout the reform process. The administration took a positive, active attitude toward NPS reform, in contrast to its lukewarm attitude toward occupational pension reform. This was because the administration knew that the NPS reform must be carried out while there were still relatively few NPS pensioners. Labor unions are usually against reform initiatives, but in this case the impact of the reform seemed too far in the future to be cause for concern. In the National Assembly, the attitudes of the governing party and the opposition party were confrontational: while the opposition party advocated bold structural reform, the governing party was afraid that structural reform might backfire and they would lose general public support as a result. Nonetheless, both parties, as well as the income-protection supporters and the sustainability supporters, agreed to compromise, pass the reform bill, and introduce the basic elderly pension (though its amount is small). With the compromise, both the governing and opposition parties freed themselves from the sensitive issue of pension reform just before the 2007 presidential election.

Conclusion

The most important challenge facing pension policy in South Korea is how the two contradicting policy objectives—income protection for the elderly and pension fund sustainability—can be harmoniously incorporated into a unique pension policy.

Though the NPS did not achieve universal coverage until 1999, it has faced a sustainability problem since the early years of its implementation and been subject to a bevy of reforms. These reforms emphasized financial sustainability through benefit reduction, and as a result the NPS may now fail in its principal obligation of providing income protection for the elderly. If the current pension system is maintained, it is likely that many current and future elderly will be left outside the old-age pension. It is possible that the income gap between the

---

[11] Under the draft reform, civil servants with more than ten years of service would be free from the benefit reduction, while those officials with fewer than ten years of service would face a benefit reduction of 1 to 8 percent. For the new joinees, the pension benefit would be 9 percent less than that of current officials and eventually would be 25 percent less (Moon 2009a, 10–11).

rich and the poor could widen further because of the paying out of unequal pension benefits.

The occupational pensions were established earlier than the NPS, and continue to provide old-age income maintenance by paying high benefits. Since these occupational pensions were ill-prepared for the future financial commitment, they now depend on government support to survive. To make these pensions self-sufficient, the benefit levels must be brought down to the level of the NPS so that government support can be minimized. Despite efforts to squeeze the civil servants' pension during the 2007 NPS reform, the 2008 occupational pension reform bill does not fully reflect proposals to make the system financially sustainable. Even if the National Assembly passes the reform bill, there will be further need for another round of reform in the near future. It is also likely that new civil servants will demand reform to correct unfair and discriminatory treatment toward them by those already in the system.

Aging is a variable that can be predicted, but the pace at which the population ages has always exceeded predictions. If labor productivity can be improved consistently through technological innovations, we should not be too concerned about the resources to support a rapidly growing senior population. If we can achieve healthy aging with improved medical technology, the pension fund depletion could be further delayed or avoided by extending the pension-eligible age.

In the future, as public pensions face a rapidly growing senior population, economic uncertainties, and changes in family structure, they must respond flexibly. In the light of the experiences of some advanced countries, we suggest that the government guarantee a minimum old-age pension and introduce a new portable retirement pension for employees in workplaces. This portable pension could be managed as either a DC plan or as a defined-benefit type pension, with clear supervision or oversight mechanisms, as well as a security arrangement to guarantee payment. Once the appropriate pension benefit is secured, total benefits should be controlled within the economy and be adequately redistributed among the different income groups. Finally, there should be concerted efforts to link pension policy with health care, employment, and social welfare to effectively address the risks of old age.

References

Bailey, Martin Neil, and Jacob Funk Kirkegaard. 2009. *U.S. Pension Reform: Lessons from Other Countries*. Washington, DC: Peterson Institute for International Economics.

Bang, Hanam, S. Kang, D. Shin, J. Ahn, J. Lee, and M. Kwon. 2008. *Gradual Retirement and Partial Pension* [in Korean]. Seoul: Korea Labor Institute.

Bodie, Zvi. 1990. "Pensions as Retirement Income Insurance." *Journal of Economic Literature* 28: 28–49.

Bureau of Statistics. 2000. *Households Consumption Survey*. Seoul, Republic of Korea.

Korea Labor Institute. 2005. *KLoSA (Korea Longitudinal Study of Aging) 2005*. Seoul.

Moon, Hyungpyo. 2009a. "Review on the Proposal for the Revision of Civil Servant Pension Law" [in Korean]. *Korea Development Policy Forum*, No. 208, Korea Development Institute, Seoul.

———. 2009b. "Demographic Changes and Pension Reform in the Republic of Korea." ADBI Working Paper Series 135, Asian Development Bank Institute, Manila.

Nam, Sang-Ho, and Soonhyun Kwon. 2008. "Asset Distribution, Inequality, and Poverty among Elderly Households in Korea." *Review of Health and Social Affairs* 28 (2): 3–32 [in Korean].

National Pension Development Committee. 2003. *Financial Evaluation and Improvement of National Pension* [in Korean]. Seoul.

Park, Inhwa, C. Kim, and S. Kim. 2007. "Financing Four Types of Pubic Pensions and its Policy Measure" [in Korean]. *Budget Issue Brief* 11, National Assembly Budget Office, Seoul.

The President's Commission to Strengthen Social Security. Report on December 21, 2001.

Tchoe, Byongho. 2000. *Liabilities of Public Pensions in Korea* [in Korean]. Seoul: Korea Institute for Health and Social Affairs.

Tchoe, Byongho, and Taewan Kim. 2005. "Redistributive Effect of Social Security System in Korea." *Social Security Review* 21 (3): 205–31 [in Korean].

THE DIABETES EPIDEMIC IN THE ASIA-PACIFIC

*Karen Eggleston, Young Kyung Do, Hong Li,
Qiong Zhang, Sauwakon Ratanawijitrasin,
Xiaoyong Wang, Syed Aljunid,
Le Thi Kim Anh, Nilay D. Shah,
Sudha Vidyasagar, Sanita Hirunrassamee,
Qingqing Lou, Chu Viet Anh, K. L. Bairy,
Jian Wang, Saperi bin Sulong, Amrizal M. Nur,
and Jeremy Goldhaber-Fiebert*

Diabetes mellitus (DM) is an important public health problem that not only compromises the length and quality of life of millions, but also offers an illuminating example of the challenges that Asia-Pacific health systems face as their populations age, move to cities, and increasingly suffer from noncommunicable diseases (NCDs). A variety of policies have been introduced to try to meet this challenge in high-income nations such as Japan and the United States (the country with the highest rate of obesity, a leading cause of NCDs). The difficulties are all the more acute for people living on less that $1 a day, as is the case for one in five residents of Vietnam.

In this chapter, we outline the DM epidemic and the associated challenges facing public health and health-care financing and delivery systems in Japan, South Korea, and China. We then compare these with the relevant experiences of other Asia-Pacific nations. Our quantitative overview of DM's prevalence and economic burden is complemented by illustrative "patient journeys" that point to opportunities for policy improvement.

The Prevalence of Diabetes in Asia and Its Associated Costs

According to the World Health Organization (WHO), the number of people in the world with DM has doubled every twenty years since 1945 and is expected to increase to well over 300 million people by the year 2030 (King, Aubert, and Herman 1998). Chan et al. (2009) estimate that in 2007, more than 110 million individuals in Asia were living with DM, a disproportionate number of them young and middle aged. DM's growth has been especially rapid in developing countries such as India and China, where it is associated with major demographic and epidemiological shifts toward aging populations and chronic diseases. India alone was home to 40 million persons with DM in 2007. By 2030, this number is estimated to rise to 79.4 million, representing about one-fifth of all people in the world with DM (International Diabetes Federation; see table 9.1). Siegel, Narayan, and Kinra (2008, 1077) argue that "in the next decade, India will lose $237 billion in national income due to DM, stroke, and heart disease, yet Indian policymakers do not yet perceive the epidemic as a priority."

Table 9.1 Prevalence of Diabetes in Select Asia-Pacific Countries

Country	Prevalence in 2010 (%)
China	9.7
India	7.1
Japan	7.3
Republic of Korea	9.0
Malaysia	10.9
Singapore	12.7
Thailand	7.7
Vietnam	2.9
United States	12.3

Sources: For China, Yang et al. 2008. For all other countries, International Diabetes Federation Diabetes Atlas, www.diabetesatlas.org/content/regional-data.

In China, studies conducted in the 1980s and early 1990s showed a DM prevalence rate of 1.5 percent or less (National Diabetes Cooperative Study Group 1981; Shanghai Diabetes Research Cooperative Group 1980; Pan et al. 1993; Hu, Li, and Pan 1993). However, later studies indicated a sharp rise (Xiang et al. 1998; Yang, Zheng and Tong 2001; Jia et al. 2002). For example, DM prevalence in urban Qingdao (Dong et al. 2005) by the early 2000s was already as high as it was in Hong Kong and Taiwan in the mid-1990s (Cockram et al. 1993; Janus et al. 2000; Chen et al. 1997). Gao et al. (2009) report that the age-standardized prevalence of DM and pre-diabetes in urban Qingdao was 12.2 percent and 15.4 percent in 2002, rising to 18.8 percent and 28.7 percent only four years later. Prevalence was lower, yet still quite high, in the rural areas of Qingdao (14.1 percent diabetic and 20.2 percent pre-diabetic in 2006). A survey of about nine hundred Beijing residents not previously diagnosed with DM (Zhou et al. 2009) reported that 11.1 percent had DM and 22.4 percent were pre-diabetic. A 2008 study of 14 provinces revealed a four-fold increase in DM prevalence in China since 1994, with a crude prevalence rate of 15.0

percent (Yang et al. 2008). A recent study shows that about 92 million Chinese adults have DM, with an age-standardized prevalence rate of 9.7 percent in 2007–2008. DM prevalence is higher (11.4 percent) among urban residents than among rural residents (8.2 percent), but the prevalence of pre-diabetes is greatest in rural areas of China (Yang et al. 2008).

Causes of the large increase in DM include not only population aging but a constellation of risk factors: rapid urbanization and changes in lifestyle that include increases in high-fat and calorie-rich diets and reductions in physical activity, alongside high rates of male smoking. Of course, increased DM prevalence is not an unmitigated evil, since it also stems from improvements in disease detection[1] and reduced mortality rates.

Recent studies have also highlighted the distinctive epidemiology and pathophysiology of DM in Asia. According to Chan et al. (2009, 2129):

> Unlike in the West, where older populations are most affected, the burden of diabetes in Asian countries is disproportionately high in young to middle-aged adults. . . . The "metabolically obese" phenotype (i.e., normal body weight with increased abdominal adiposity) is common in Asian populations. The increased risk of gestational diabetes, combined with exposure to poor nutrition in utero and overnutrition in later life in some populations, may contribute to the increasing diabetes epidemic through "diabetes begetting diabetes" in Asia. While young age of onset and long disease duration place Asian patients with diabetes at high risk for cardiorenal complications, cancer is emerging as an important cause of morbidity and mortality.

The increase in DM prevalence, especially among youth, foreshadows a large increase in morbidity, disability, and premature mortality, as well as a growing economic burden from lost productivity and medical spending on the management of DM and its complications.

Patients with chronic conditions such as DM usually require regular outpatient visits and daily medication as well as periodic inpatient treatment. Providing these services can represent a substantial economic burden, especially among low-income households. For example, according to one study of medicine availability in Shandong Province in China, a patient with DM taking innovator brand rosiglitazone would need to spend a month's wages on a month's treatment. Older drugs such as metformin absorb almost eleven days' wages, and generics are not generally available (Sun 2005, 6). As China puts in place plans for universal health insurance coverage and promises grassroots health-care organizations better coverage of drugs on the essential drug list (EDL),

---

[1] However, there is still considerable room for improvement: estimates suggest that about half of the people living with diabetes in Hong Kong and Taiwan, and as much as two-thirds in Mainland China, are undiagnosed (Chan et al. 2009, 2130).

patient access could improve. But the social burden of financing the treatment of a growing population remains.

The economic burden is even more pronounced for patients requiring inpatient treatment. Looking across outpatient and inpatient care settings in urban China, Wang et al. (2009) estimate that the median, annual direct medical cost per patient with type 2 diabetes is 4,800 RMB, or almost 40 percent of the per capita disposable income in a city such as Chengdu. Spending for patients with complications averages about 70 percent more than that for patients without complications (6,056 versus 3,583 RMB).

According to one recent comparative study (Goldhaber-Fiebert et al. 2010), the cost of a single hospitalization (for an adult, type 2 DM patient with no complications, hospitalized between 2005 and 2008 in one of five tertiary hospitals) ranged from 11 percent to 75 percent of 2007 per capita income in China, India, Malaysia, and Thailand. Spending for patients with complications was anywhere from 6 percent to over 300 percent more than spending for patients without complications treated in the same hospital. HbA1c, a key marker of diabetes control, was significantly higher for uninsured patients than for insured patients in India and China, suggesting that uninsured patients were not managing their condition as well. Yet when comparing expenditures across both India and China, the study showed that the uninsured spent consistently less than the insured. The authors conclude that the returns on investment in preventing diabetic complications appear substantial. Countries with large out-of-pocket financing burdens, such as India and China, are associated with the widest gaps in resource use between insured and uninsured patients, likely reflecting both overuse by the insured and underuse by the uninsured.

To provide a comparison, we obtained data on hospitalization expenditures for DM patients in the United States from the 2006 National Inpatient Sample, with weights applied to represent the U.S. population. We reported ratios of inpatient spending to gross national income per capita of $44,710 for the United States in 2006 (World Bank, World Development Indicators). Patients in the low- and middle-income Asian countries spend more on hospitalization due to DM, relative to per capita income, than U.S. patients do. In 2006 spending for a U.S. diabetic inpatient without complications was 7.9 percent of per capita income on average, increasing to 19.3 percent on average for patients with complications (figure 9.1).

In sum, the rising prevalence of DM in the Asia-Pacific is a harbinger of the challenges for societies in which the primary causes of morbidity and mortality are chronic NCDs. Japan, South Korea, and China are at the forefront of this wave. To better understand how they are responding, we discuss each country in turn.

Japan

The number of patients with DM in Japan has continuously increased since at least 1970, predominantly due to changes in people's lifestyle and social environment. The Funagata diabetes study in 1990 showed that the prevalence

Figure 9.1 Hospitalization Expenditure as a Percentage of Gross National Income Per Capita in the United States

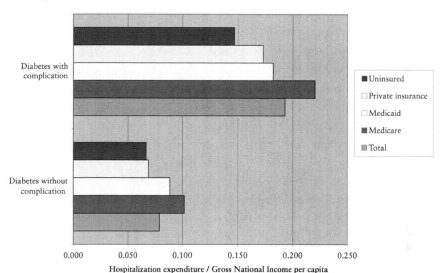

Source: National inpatient sample; weights were applied to represent the U.S. population. *Note*: Gross national income per capita (Atlas method) for the United States in 2006 was $44,710 (World Bank World Development Indicators). Statistical significance of difference in mean expenditures, comparing each category of insurance to the grand mean, 1-tail t-test: * for 10% level (p<0.1); ** for 5 percent level (p.<0.05); *** for 1 percent level (p<0.01).

of DM (defined as a fasting blood glucose sample with plasma value ≥ 200 mg/ dl) in a rural area of Japan was 9.1 percent and 10.8 percent among men and women over 40, respectively (Sekikawa et al. 2000). In November 1997 a survey revealed that the total number of Japanese with DM was nearly 14 million, or about 7 percent of the total population, somewhat analogous to DM and pre-diabetes incidence in the United States. By 2002 the Ministry of Health, Labor, and Welfare (MHLW) announced that over 16 million Japanese people were either "probable" or "suspected" cases (8.8 million people were candidates for DM, and 7.4 million people were strongly suspected to already be diabetic). Three years later, national data indicated roughly 1,933 diabetics per 100,000 (AWI 2009). Most recently, the "Outline of the National Health and Nutrition Survey, Japan 2006" estimated that 8.2 million people had full-blown DM and another 10.5 million had moderate symptoms—a total of 18.7 million probable cases[2] (see figure 9.2).

---

[2] www.nih.go.jp/eiken/english/research/pdf/nhns2006_outline.pdf.

143

Figure 9.2 Prevalence of DM Cases in Japan, 1997 and 2002

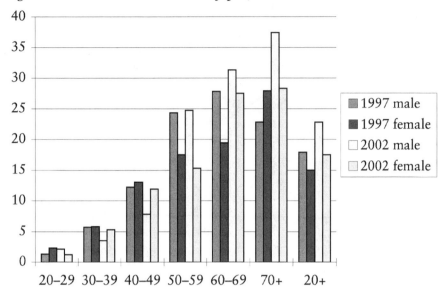

Source: FY 2002 Diabetes Survey Report, Japan Ministry of Health, Labor and Welfare (2004).

The cost implications of the increasing incidence of DM are enormous. In 1998 the total annual direct cost of DM in Japan reached $16.94 billion (6 percent of the total health budget) (Mohan et al. 2004). The economic burden is even larger if one takes into account the indirect losses associated with morbidity, decreased labor-force participation, and premature mortality.

The risk factors of DM and the ways of effectively preventing or reducing its progression in Japanese with impaired glucose tolerance (IGT) have been studied extensively, but convincing results are still elusive. For example, U.S. and European researchers suggest that moderate alcohol consumption is a protective factor against DM for patients with European heritage, while others report that alcohol intake may in fact be a risk factor, especially among low body mass index (BMI) Japanese (Iwasaki et al. 2003).

Japan's "National Health Promotion Movement in the 21st Century (Healthy Japan 21) for the period 2001–2010" set specific goals for improving people's lifestyles to reduce the overall burden of NCDs in Japan, including the primary prevention and early detection of DM and consistent adherence to its treatment. The annual budget for the prevention of DM was ¥11.74 billion in 2001.[3]

---

[3] http://fikb.firdi.org.tw/firdi_news/common/FileDownLoad.aspx?Fid=632.

In 2004 the Liberal Democratic Party created "A Strategy for Health Frontier," which principally aimed to prolong life and prevent disease and frailness. Later, the strategy formally became a part of government policy. A program on DM and the pre-diabetes metabolic syndrome was established in 2005 to promote regular checkups and to focus on research. The program's targets included halving the rate of transition from pre-diabetes to actual DM, increasing treatment adherence, and reducing diabetic complications by 30 percent (AWI 2009).

Meanwhile, the MHLW continues to support food for specified health uses (FOSHU), which producers claim can reduce or control blood glucose levels. Japan's Mitsubishi Research Institute estimates that Japan's health-food market was worth ¥677.9 billion in 2005 and had experienced an average annual growth rate of 13 percent since 2001. Products associated with blood glucose control represent a ¥55.2 billion market, with a much higher average annual growth rate (over 30 percent). According to the MHLW, a total of sixty-four health-food products related to blood glucose had been approved by May 30, 2005, produced by twenty-five different health-food manufacturers.[4]

Despite authorities' attempts to promote healthy lifestyles, good nutrition, and regular screening, the rate of increase in NCDs such as DM does not appear to be falling. A midterm evaluation of "Healthy Japan 21" in 2007 revealed that the prevalence of obesity among male adults and of DM among all adults had increased (Kinugasa Research Institute 2007). The 2007 National Health and Nutrition Examination Survey showed that 22.1 million Japanese adults were suspected to have DM—1.6 times more than in 1997 (MHLW 2008).

Of course, the Japanese enjoy the highest life expectancy in the world, and because Japan's population is aging rapidly, even the most valiant efforts to prevent and control NCDs can only hope to slow the rate of overall increase, not reverse the trend. Nevertheless, a reduction in the age-specific prevalence of DM would contribute greatly to a better quality of life and a lower health-care financing burden in the coming decades.

South Korea

South Korea faces many of the same challenges as Japan in coping with the epidemic of NCDs such as DM. To illustrate, we describe the treatment path of Mr. Kim, a hypothetical 56-year-old office worker living in rural Korea.

Five years ago, Mr. Kim had his biennial checkup, provided by the national health insurance program. One week later, he received a report that stated his blood glucose level was high and recommended that he have a follow-up examination for DM. In subsequent tests and medical visits, he was diagnosed with type 2 diabetes. He chose to visit his county's public health center, where he could receive outpatient care at a much lower price than at a private doctor's office. Fortunately, for the first year following diagnosis, oral hypoglycemic

---

[4] http://fikb.firdi.org.tw/firdi_news/common/FileDownLoad.aspx?Fid=632.

145

therapy successfully kept his blood glucose levels under control, and he did not have any diabetes-related symptoms. Then he decided that his condition did not require further medication. Instead, he decided to take silkworm powder, which was advertised in the media as lowering blood glucose levels. With advice from many relatives and friends, he also tried raw salts and several other kinds of alternative medicine.

About two years after missing his follow-up visit, Mr. Kim started to suffer extreme fatigue. One night, he had coma-like symptoms and was admitted to the emergency department of a local hospital. In a subsequent outpatient visit to the public health center, he was told that he would need insulin therapy, as well as close attention to his diet and exercise. He chose not to go on insulin, both because he thought that it was addictive and because the public health center could not provide care to patients on insulin therapy. Moreover, he was befuddled by the complexity of the recommendations on insulin, diet, and exercise. Since, he occasionally takes oral hypoglycemic drugs with silkworm powder and has had to make several more emergency department visits. Over time, he has had to go on sick leave more often. He has also noticed that his vision has worsened and that his foot wounds are not healing well.

Mr. Kim now sees an endocrinologist at a tertiary hospital in Seoul and is spending money on various treatments and transportation. His doctor tells him that his nephropathy will progress to end-stage renal disease, even though his blood glucose levels are controlled. He is concerned that his kidney condition will place a great financial burden on his family.

While there are many success stories of DM management in Korea, this fictitious case illustrates the most salient barriers to effective DM care in the country: problems associated with health-care delivery and the health-care financing (and payment) system.

In South Korea, as in many countries, the delivery system supports effective DM care only when the patient is willing and able to adhere to the recommended treatment. In the case of Mr. Kim, the patient had two periods when the delivery system functioned: the period of initial success in oral hypoglycemic therapy and the later period of specialty care for complications. For much of the disease course, however, the delivery system was ineffective: it provided neither the continuity of care nor the skills for self-management that would have prevented Mr. Kim from developing diabetic complications. This void is too often filled by a variety of popular misconceptions about DM care and the use of alternative medicines with little clinical evidence of effectiveness.

Given such weaknesses in primary health care in South Korea, the quality of DM care depends largely on the patient's own ability to seek the right care and to acquire effective self-management skills. As a result, measures for DM care reveal disparities across socioeconomic levels, in particular education levels.

The health-care financing system also has important implications for DM care in South Korea. Since Korea has universal coverage, one might think that financial barriers are not a major concern for patients with DM. This is far from the truth. For a country with Korea's level of social insurance and national income, the health-care financing system is heavily dependent on out-of-pocket expenditures. This feature has two critical implications for DM care. First, patients with DM face substantial out-of-pocket spending if their disease progresses beyond well-controlled and uncomplicated DM. Since risk factors such as obesity and physical inactivity lead to multiple chronic diseases, patients with DM often have co-morbidities, as well as multiple diabetes-related complications. Moreover, many complications predictably progress over time even with aggressive disease management. As a result, patients face rapidly escalating out-of-pocket payments as their disease progresses. Reduced earnings, both for the patient and for family members who help with patient care, further burden households.

Because the out-of-pocket payment is largely *proportional* to the incurred medical expenditure across income levels, the out-of-pocket spending is *regressive*. In other words, given the same medical expenditure, lower-income patients pay a higher percentage of their income in out-of-pocket payments than do higher-income patients. This burden is compounded by the fact that lower-income patients with DM are likely to have poorer health status than their higher-income counterparts, and therefore incur higher expenditures. Given that DM care requires continued management, even a small amount of out-of-pocket spending per visit may add up to a considerable amount. Although there is no evidence that financial barriers affect the quality of DM care in South Korea, many low-income patients will likely forego necessary intensive management because of the burden of out-of-pocket spending.

Another challenge is that provider payment in South Korea, as in the United States and many other countries, is usually a fee for service. The fee-for-service system does not provide any financial incentive to improve the quality of DM care; providers receive a fee regardless of whether patient health improves or not. This payment system does little to spur improved continuity of care or coordination in the delivery system. The quality of care might benefit from introducing other forms of payment that link reimbursement to outcome or that provide incentives to invest in disease prevention.

In summary, South Korea's health-care delivery, financing, and payment systems pose many critical challenges for providing quality DM care. Although the system assures a level of access to screening, primary care, and specialty care that many lower-income countries still aspire to attain, these developments largely reflect South Korea's overall accomplishments in treating patients with acute health episodes such as heart attacks. Chronic disease requires a different approach, often addressed in policy but rarely put into practice. Thus, the South Korean health-care system still faces the challenge of how to reform and address the epidemic of DM and other chronic diseases.

China

Health-care spending, resource allocation, and the distribution of health-care facilities and professionals vary widely between China's rural and urban areas. Health insurance coverage is assured for most urban government employees, college students, and state enterprises. In rural areas most people were uninsured until only recently. In 2003 China introduced and expanded rural residents' coverage under the New Cooperative Medical System (NCMS), and in 2007 it established Urban Residents Basic Medical Insurance, which covers approximately half the urban residents without workplace-based coverage (such as children, the elderly, and the self-employed).

Although China has an extensive network of grassroots health-care organizations (village clinics, township health centers, urban clinics, and community health centers), it does not have an integrated primary-care system. In other words, no primary physician decides patients' health-care plans, and referrals are not required. Patients decide on their own when to see a doctor, which hospital to visit, and what specialist to see. Care is often episodic and uncoordinated. As a result, the diagnosis and treatment of DM is delayed for many patients, especially the uninsured. Screening for DM and other chronic diseases is not very common and until recently had not been covered by social health insurance. Community DM screening is only carried out in some large firms and communities in major cities.

Patients with DM are typically diagnosed at hospitals, either as outpatients or inpatients. In large hospitals, an endocrinologist will make the diagnosis, but in smaller hospitals the physician is usually a specialist in internal medicine. There are four primary pathways to diagnosis: (1) a regular physical examination (typically paid for out of pocket or by an employer) reveals high fasting blood glucose, resulting in a referral to an endocrinologist or general physician for the diagnosis; (2) the patient visits a physician for particular DM symptoms (such as polyuria, polydipsia, or polyphagia) and is then diagnosed as diabetic; (3) the patient presents himself at an emergency room for an acute DM complication, and only then is the underlying DM detected; and (4) in the process of treatment for a different medical condition, lab tests reveal high blood glucose, so the patient is referred to an endocrinologist.

Services and protocols vary across China. To illustrate current practice in Hangzhou, China, we describe the journey of a fictitious patient, Susan, a 54-year-old with type 2 diabetes. She has a foot ulcer, some retinopathy, and is moderately obese. She has been unemployed for three years and receives social assistance benefits with limited insurance coverage. Since DM is typically asymptomatic in its early stages, diagnosis of her DM is probably delayed. She will probably see a general surgeon or a dermatologist for her foot ulcer only after two or three months go by without it healing. Only after the lab report comes out will her underlying high blood glucose be detected and the diagnosis of DM confirmed by an endocrinologist.

Susan will very likely need to be admitted to the hospital for her high blood glucose and foot ulcer. Unfortunately, she will have to pay a major portion of the costs on her own, with her family's support. Physicians screening her for complications will refer her to an ophthalmologist, and insulin treatment might be initiated. Very few hospitals provide bedside teaching for DM inpatients, and only a few hospitals offer group DM education programs. If Susan is lucky enough to be admitted to one of the hospitals with a diabetes nurse, she might get diabetes education without extra charge and will also be instructed on weight loss. Depending on the resources available at the hospital, Susan might also consult with a dietician and a wound-care nurse (China does not have podiatrists). The duration of her hospital stay may range from a few days to over a month. When she is discharged, Susan will be asked to make follow-up visits to an endocrinology clinic on a regular basis, usually once a month, but many patients do not, usually because of the associated economic burden.

Meanwhile, in Shandong Province, Meili Wang is a 53-year-old rural resident enrolled in the NCMS. She has blurred vision and is moderately obese. When she went to see an ophthalmologist in a provincial general hospital, the eye fundus examination showed retinopathy and moderate cataracts. A blood glucose test confirmed diabetic retinopathy. Meili was referred to the department of endocrinology, where physicians admitted her and developed a comprehensive treatment plan. Depending on the hospital, as in Hangzhou, DM self-management guidance may be provided. There is no system of coordinated follow-up, however, and Meili will have to decide whether or not to make the long journey to the provincial hospital for regular follow-up visits or to rely on local providers with less formal training. Depending on where she lives, she may benefit from expanding efforts to integrate community health-service centers and hospitals into a more coordinated network for the prevention and control of NCDs, including DM.

The expansion of medical insurance coverage in China, alongside other reforms announced in April 2009 in the national reform plan (such as more government subsidies for public health services, including NCD prevention and control), may help patients in China detect DM sooner than Susan or Meili did and face less financial hardship in adhering to follow-up care regimens. But as the population continues to age, move to cities, and change lifestyles, the growing number of patients with DM will present a significant challenge to China's health-care delivery and finance systems.

By way of comparison, we will follow typical patient care paths in Thailand, Malaysia, Vietnam, and India.

Thailand

The journey of a patient with chronic illness through the Thai health system can be illustrated by the fictitious case of Boonma, a 54-year-old woman with type 2 diabetes, chronic obstructive pulmonary disease (COPD), a leg ulcer, and moderate retinopathy. Boonma is slightly overweight, unemployed, and lives alone.

In Thailand a patient can choose to visit a health center, private clinic, or hospital—regardless of the level of referral. As in Japan, South Korea, and China, hospitals in Thailand provide both outpatient and inpatient services. Since Boonma is unemployed, she is likely to be covered by the 30-Baht Health Insurance Scheme. In this case, she must first get a diagnosis from the health-care setting where she is registered to acquire free services. She also needs a referral letter before her insurance will cover specialist services in another health-service setting.

Where Boonma gets her diagnosis depends on where she lives. In rural areas, she is likely to seek care from the health center in her subdistrict. Health centers are staffed by nonphysician health workers who are trained to screen for DM. Once the health worker determines that Boonma probably has DM, she will be transferred to the district hospital for tests and treatment. Alternatively, if Boonma resides in a town or a city, she will most likely go to a hospital for initial care. (In Bangkok, she may also receive her initial diagnosis at a Bangkok Metropolitan Health Center with in-house physicians.) It would not be unusual for Boonma to first seek care at a hospital when the COPD symptoms appear and then have her DM diagnosed in the process.

In a district hospital, the diagnosis, initial treatment, and follow-up are generally made by a general practitioner (GP). For her leg ulcer and retinopathy, Boonma will be referred to a provincial or regional hospital for specialist services. After her condition stabilizes, she will either go back to the district hospital or continue receiving care from the higher-level hospital. If she first seeks care at a higher-level hospital and is diagnosed there, the GP will coordinate her care and consult specialists in the same hospital for the treatment of any co-morbidities and complications. In a higher-level hospital, a DM patient covered by the Civil Service Medical Benefits or a private health insurance policy—or one who can afford to pay out of pocket—will be referred to an endocrinologist or an internal medicine specialist who will provide treatment and manage her case.

In Thailand a DM patient generally visits her doctor once every three months. During each visit, basic checkups are carried out. For example, blood pressure and fasting plasma glucose (FPG) tests are done almost every time a patient visits the hospital. However, certain tests may not be performed regularly. In larger hospitals, DM patients generally receive HbA1C tests at least once a year, but because of limited funds only a small percentage of patients in district hospitals get their annual HbA1C tests. Tests for lipid profile, urine albumin, and eye health follow a similar pattern. Only some hospitals offer education sessions to new DM patients.

Malaysia

The Malaysian health-care system does not provide regular screenings for chronic diseases such as DM or hypertension unless patients present themselves in health-care facilities for treatment or for pre-employment medical examinations. Women might be screened if they are pregnant or are receiving antenatal checkups.

We use the same patient profile (of a 54-year-old woman with type 2 diabetes) to describe the typical patient care path in Malaysia. The patient might be treated at a primary health clinic owned by the government and receive treatment for DM and its complications from the medical officer or staff nurses without charge. Clinics provide first-line medications for DM and simple procedures such as wound dressing. Patients usually have to go for regular follow-up visits every six months.

The patient might also choose to go to a private GP for the same treatment, but she will have to pay out of pocket unless the visit is covered by her employer's benefit scheme (through a company panel doctor, managed care organization, or private insurance). GP clinics are run by medical doctors who usually manage the cases themselves and rarely refer patients to specialists in the private sector for fear of "losing" them (patients will rarely be referred back to the GPs).

In Malaysia a patient with DM might first receive treatment at the primary health clinic or GP, and later be referred to the specialist clinic at the government hospital for a minimal charge (about $2 for all treatments). This is the case when DM is not well controlled, or when complications, such as leg ulcers and retinopathy, need further treatment at the hospital level. The patient will be given a regular dressing and referred to an ophthalmologist for management of the retinopathy. The patient will also be taught about proper diet, healthy lifestyle, and other self-management skills. A regular checkup every four months is typical.

Vietnam

In Vietnam, the number of people living with DM has increased rapidly, especially in urban areas. In 1990 the prevalence of DM in big cities such as Hanoi, Hue, and Ho Chi Minh City was 1.2 percent, 0.96 percent, and 2.52 percent, respectively (Trach and Thy 1998). By 2001 the prevalence of type 2 diabetes had increased to about 4 percent in the big cities, with an additional 5.1 percent with impaired glucose tolerance (Binh 2001). A national survey in 2002 (Binh 2002) indicated that 2.7 percent of Vietnamese between the ages of 30 and 64 had DM. Prevalence in big cities was higher, at 4.4 percent. Prevalence rates increased with age; for those aged 60 and above, the prevalence of DM ranged from 7.8 percent in remote rural areas to 13.4 percent in large cities (Binh 2002). Moreover, clinical studies indicated an increase in the percentage of newly diagnosed patients who already had diabetes-related complications (Binh and Hideshi 2006).

Most DM patients in Vietnam, especially those with severe symptoms or complications, are diagnosed either by urban medical centers (29.1 percent) or national health centers (63.7 percent) (Binh 2001). Here we describe a typical patient journey based on the experience of a real Hanoi resident, a 54-year-old woman with type 1 diabetes. One day in 1999 she felt very dizzy after coming home from the market. She realized that she had been experiencing fatigue for two months. She continued to work as she had before and did not notice any

151

other unfamiliar feelings; she assumed her exhaustion was due to hard work. A nurse from Bach Mai hospital (a large general hospital in Hanoi) advised a fluid transfusion; but after taking two bottles of glucose (5 percent), the patient felt even more exhausted and was admitted to the hospital, where she was diagnosed with type 1 diabetes. Since then, she has tried to adhere to a diabetic regimen with insulin, as well as some folk medicines such as bitter melon. She checks her blood glucose two to three times a week herself and engages in moderate exercise every day, but she does not follow up with regular health examinations. Her only clinical contact has been two emergency visits because of hypoglycemia.

There are few studies on the economic burden of DM in Vietnam, although it is clear that patients, households, and the overall economy face significant and increasing financial burdens. One study in 2001 found that the average total cost of diabetes-related hospitalizations was 50 percent higher than that for other diseases, with substantially greater spending among patients with complications such as cardiovascular disease, diabetic foot lesions, and severe infections (Lan et al. 2004). The average cost of a hospitalization was only $61, but this represented 15 percent of the per capita gross domestic product (GDP) in 2001, and the total, including travel and accommodation costs for the patients and their families, was $134 per hospitalization—or one-third of average per capita income (Binh 2001). Moreover, DM inpatients lost earnings for about twelve working days on average (Lan et al. 2004). Since about 50 percent of patients are uninsured—and even those with insurance pay 15 to 30 percent of expenses—a single hospitalization can represent a large burden for the average Vietnamese DM patient.

India

We present a final, fictitious but representative "patient journey" to introduce the challenges facing patients living with diabetes in India.

A 60-year-old farmer begins feeling unusually tired and loses considerable weight (4 kilograms over four months). Although both his father and two brothers have been previously diagnosed with DM, he is only brought to a medical provider—the nearby government hospital—when a cellulitis in the right leg begins spreading to the thigh. He is then diagnosed with type 2 DM that is badly out of control (fasting blood sugar 244mg/dl; post-prandial sugars 345 mg/dl; glycosylated haemoglobin 10 percent). The patient is treated with antibiotics for the cellulitis and insulin for the raised sugars. He is apprehensive of the idea of lifelong insulin because of the associated cost burden, since he must pay for care out of pocket (he is not insured). He is reassured that insulin may only be essential until the infection heals. The physician also performs additional tests; advises the patient about diet, exercise, and foot care; refers him to an ophthalmologist; and recommends that he come back for regular follow-up care.

In India, routine health checkups are not common for rural residents, and people approach hospitals only when they are sick. It is quite common for patients to be diagnosed as diabetic only after they have developed some complications from the disease. Awareness of type 2 DM is gradually increasing, especially in urban areas, because of media efforts as well as an increase in the sheer number of Indians with the disease. Medical insurance is not widespread, and affordability is a major determinant of access to medical treatment, drug therapy, and follow-up care. Socioeconomic status also influences how a patient understands the implications of the diagnosis and how diligently the patient will follow the physician's instructions.

Conclusion

Throughout the Asia-Pacific, health financing and delivery systems—originally designed to control infectious diseases and treat episodic, acute medical conditions—face a new challenge: the primary and secondary prevention of chronic disease. Such systems need to reorganize to emphasize patient education in self-management skills and community-based primary care for the growing number of patients with NCDs such as DM. The scope of the DM epidemic in the region necessarily draws attention to these and other challenges. In the low- and middle-income countries, in particular, patients face significant barriers to early DM diagnosis, which would help prevent or delay the onset of complications. Reliance on out-of-pocket financing, urban-rural disparities, and a general lack of DM-related knowledge exacerbate barriers to self-management and coordinated care. Creative and evidence-based policies to prevent and control DM should be a high priority for public health policymakers in Japan, South Korea, China, and their counterparts—including the United States. The effective diffusion of best practices could help to prevent further escalation of the personal and social burden associated with diabetes in the Asia-Pacific.

References

AWI (Association of Pacific Rim Universities World Institute). 2009. "Public Health Research Project Phase I Report on Japan." Template for Baseline Assessment of Research, Policies and Programs on Chronic, Non-Communicable Diseases (NCD), submitted by University of Tokyo.

Binh, Ta Van. 2001. *Epidemiology of Diabetes, Risk Factors of the Disease and Factors Related to Diabetes Disease Management in 4 Cities (Ha Noi, Hai Phong, Da Nang, and Ho Chi Minh City) in 2001.* Typical research of national projects implemented in the National Hospital of Endocrinology. Hanoi: Vietnam Medicine Publisher, 173–99.

———. 2002. *Epidemiology of Diabetes in Vietnam, Treatment Methods and Preventive Measures.* Hanoi: Vietnam Medicine Publisher.

Binh, Ta Van, and Kuzuya Hideshi. 2006. *Follow-up Study on Diabetic Complications in Patients since their First Presentation at National Hospital of Endocrinology.* Hanoi: Vietnam Medicine Publisher.

Chan, Juliana C. N., Vasanti Malik, Weiping Jia, Takashi Kadowaki, Chittaranjan S. Yajnik, Kun-Ho Yoon, and Frank B. Hu. 2009. "Diabetes in Asia: Epidemiology, Risk Factors, and Pathophysiology." *JAMA (Journal of the American Medical Association)* 301 (20): 2129–40. doi:10.1001/jama.2009.726.

Chen, H. D., C. K. Shaw, W. P. Tseng, H. I. Chen, and M. L. Lee. 1997. "Prevalence of Diabetes Mellitus and Impaired Glucose Tolerance in Aborigines and Chinese in Eastern Taiwan." *Diabetes Research and Clinical Practice* 38 (3): 199–205.

Cockram, C. S., J. Woo, E. Lau, J. C. Chan, A.Y. Chan, J. Lau, R. Swaminathan, and S. P. Donnan. 1993. "The Prevalence of Diabetes Mellitus and Impaired Glucose Tolerance among Hong Kong Chinese Adults of Working Age." *Diabetes Research and Clinical Practice* 21 (1): 67–73.

Dong, Y., W. Gao, H. Nan, H. Yu, F. Li, W. Duan, Y. Wang, B. Sun, R. Qian, J. Tuomilehto, and Q. Qiao. 2005. "Prevalence of Type 2 Diabetes in Urban and Rural Chinese Populations in Qingdao, China." *Diabetic Medicine* 22 (10): 1427–33.

Gao, W. G., Y. H. Dong, Z. C. Pang, H. R. Nan, L. Zhang, S. J. Wang, J. Ren, F. Ning, and Q. Qiao (for the Qingdao 2006 Diabetes Survey Group). 2009. "Increasing Trend in the Prevalence of Type 2 Diabetes and Pre-diabetes in the Chinese Rural and Urban Population in Qingdao, China." Accepted article forthcoming in Diabetic Medicine. doi: 10.1111/j.1464–5491.2009.02832.x.

Goldhaber-Fiebert, J. D., H. Li, S. Ratanawijitrasin, S. Vidyasagar, X. Y. Wang, S. Aljunid, N. Shah, Z. Wang, S. Hirunrassamee, K. L. Bairy, J. Wang, S. Saperi, A. M. Nur, and K. Eggleston. 2010. "Inpatient Treatment of Diabetic Patients in Asia: Evidence from India, China, Thailand, and Malaysia." *Diabetic Medicine* 27 (1): 101–8.

Hu, Y. H., G. W. Li, and X. R. Pan. 1993. "Incidence of NIDDM in Daqing and Forecasting of NIDDM in China in 21st Century." *Zhonghua Nei Ke Za Zhi* [China journal of internal medicine] 32: 173–75.

International Diabetes Federation. *Diabetes Atlas*. www.eatlas.idf.org/Prevalence/index. cfm?data=table&tableId=25.

Iwasaki, N., N. J. Cox, Y. Q. Wang, P. E. Schwarz, G. I. Bell, M. Honda, M. Imura, M. Ogata, M. Saito, N. Kamatani, and Y. Iwamoto. 2003. "Mapping Genes Influencing Type 2 Diabetes Risk and BMI in Japanese Subjects." *Diabetes* 52 (1): 209–13.

Janus, E. D., N. M. S. Wat, K. S. L. Lam, C. S. Cockram, S. T. S. Siu, L. J. Liu, and T. H. Lam. 2000. "The Prevalence of Diabetes, Association with Cardiovascular Risk Factors and Implications of Diagnostic Criteria (ADA 1997 and WHO 1998) in a 1996 Community-based Population Study in Hong Kong Chinese." *Diabetic Medicine* 17 (10): 741–45.

Jia, W., K. Xiang, L. Chen, J. Lu, and Y. Wu. 2002. "Epidemiological Study on Obesity and its Co-morbidities in Urban Chinese Older than 20 Years of Age in Shanghai, China." *Obesity Reviews* 3 (3): 157–65.

King, H., R. E. Aubert, and W. H. Herman. 1998. "Global Burden of Diabetes, 1995–2025: Prevalence, Numerical Estimates, and Projections." *Diabetes Care* 21 (1998): 1414–31.

Kinugasa Research Institute. 2007. *Midcourse Review of Health Japan 21*. Kyoto: Ritsumeikan University. www.hpm.org/en/Surveys/Ritsumeikan_University_-_ Japan/09/Midcourse_review__of__Health_Japan_21_.html.

Lan, Pham Thi, Pham Huy Dzung, Ta Van Binh, Le Quang Toan, and Nguyen Vinh Quang. 2004. *Study on the Payment Burden of Diabetes Inpatients at the National Hospital of Endocrinology in 2001*. Summary record of the Second National Conference of Endocrinology and Metabolic Diseases. Hanoi: Vietnam Medicine Publisher, 303–12.

MHLW (Ministry of Health, Labor and Welfare), Japan. 2004. *Fiscal Year 2002 Diabetes Survey Report*. www.mhlw.go.jp/shingi/2004/03/s0318-15.html.

———. 2008. *Annual Health, Labor and Welfare Report 2007–2008*. www.mhlw. go.jp/.

Mohan, V., Z. Madan, R. Jha, R. Deepa, and R. Pradeepa. 2004. "Diabetes: Social and Economic Perspectives in the New Millenium." *International Journal of Diabetes in Developing Countries* 24 (2): 29–35.

National Diabetes Cooperative Study Group. 1981. "A Mass Survey of Diabetes Mellitus in a Population of 300,000 in 14 Provinces and Municipalities in China." *Clinical Journal of Internal Medicine* 20: 678–83.

Pan, X., Y. Hu, G. Li, P. Liu, P. Bennett, and B. Howard. 1993. "Impaired Glucose Tolerance and its Relationship to ECG-indicated Coronary Heart Disease and Risk Factors among Chinese. Da Qing IGT and Diabetes Study." *Diabetes Care* 16 (1): 150–56.

Sekikawa, A., H. Eguchia, M. Tominagaa, K. Igarashia, T. Abea, H. Manakaa, H. Sasakia, H. Fukuyamab, T. Katoa, Y. Kiyoharac, and M. Fujishimac. 2000. "Prevalence of Type 2 Diabetes Mellitus and Impaired Glucose Tolerance in a Rural Area of Japan: The Funagata Diabetes Study." *Journal of Diabetes and Its Complications* 14 (2): 78–83.

Shanghai Diabetes Research Cooperative Group. 1980. "A Survey of Diabetes Mellitus among the Population in Shanghai." *Chinese Medical Journal* 60: 323–29.

Siegel, Karen, K. M. Venkat Narayan, and Sanjay Kinra. 2008. "Finding a Policy Solution to India's Diabetes Epidemic." *Health Affairs* 27 (4): 1077–90. doi:10.1377/hlthaff.27.4.1077. Accessed

Sun, Q. 2005. "A Survey of Medicine Prices, Availability, Affordability, and Price Components in Shandong Province, China." October 2005. www.haiweb.org/medicinepdces/surveys/200411CN/survey_report.pdf. Accessed October 13, 2010.

Trach, Mai The và Khe, and Nguyen Thy. 1998. *Diabetes Mellitus. Basic Endocrinology.* Ho Chi Minh City Publisher, 467–554.

Wang, Weibing, Chao Wei Fu, Chang Yu Pan, Weiqing Chen, Siyan Zhan, Rongshen Luan, Alison Tan, Zhaolan Liu, and Biao Xu. 2009. "How Do Type 2 Diabetes Mellitus-related Chronic Complications Impact Direct Medical Cost in Four Major Cities of China?" *Value in Health*, forthcoming.

World Bank. *World Development Indicators.* http://ddp-ext.worldbank.org/ext/DDPQQ/member.do?method=getMembers&userid=1&queryId=6. Accessed October 13, 2010.

Xiang, H. D., W. Wu, C. Q. Liu, K. Li, J. G. Feng, Y. T. Zhang, F. Q. Wang, S. L. Yan, C. J. Wang, Y. C. Xu, D. R. Xu, Z. Z. Fu, Z. Y. Liu, T. L. Li, J. Bai, Z. Y. Fu, and K. A. Wang. 1998. "An Epidemiological Study on Diabetes Mellitus 1995–1996, in China." *Chinese Journal of Diabetes* 6: 131–33.

Yang, Z., H. Zheng, and Z. Tong. 2001. "Prevalence of Diabetes and IGT in Elderly Population of Beijing in 1997." *Chinese Journal of Geriatrics* 20: 290–93.

Yang, W., J. Liu, J. Weng, W. Jia, L. Ji, and J. Xiao. 2008. "Diabetes Impact Study Results in 14 Provinces in China." DM Survey Series 0467. *Clinical Journal of Internal Medicine* (in Chinese).

Zhou, X. H., L. N. Ji, Y. Y. Luo, X. Y. Zhang, X. Y. Han, and Q. Qiao. 2009. "Performance of HbA1c for Detecting Newly Diagnosed Diabetes and Pre-diabetes in Chinese Communities Living in Beijing." *Diabetic Medicine.* doi: 10.1111/j.1464-5491.2009.02831.x.

Families Dealing with Dementia: Insights from Mainland China, Hong Kong, and Taiwan

Dolores Gallagher-Thompson, Marian Tzuang, Alma Au, Dahua Wang, Teresa B. K. Tsien, Peng Chih Wang, and Yifan Huang[1]

Average life spans are increasing around the world, nowhere more than in the Asia-Pacific region. Across Mainland China, Hong Kong, and Taiwan, the number of people aged 65 and above is expected to grow dramatically over the next fifty years. Table 10.1 provides an overview of the three regions' populations, age ratios, and life expectancies.

First we turn our attention to Mainland China. In 2005 a 1 percent sample survey of the populace (conducted by the National Bureau of Statistics of China) put China's total population at 1.306 billion (excluding Hong Kong and Macao), of whom those 65 years or older accounted for about 100 million (7.69 percent). China's population is aging rapidly. It is estimated that by 2040, China's elderly will number 397 million, equivalent to the total population of Germany, France, the United Kingdom, and Japan (Jackson 2009). The China National Committee on Ageing (CNCA) (2009) reports that it will take only 27 years for the proportion of the population aged 65 years and older to increase from 7 to 14 percent, compared with 69 years for the United States, 85 years for Sweden, and 115 years for France. Meanwhile, the ratio of working-age adults available to support their elders is reported to be declining rapidly, from 9 workers to support 1 elder in 2005 to a projected 2.8 workers per elder in 2050. This is due (for the most part) to declining birth rates throughout the world.

China also faces some other relevant challenges.

- *The one-child policy has led to a disproportionate ratio of males to females.* The projected shortage of women will translate into fewer

[1] Preparation of this chapter was substantially supported by grants from the Department of Health and Human Services, Health Resources & Services Administration (HRSA), Bureau of Health Professions (D31HP08825), and from the national office of the Alzheimer's Association, Chicago, IL, USA (IIRG-04-1109) to Dolores Gallagher-Thompson, principal investigator.

157

daughters-in-law, the traditional caregivers for the elderly.

- *As workers emigrate to cities, rural elderly are left alone.* Young rural workers are leaving en masse for the cities, where per capita income is three times as high as it is in the countryside. Twelve million migrant workers come to the cities annually to try and make a living. This leaves older people in rural areas without the traditional network of children to care for them as they age.
- *Disparities between urban and rural areas put the rural elderly at a disadvantage.* Rural areas face mounting challenges. The CNCA (2009) reports that almost 66 percent of China's elderly live in rural areas, where social insurance systems and medical care systems are inadequate or nonexistent. The rural poor are particularly hard hit, as they are unable to pay for health care, however scant it may be.
- *Infrastructure is not in place.* Institutions that specialize in elderly care serve less than 1.2 percent of the aging population, compared with 8 percent in developed countries. Moreover, the health-care workforce is inadequately trained, and there are no formal fellowships or national board certifications in geriatrics.

Table 10.1 Demographic Information: Mainland China, Hong Kong, and Taiwan

	China	Hong Kong	Taiwan
Total population	1.3 billion	7.01 million	23.05 million
Age ratio (% of people 65+)	7.69%	7.7%	10.43%
Life expectancy, male (years)	72.0	78.8	74.9
Life expectancy, female (years)	75.0	84.5	81.4
Elderly dependency ratio (Ratio of the number of elderly persons at an age when they are generally economically inactive divided by the number of persons of working age.)	10.7	16.5	13.6

Sources: The World Health Organization, Taiwan Department of Health and the Legislative Council, and Hong Kong Special Administration Region of the People's Republic of China.

Similar trends are at play in Taiwan and Hong Kong. Taiwan's Ministry of the Interior projected that by 2014, 11.6 percent of the population would be over 65 years of age, and that this number would rise to 16.5 percent by 2021 and to 20 percent by 2030. Currently, six to seven people aged 15 to 64 are available to provide support for every elder. But as in Mainland China, this number is expected to drop in the coming years.

Judging from the results of the 2006 Hong Kong Population By-census, the proportion of the population aged 15 and under has fallen markedly, reflecting a sustained drop in fertility rates. By contrast, the proportion of those aged 65 increased from 8.7 percent (502,400) in 1991 to 12.4 percent (853,000) in 2006 and is projected to increase to 14.4 percent (1 million) in 2016 and 24.3 percent (2.1 million) in 2031.

What Is Dementia?

Dementia is a disease characterized by the loss or decline of memory and other cognitive abilities. While there are different types of dementia, Alzheimer's disease is the most common, accounting for 70 percent of all cases in older Americans (Alzheimer's Association 2009). This disease is a progressive one, with the early stages characterized by episodic forgetfulness. Later, patients become unable to perform even simple tasks such as dressing and grooming. They also begin to have difficulty in speaking and understanding, and typically exhibit emotional and behavioral problems, including depression, agitation, aggressiveness, and wandering. Physical and mental functions can deteriorate to the point where total care is needed.

Statistics on Dementia

In 2003 the estimated number of people with dementia worldwide was 27.7 million. China was home to more of these people (about 5 million) than any other country in the world (Wimo, Jonsson, and Winblad 2006). According to Alzheimer's Disease International (2009), there is one new case of dementia every seven seconds.

Although a well-accepted risk factor for dementia is age,[2] dementia is neither an inevitable consequence of age nor a disease that affects only older adults. The likelihood of dementia increases from around 0.1 percent for people under 65 to 1 percent for people in their sixties to nearly 25 percent for people aged 85 and older (Alzheimer's Disease International 2009). Therefore, we can reasonably predict that persons and families affected by dementia will increase dramatically as the population ages.

At present, the prevalence of dementia in Mainland China can only be estimated; no nationwide survey data are available. The consensus estimate for Mainland China is that 4 percent of those 60 and older have dementia (Ferri et al. 2005); accordingly, the estimated number of people with dementia in Mainland China is about five million. In Hong Kong, this number is around sixty thousand.

---

[2] The term *dementia* is used here to include Alzheimer's disease (by far the most prevalent form) and other related disorders, such as vascular dementia, dementia with Lewy bodies, frontotemporal dementia, and so on. Throughout this chapter, we use the abbreviation ADOD—Alzheimer's disease and other dementias—to refer to this group of diseases.

The Taiwanese Ministry of the Interior calculated that 24,217 persons, or 0.11 percent of Taiwan's total population, had dementia at the end of 2007. Studies have shown that the prevalence of dementia among Taiwan's elderly is approximately 1.7 to 4.3 percent and that the most common cause of dementia is Alzheimer's disease (Fuh and Wang 2008). But the Taiwan Alzheimer's Disease Association (2009) reported that only one-fifth of people with dementia had received a formal diagnosis, meaning that there are many more undiagnosed cases. The public needs to be educated about dementia, especially its early symptoms, so they can receive timely treatment for the disease.

There are three reasons why dementia is so widely underreported in Taiwan, Mainland China, and Hong Kong. First, DSM-IV (the Diagnostic and Statistical Manual of Mental Disorders, fourth edition) (American Psychiatric Association 2000) states that a diagnosis of dementia should be given only when there is significant impairment in social or occupational functioning. However, because older adults in Chinese culture are frequently freed from household responsibilities, their families may not identify any decline until the condition is severe. Second, Chinese culture is known for respecting its aged; families may overlook or fail to recognize mild cognitive deficiencies in their elders. Third, traditional Chinese populations treat memory decline as a normal part of the aging process (Fuh and Wang 2008). Thus, epidemiological surveys, relying mostly on informants' reports, underestimate the prevalence of dementia. This in turn leads to delayed diagnosis and treatment.

Common Beliefs about Dementia in Chinese Culture

Dementia is commonly viewed as a mental illness in Chinese culture, and like other mental illnesses it is considered shameful. People with mental illness often carry the stigma of being "crazy" or "catatonic." As a result, families usually keep them, or at least their condition, hidden (Guo et al. 2000).

Family values and roles are guided by the traditional Chinese virtue of filial piety, whose importance is summed up by the Chinese proverb *Bai shan xiao wei xian* (Of a hundred good characteristics, filial piety is the most important). Sung (1995) defines filial piety as a two-dimensional construct: behavioral (making sacrifices, taking responsibility) and emotional (harmony, love, respect). In the case of dementia care, filial piety dictates that family members—not doctors or institutions—should take care of dependent relatives. Other unique features of dementia care (and family caregiving in general) in Chinese culture include the placing of families' interests above those of individuals; the emphasis on interpersonal harmony over individual expression; and, lastly, the tendency to deal with family problems privately (Zhan 2004). The eldest son, when single, is often the primary caregiver of his parents. When the eldest son is married, his wife also becomes responsible for the care of her in-laws. A saying still widely embraced by today's older population is *Yang er fang lao* (To raise a son is to protect yourself in your old age). Other children or family members share secondary responsibility in caring for disabled or sick family members (Huang et al. 2009).

Although there is still pressure to perform acts of filial piety today, this traditional virtue has been heavily affected by societal trends—modernization, urbanization, and globalization. Indeed, while the practical expression of these trends is evolving, it seems clear that filial piety is much less influential now than it was in the past (Lan 2002). In Hong Kong, for example, recent data indicate that many adult children no longer consider their parents their first priority (Ng 2002) because greater opportunities for education and career advancement leave them with no time for looking after the elderly. Changing social values (such as desire for more independence) and changing family patterns also affect the provision of care and income security for older people, particularly in countries where family support has traditionally played a major role. This intergenerational conflict leads to an inevitable question: Who will care for the elderly if their adult children cease to do so?

Dementia Caregiving

Most studies of dementia caregiving have been done in the United States, with the following results. Families, broadly defined, provide most of the care for persons with dementia: 8.9 million caregivers (20 percent of adult caregivers) care for someone who is 50 or older and has dementia (Alzheimer's Association and National Alliance for Caregiving 2009). These family caregivers are family members, friends, and neighbors who provide unpaid, ongoing, consistent care to the person who needs help. Their situations vary widely: they can be primary or secondary caregivers, they can work as caregivers full time or part time, and they can live with the person being cared for or live separately.

Among caregivers of people with Alzheimer's disease and other dementias (ADOD), 60 percent are women, typically adult children taking care of their parent or parent-in-law (Alzheimer's Association 2009). Family caregivers' tasks are determined by the evolving needs of the person with ADOD. In the early stages of the disease, caregivers perform relatively simple duties, such as preparing meals, providing transportation, helping with medications, and managing finances. But as the disease progresses, these tasks become more complex and time-consuming; they may include supervising the person so that he or she avoids unsafe activities (such as wandering), arranging doctors' visits, and helping with personal care (such as bathing, feeding, dressing, and toileting). The total duration of caregiving varies, but at any one time, 32 percent of family caregivers of people with ADOD have been providing care for five or more years and 39 percent have been providing care for one to four years (Alzheimer's Association and National Alliance for Caregiving 2009).

Caring for a person with ADOD is known to have multiple, adverse effects on the primary caregiver. Dementia family caregivers are at an increased risk for both physical illness and psychiatric disorders, including increased levels of

161

depressive symptoms and a higher prevalence of clinical depression and anxiety (Connell, Janevic, and Gallant 2001; Schulz and Martire 2004). They also experience social isolation (due to the time-consuming nature of caregiving), reduced social support, and stress due to conflicting expectations based on their various roles (e.g., parent, employee, caregiver) (Schulz and Martire 2004). Dementia caregiving is also known to have negative impacts on a caregiver's employment and financial security. The Alzheimer's Association estimated the economic value of the total care provided by family caregivers in the United States at $94 billion in 2008. In addition, studies conducted in the United States found that Asian American (particularly Chinese American) caregivers had higher levels of depression than their Caucasian counterparts, and that these caregivers attributed significant levels of burden and distress to the caregiving role (Pinquart and Sorensen 2005). Thus, despite the presence of a strong cultural norm to provide caregiving without complaining of its being a burden, research shows that Chinese and Chinese Americans experience similar (if not greater) distress as others in the caregiving role.

Successful Interventions to Reduce Caregivers' Distress

A number of studies in the past decade have described (and often evaluated) a variety of interventions to improve caregivers' quality of life. These interventions have ranged from intensive home-based programs such as the REACH II national collaborative study—a randomized controlled trial that enrolled more than six hundred caregivers in the United States (REACH II Investigators 2006)—to community-based support groups that have been subject to little empirical scrutiny. Using a strict definition for what qualifies as an "evidence-based" intervention, Gallagher-Thompson and Coon (2007) found that psychoeducational skill-training programs, the most frequently researched form of intervention, generally succeeded in reducing depressive symptoms, while also improving caregivers' coping skills so they could better manage difficult behaviors and the everyday stress of their situations.

Pinquart and Sorenson (2005 and 2006) reviewed interventions for dementia caregivers (and their effectiveness) in updated meta-analyses that used less stringent criteria for determining if an intervention was evidence-based. In both reviews the authors reported that psychoeducational programs and psychotherapeutic interventions were the most effective means of reducing distress and improving caregivers' quality of life. Other interventions that were reviewed—such as support groups, respite care, multicomponent interventions, programs focused on the care recipient, and programs that modified the home environment for the dementia patient and used the skills of occupational therapists to promote positive engagement—were found to be less successful overall and to be "domain-specific" in their effects. In other words, their effects tended to be confined to specific outcome measures of relevance to the particular study.

This large and growing body of literature offers some conclusions about what psychoeducational programs do best. Such programs, which are generally small-group programs offered in community settings with appropriate linguistic and cultural modifications to meet the needs of the participants, are being recommended for a broad range of problems. But their content varies greatly, so one must be mindful to select one that is targeted appropriately to the caregivers in need.

Unfortunately, very few of these empirical studies have been conducted with Chinese or Chinese American caregivers, and those that have been done have tended to use small convenience samples. Larger, more comprehensive studies are clearly needed. That said, we will briefly describe the studies that have been done in the United States and Hong Kong as background for the facts and figures that follow. It is our belief that this body of data will be transferable (with appropriate linguistic and cultural modifications) and provide a starting point for China to develop comprehensive plans for caregivers' services.

Two studies were completed in the United States with Chinese American caregivers: the first was an in-home program that used cognitive-behavioral therapy to teach relevant coping skills over a four-month period (Gallagher-Thompson et al. 2007). Out of 51 women who enrolled, 44 completed the program. During the program, random assignment (by chance) to conditions was done, a standardized protocol was followed, treatment was provided in Mandarin or Cantonese by trained interventionists, and progress was tracked. The program consisted of several "modules," or areas of focus, which were given more or less emphasis according to the needs of the particular caregiver (for example, managing a care recipient's disruptive behavior, challenging unhelpful negative thinking patterns, learning to ask for help from family members, and so on). Researchers found that the participants in the active treatment group showed fewer depressive symptoms and used adaptive coping skills more frequently after the program than did those in the control group, who received brief, periodic phone calls to "check in" on their situation and were mailed information (in Chinese or English as preferred) that would address their problems. In the second study, the skills that were rated as "most helpful" to participants in the first study were selected for inclusion in a new, two-hour DVD that the researchers created (in Mandarin Chinese with English subtitles); an accompanying workbook (in English and Chinese) amplified points made on the DVD (Gallagher-Thompson et al. 2010). The strategy was to show a variety of typical caregiving situations (for example, the care recipient repeating over and over, "When are we going to eat?") and a caregiver's ineffectual response to them (for instance, becoming angry). This was followed by a discussion about appropriate ways to tackle the situation, and then the scene was redone, with the caregiver handling the care recipient in a more effective way (such as by distracting her or otherwise redirecting her attention).

A new sample of about one hundred caregivers was recruited for this project, and seventy completed it. Again, random assignment was used: the comparison condition was a DVD (also in Mandarin Chinese) that provided information about ADOD but did not teach coping skills. Comparison of pre- and post-data after a three-month period of intervention, which consisted of a review of the DVD with periodic phone calls to ask about use and helpfulness, indicated that those in the skill-training group reported less distress from their care recipient's behavioral problems than those in the control group. The former also rated the intervention higher in helpfulness and relevance to their everyday lives. These results are encouraging and seem to support the positive impact that cognitive-behavioral principles and techniques can have, even when they are delivered by DVD, a much less expensive and more convenient medium than the small group setting. Further research is needed to determine if the results of these studies can be replicated with larger samples and in other locations, such as Mainland China and Taiwan, where, to our knowledge, no research of this nature has been conducted.

The final study was conducted in Hong Kong by Au et al. (2009) using the group psychoeducational approach discussed earlier. The "coping with caregiving" program was adapted for the culture of Hong Kong, translated, and offered in a randomized trial to twenty-seven female caregivers who participated in thirteen weekly group sessions held in the community. Following the class, participants showed significantly more self-efficacy in managing the disruptive behaviors of the care recipient and more control in managing their own negative thoughts than those in the control group (those on the waitlist). They also reported an increased use of problem-focused coping strategies in their daily lives. These results are consistent with those of the U.S. studies and encouraging for caregivers in Hong Kong. Again, however, further research is needed to replicate and extend these promising findings in other regions of China. In addition, cost-effectiveness studies are needed to determine the costs versus benefits of these programs.

Dementia Caregiving in Mainland China and Taiwan

The largest dementia study to date in China—carried out in Beijing, Xian, Shanghai, and Chengdu—found that the vast majority of dementia patients (96 percent) were cared for at home (Zhang et al. 2004). More specifically, 44 percent of the primary caregivers are sons and daughters-in-law, 31 percent are spouses, 15 percent are daughters and sons-in-law, 6 percent are grandchildren, and less than 1 percent are parents. Partly due to their scarcity and partly due to their high costs, elder-care institutions are rarely used.

Based on a nonrandomized survey of 626 family caregivers carried out by the Family Caregiver Association (2009) in Taiwan, 15 percent of Taiwanese caregivers were taking care of a family member with some kind of dementia, on average providing care for 11.72 hours per day over a span of 5.97 years. The same report found that as many as 67 percent of the caregivers receive no assistance from other family members, and about 35 percent of them quit their jobs to take on the caregiving role. With regard to the social support structure, Taiwanese society tends to promote informal assistance over formal services. Family interactions are frequent and instrumental, and a high percentage of older persons reside with and/or are cared for by their children. An older individual is likely to live in an institutional care facility only when network support is lacking, regardless of his or her health status (Zimmer, Ofstedal, and Chang 2001).

In Chinese cultures, families continue to play an important role in providing care to a family member with dementia. However, services to assist these caregivers in their role have been slow to develop. This is due, in large part, to the tendency of Chinese families to hide a family member's disability as well as to the strongly held cultural norm of filial piety, which dictates that the care of an elder with dementia be provided primarily (perhaps exclusively) by the family and not the government. The next section attempts to calculate the economic burden of dementia caregiving.

The Economic Burden of Dementia

The economic burden of dementia generally includes two components:

- Medical (formal) expenses, such as treatment and medicines
- Caregiving (informal) expenses, such as the cost to the family of having a family member take primary caregiving responsibility

However, there are differing opinions of what cost categories are to be included in the calculation, leading to an inclusion of a wide range of costs in some reports but not in others. While unpaid informal care forms a major part of the total costs, accurately establishing the monetary value of such care is complicated and controversial (Wimo, Ljunggren, and Winblad 1997).

Back in 1993, Liu estimated that the cost of long-term care (LTC) of the elderly in Taiwan would reach $1.3 billion by 2040, with 30 to 40 percent of this amount paid for by the government. A more recent study (Chiu and Shyu 2001) estimated the costs of home and nursing-home care for families of patients with either Alzheimer's disease or vascular dementia in Taiwan. The study found that the estimated cost of home care per patient per month was $2,664, with labor costs accounting for 96 percent of the total. When the cost of labor was deducted from the calculation, the cost of home care per patient per month was only $127. For patients receiving nursing-home care, the cost per patient per month was estimated at $905. Another study showed that unpaid informal care, and nonmedical treatment costs, constitutes a major part of the total cost of caring for dementia patients, and the economic costs for one dementia patient per year varied from a substantial $6,447 to $22,211 (Chou et al. 2001).

It is difficult to estimate the economic burden of dementia care in China because it varies greatly according to the treatment setting. For instance, the expenses for hospital inpatient care are significantly higher than those for institutionalized patients, whereas the expenses for people with dementia living at home are far lower. Hu, Tang, and Zheng (2008) compared the expenses of caring for older people with dementia in three places: hospitals, institutions, and communities. The average expenses per month for a patient were $1,427,

$200, and $81, respectively, and the most important predictor of the cost was the method of payment. Those without medical insurance are less likely to seek medical treatment than those with insurance. Those who have medical insurance usually go in for treatment and medical care. Using a small dementia sample (fifty-five persons) from a Beijing community to estimate the medical and nonmedical (for example, caregiving) expenses taken on by patients, the average cost for a dementia family per month was between $82 and $298 (An and Yu 2005). The results also indicated that cost positively correlates with lower Mini-Mental Status Examination (MMSE) scores and with the concurrence of behavioral and psychological symptoms. Based on these studies, Wang (2009) estimated the total economic burden on Chinese families at roughly $11.7 billion per year. In comparison, in the United States, the economic value of the care provided by the family and other unpaid caregivers of people with ADOD was estimated at about $94 billion (Alzheimer's Association 2009).

Existing Services for People with Dementia and Their Families

A range of services for persons with dementia and their families exists in Mainland China, Taiwan, and Hong Kong. Table 10.2 provides a brief overview of medical and LTC services for this population in each region.

Medical Services

Medical services in Mainland China are paid for through socialized medicine (publicly funded health care), medical insurance, or out of pocket. Those retired from public organizations such as public universities usually enjoy socialized medicine. Depending on the plan, between 50 and 100 percent of their treatment and medicine are covered by the state. Those retired from private enterprises such as companies or factories are usually covered by medical insurance. Older people who have never been employed buy commercial medical insurance or pay for medical expenses themselves. However, the third National Health Service Investigation and Analysis, conducted by the Information Statistics Centre of Ministry of Health, indicates that more than 50 percent of all urban residents and more than 80 percent of all rural residents have *no* medical insurance and thus have to pay all costs out of pocket. Another study that surveyed 295 families of people with dementia showed that 62.4 percent could not afford the $1.38 per day necessary for medicine expenses (Zhang et al. 2004). The fact that the price of dementia medicines is much higher than they can bear often results in delayed treatment or none at all.

Taiwan's National Health Insurance (NHI) provides coverage for the entire population, and includes preventive services and most inpatient, outpatient, and in-home medical care. Insurers are required to pay monthly premiums (shared by employers and the government), as well as modest copayments for the services received. Pharmacological therapy for dementia has been covered by the NHI since 2000. If a middle- or low-income elderly citizen is hospitalized due to a severe case of dementia, the NHI subsidizes up to $30 per day for nursing care. Special-care allowances (up to $100 per month) are given every month to middle- to low-income elderly citizens who have not been placed in institutions and suffer from chronic diseases such as ADOD (Chien et al. 2008).

In Hong Kong, nine memory clinics and eight community-based assessment centers provide psychosocial and medical assessment services for people with cognitive impairments. Both geriatric and psychogeriatric services are funded by the government. The government also funds screening services conducted by the clinics, but not the screening programs conducted in the community. Users must pay for these services, which are subsidized by funds from the community chest or private foundations. Available medical services include outpatient services, domiciliary care, outreach services to nursing homes and day-care centers, day hospitals, inpatient units, and LTC.

Long-term Care Facilities

Institutions that can provide LTC for people with dementia in Mainland China include social welfare institutions for the aged (SWIAs), homes for the aged, and nursing homes. The SWIAs are funded and run by the state and mainly provide care to older adults who have no economic sources, families, or the ability to earn a living. The houses for the aged and nursing homes are usually run by social service organizations and provide care for the elderly, from independent older adults to those who need nursing care. However, current capacity does not meet the rocketing demand. Optimistically, the present capacity may accommodate only 4 percent (or less) of people with dementia.

There were 310 nursing homes in Taiwan as of 2006, a number that has grown rapidly in recent years according to the Department of Health (2009). There is a partial premium subsidy from the NHI for the disabled (including people with dementia), the elderly, and the jobless. However, long-term institutional care is not funded under the NHI.

In Hong Kong, institutional care for people with dementia is provided by public residential care homes, infirmary wards, and private residential homes. An annual supplement of $4,230 per elderly person diagnosed with an advanced stage of dementia is provided to residential care homes, compared with $7,049 per dementia patient in infirmary wards. This additional sum is granted to the facility to employ professional staff or purchase necessary equipment to provide better care and training. As for people living in the community, those who have been certified by a medical doctor as having ADOD are entitled to receive a monthly disability allowance between $160 and $294 from the government, depending on the degree of disability.

A range of LTC services is available in both Taiwan and Hong Kong, including home-care services, day care, respite, and caregiver support groups (see table 10.2). Respite is a very common term in the caregiving field. It means a service or program that allows the caregiver some "time out" from his or her responsibilities—for example, the caregiver hires a home health aide who comes

Table 10.2 Brief Overview of Services for Persons with Dementia and Their Families: Mainland China, Taiwan, and Hong Kong

	Medical Services	Long-term Care Facilities
China	• 3 methods of payment for medical expenses: socialized medicine, medical insurance, and private pay.	Limited beds available by social welfare institutions for the aged, homes for the aged, and nursing homes.
Taiwan	• National Health Insurance (NHI) covers or subsidizes: (1) Pharmacological therapy. (2) Up to approx. $30 per day of nursing care for middle- to low-income elderly citizens. • Special care allowance (up to $100 per month) given to middle- to low-income community-dwelling elderly citizens with dementia.	• NHI does NOT cover long-term institutional care. • Intermediate care facilities, nursing homes, and veterans' home are available. Occupancy rate is around 73%.
Hong Kong	• 9 memory clinics and 8 community-based assessment centers do psychosocial and medical assessments for dementia. • The government funds screening services in memory clinics.	• An annual "dementia supplement" is given to residential care homes and infirmary wards for persons with advanced-stage dementia. • Public residential care homes and infirmary wards, and private residential homes are available.

Source: Authors' summary.

Table 10.2 continued

Long-term Care Services
Limited and concentrated in urban areas. Drop-in home care available in a few communities.

• NHI partially covers home nursing care.
• Local government provides subsidies of around $31 daily for up to 7 days per person per year for respite care.
• Missing elders' search center.
• Emergency rescue hotline.
• 25 long-term-care resource centers refer services including:
  (1) ID bracelet program
  (2) In-home rehabilitation
  (3) Friendly visit or phone call
  (4) Home-delivered meals
  (5) Home modification
  (6) Home-care service
  (7) Day-care service
  (8) Respite
  (9) Transportation
  (10) Caregiver support groups
  (11) Case management

Hong Kong Alzheimer's Disease Association (HKADA) provides: • Day-care service • Respite • Early detection program • Counseling • Case management • Caregiver support groups • Hotline service • Educational programs for professionals • Resource centers

in and "relieves" the caregiver; or the caregiver places a loved one in a facility like a nursing home for a weekend or a week (on a temporary basis) while he or she takes care of personal needs. In Taiwan, twenty-five long-term regional care resource centers are the primary conduits of information and community resources, including referrals for assistive devices (such as grab bars in the bathroom), consultation on issues from providing care at home to placement, and the training of health-care professionals and family caregivers. The staff of such centers is mostly comprised of social workers and nurses.

Noninstitutional Long-term Care Services

In Hong Kong, services for people with dementia and their families are primarily provided by the Hong Kong Alzheimer's Disease Association (HKADA). The association does not receive any public funding and is supported mainly by donations. A unique service that the HKADA provides is early detection, using a community-based approach that provides comprehensive psychosocial assessment and screening for people with cognitive impairments. Referrals for medical assessment or community support services are then provided. The HKADA also organizes a variety of trainings on dementia care in different disciplines for professionals, family members, volunteers, and caregivers, as well as campaigns to increase public awareness and destigmatize ADOD.

As in the case of Mainland China, literature has shown that in bigger and wealthier cities, older residents enjoy more welfare services, offered by local governments as well as burgeoning nongovernmental organizations (Tian 2006). Recently, a few rural communities have implemented drop-in home care, in which practitioners from local hospitals or medical centers visit patients regularly and provide medical intervention as well as consultation services. More support from both the state and local organizations is needed to expand this service in rural areas.

Plans for the Future

Mainland China, Taiwan, and Hong Kong are gearing up to meet the challenges of their aging societies. We will now detail a number of strategies being proposed to meet their projected needs.

Mainland China

1. *Expand medical insurance coverage for all citizens.* In recent years, the central government has made much progress in improving public medical insurance, and more people are now covered. In 2002 only 55 percent of urban residents and 21 percent of rural residents enjoyed medical insurance, but by 2008, about 91.5 percent of the total rural population had been covered (Information Statistics Centre of Ministry of Health 2009). A new medical reform was announced in April 2009 by the State Department of China, aimed at benefiting all people by the year

2011. In the next three years, both the central and local governments will invest $125 billion to support this new plan (Information Statistics Centre of Ministry of Health 2009).

2. *Dementia-specific health plans.* Although no dementia-specific government plans have been announced so far, some ordinances on mental health have pointed to this issue. In 2002 the Working Plan of Mental Health in China from 2002 to 2010 was announced. Dementia was listed as a priority for disease prevention and treatment. The plan aimed to set up at least one prevention center in each province by 2005, where 50 percent of patients would be identified and treated. This goal has been reached. With respect to improving public awareness of dementia, it is believed that with the expansion of scientific education, at least half of all families will be aware of the disease by 2010. Some of the subgoals of the plan include the following:

   a. The plan will center on clinicians. Nationwide training courses, workshops, seminars, case reports with pathological discussion, and increasing exchanges with international partners (Harvard University, University of California–Los Angeles, University of California–San Francisco, Stanford, and so on) were offered by these experts to increase clinicians' knowledge. More focus is now placed on early detection methods, the publishing of relevant articles in Chinese medical journals and textbooks, and the revision of neuropsychological tests so that the diagnosis of dementia takes Chinese cultural issues into account.

   b. With the goal of improving access to health care, the plan is to establish eight dementia clinics and forty memory-disorder-specific outpatient clinics in China.

   c. A number of educational events and outreach efforts have been put in place in order to raise public awareness of ADOD. For example, "World AD Day" activities have been held annually since 2001.

   d. Research is increasing, supported by the government to inform policy and the allocation of resources for improved health and welfare.

Taiwan

In April 2007 the Executive Yuan of Taiwan ratified the Ten-year National Long-term Care Plan (2007–2016). Its overarching goal is to construct a long-term care system that offers quality services to older adults and people with disabilities in their homes and communities to maximize their independence and quality of life. Subgoals include making services more affordable for the public via subsidy, and increasing manpower and infrastructure to meet the growing need for LTC. Under the plan, subsidized services will be available for eligible recipients who need assistance in their daily lives, including people with dementia. Services provided will include home-care services, in-home nursing, in-home rehabilitation, the purchase and lease of mechanical aids, home modifications, respite services, transportation, and provision of nutritious meals. The government is investing $2.5 billion in this plan over the next ten years, offering twelve thousand new jobs.

The Ministry of the Interior has a project named "Construction for the Long-term Care System Ten-year Project" under this overarching plan. It contains several objectives that relate to dementia care:

1. *Convert empty beds and spaces at nonprofit institutions into dementia-care units.* This is partly in response to a finding that the beds in nonprofit institutions are, on average, 35 percent unoccupied. The government will pay partial costs for the dementia-care unit, including remodeling the facility and paying the wages of case managers, care attendants, and nurses.
2. *Set up more day-care centers, especially in areas where services are scarce.* The goal is to have at least one day-care center at the village level by 2016.
3. *Subsidize 25 to 90 hours of home nursing care according to the severity of disability per month.* The government will also subsidize one in-home rehabilitation service per week for patients who are too disabled to utilize transportation services to go to rehabilitations centers. In addition, subsidized days of respite care will increase from the current 7 days to 14 to 21 days depending on the severity of the disability. And there will be more flexibility for families to choose from agencies or home-care aides. There will also be one-time subsidies for patients and their families to purchase or rent assistive devices or for home modifications over a span of ten years. People who are severely disabled and live in remote areas will be subsidized for up to four round-trip transportation fees. Other subsidies are planned for low-income elderly to receive home-delivered meals and institutional care.

The present government is inclined to adopt a national LTC insurance program that will require all citizens to pay the insurance premium to augment the existing NHI system. Under the current plan, it is estimated that the monthly premium rate for the LTC insurance may account for around 1 percent of a person's wages or about one-sixth of the NHI rate. It is hoped that the LTC insurance will help generate demand for domestic-licensed care workers, instead of unlicensed foreign workers, reducing the unemployment rate of Taiwanese citizens. It is projected that demand for nurses, therapists, and social workers will increase sharply once the program is launched, which might happen as early as 2011. However, the plan is still in rudimentary form and needs to be reviewed by the Executive Yuan and approved by the Legislative Yuan.

Hong Kong

There are several directions for future policies and services in Hong Kong (Tsien 2007).

1. *Education.* More training in dementia is planned for health-care professionals, which might help improve the early detection of the disease. In addition to raising awareness through more public campaigns, more dementia-related content is being included in the curricula of schools of medicine, occupational therapy, physiotherapy, nursing, and social work. Continuing education opportunities will also increase.
2. *Technology.* Online screening tests for dementia, memory-training exercises, and portable multisensory stimulation are being developed for people who are homebound. Increased use of global positioning system (GPS) devices may help to track missing people with dementia and give their family members peace of mind.
3. *Specialized services.* Specialized services such as day-care services and residential care will be improved to more specifically address the needs of people with dementia. Better-structured programs to support the well-being of caregivers are also being developed. At the moment, the Hong Kong government funds neither dementia-specific day-care services nor other dementia-specific community services. This leaves the door open for more advocacies on behalf of ADOD patients and their families.

Conclusion

Although the family is still thought to be the most reliable source of care for the demented elderly in Asia, more public resources are needed in this area as traditional belief in the importance of filial piety erodes.

Dementia is one of the most disabling of all chronic diseases. ADOD could have a devastating economic and social impact on Mainland China, Taiwan, and Hong Kong, just as it is expected to have in the United States and Western Europe. How the disease burden translates in terms of cost will vary greatly depending on the country and the mix of care services provided. It is foreseeable that costs will rise relative to the gross domestic product as prevalence increases. As we have learned, Mainland China, Hong Kong, and Taiwan have extensive plans to address the increasing needs of ADOD patients and their families. Backed by well-formulated government policies, in collaboration with community organizations, it is hoped these efforts will be successful and provide international leadership on this emerging global public health issue.

References

Alzheimer's Association. 2009. *Alzheimer's Disease Facts and Figures.* www.alz.org/news_and_events_2009_facts_figures.asp.

Alzheimer's Association and National Alliance for Caregiving. 2009. *Families Care: Alzheimer's Caregiving in the United States, 2004.* www.alz.org/national/documents/report_familiescare.pdf.

Alzheimer's Disease International. 2009. *Annual Report 2007–2008.* www.alz.co.uk/adi/pdf/annrep08.pdf.

American Psychiatric Association. 2000. *Diagnostic and Statistical Manual of Mental Disorders, text revision.* 4th ed. Arlington: American Psychiatric Association.

An, C. X., and X. Yu. 2005. "Economic Burden and Related Factors in Patient with Dementia." *Chinese Mental Health Journal* 19 (9): 592–94.

Au, A., S. Li, K. Lee, P. Leung, P. C. Pan, L. W. Thompson, and D. Gallagher-Thompson. 2009. "The Coping with Caregiving Group Program for Chinese Caregivers of Patients with Alzheimer's Disease in Hong Kong." *Patient Education and Counseling.* doi: 10.1016/j.pec.2009.06.005.

Chien, I., Y. Lin, Y. Chou, C. Lin, S. Bih, and C. Lee, and P. Chou. 2008. "Treated Prevalence and Incidence of Dementia among National Health Insurance Enrollees in Taiwan, 1996–2003." *Journal of Geriatric Psychiatry and Neurology* 21 (2): 142–48.

China National Committee on Ageing. 2009. *Report on the Chinese Elderly Population* [in Chinese]. http://59.252.131.7:800/cncaweb/forum/119.html;jsessionid=E496FC3D288FFD6F5CC335497E555BC6.

Chiu, L., and W. C. Shyu. 2001. "Estimation of the Family Cost of Private Nursing Home care Versus Home Care for Patients with Dementia in Taiwan." *Chang Gung Medical Journal* 24 (10): 608–14.

Chou, L. F., C. W. Chang, J. L. Fu, and S. J. Wang. 2001. "The Economic Costs of Dementia in Taiwan." *National Chengchi University Journal* 82: 1–25.

Connell, C. M., M. R. Janevic, and M. P. Gallant. 2001. "The Costs of Caring: Impact of Dementia on Family Caregivers." *Journal of Geriatric Psychiatry and Neurology* 14 (4): 179–87.

Department of Health. 2009. *Health Statistics in Taiwan 2006.* www.doh.gov.tw/EN2006/DM/DM2.aspx?now_fod_list_no=9085&class_no=390&level_no=1.

Family Caregiver Association. 2009. *2007 Family Caregiver Survey.* www.familycare.org.tw/fcgnew/prom_doc_list.aspx?art=research.

Ferri, C. P., M. Prince, C. Brayne, H. Brodaty, L. Fratiglioni, M. Ganguli, K. Hall, K. Hasegawa, H. Hendrie, Y. Huang, A. Jorm, C. Mathers, P. R. Menezes, E. Rimmer, and M. Scazufca. 2005. "Global Prevalence of Dementia: A Delphi Consensus Study." *The Lancet* 366 (9503): 2112–17.

Fuh, J. L., and S. J. Wang. 2008. "Dementia in Taiwan: Past, Present, and Future." *Acta Neurologica Taiwanica* 17 (3): 153–61.

Gallagher-Thompson, D., and D. W. Coon. 2007. "Evidence-based Psychological Treatments for Distress in Family Caregivers of Older Adults." *Psychology and Aging* 22: 37–51.

Gallagher-Thompson, D., P-C. Wang, W. Liu, V. Cheung, R. Peng, D. China, and L. W. Thompson. In press. "Effectiveness of a Psychoeducational Skill Training DVD Program to Reduce Stress in Chinese American Dementia Caregivers: Results of a Preliminary Study." *Aging and Mental Health* 14 (3): 263–73.

Gallagher-Thompson, D., H. Gray, P. Tang, C. Y. Pu, C. Tse, S. Hsu, L. Leung, P. Wang, E. Kwo, H-Q. Tong, J. Long, and L. W. Thompson 2007. "Impact of In-home Intervention versus Telephone Support in Reducing Depression and Stress of Chinese Caregivers: Results of a Pilot Study." *American Journal of Geriatric Psychiatry* 15: 425–34.

Guo, Z., B. R. Levy, W. L. Hinton, P. F. Weitzman, and S. Levkoff. 2000. "The Power of Labels: Recruiting Dementia Affected Chinese-American Elders and their Caregivers." *Journal of Mental Health and Aging* 6: 103–12.

Hu, W. S., M. N. Tang, and H. B. Zheng. 2008. "Study on Economic Burden of Senile Dementia in Community." *Journal of Practical Medicine* 24 (10): 1821–23.

Huang, C-Y., V. D. Sousa, S-J. Perng, M-Y. Hwang, C-C. Tsai, M-H. Huang, and S-Y. Yao. 2009. "Stressors, Social Support, Depressive Symptoms and General Health Status of Taiwanese Caregivers of Persons with Stroke or Alzheimer's Disease." *Journal of Clinical Nursing* 18: 502–11.

Information Statistics Centre of Ministry of Health. 2005. "Abstract of the report on the 3rd National Health Service Investigation and Analysis." *Chinese Hospital* 9 (1): 3–11 [in Chinese].

———. 2009. "National Health Reformation and Development in Year 2008." www. gov.cn/gzdt/2009-02/17/content_1233236.htm [in Chinese].

Jackson, R. 2009. *Preparing for China's Aging Challenge 2005*. www.csis.org/index. php?option=com_csis_pubs&task=view&id=885.

Lan, P. C. 2002. "Subcontracting Filial Piety: Elder Care in Ethnic Chinese Immigrant Families in California." *Journal of Transcultural Nursing* 13: 202–09.

Liu, L. H. 1993. "Effects of Population Composition on Finance of National Health Insurance." Master's thesis, School of Public Health, National Taiwan University, Taipei.

Ministry of the Interior. 2007. *Older Adults and People with Disabilities Data* [in Chinese]. http://sowf.moi.gov.tw/17/97/index.htm.

National Bureau of Statistics of China, ed. 2006. *China Statistical Yearbook*. Beijing: China Statistics Press.

Ng, S. H. 2002. "Will Families Support their Elders? Answers from Across Cultures." In *Ageism: Stereotyping and Prejudice against Older Persons*, edited by T. D. Nelson. Boston: MIT Press.

Pinquart, M., and S. Sorenson. 2005. "Ethnic Differences in Stressors, Resources, and Psychological Outcomes of Family Caregiving: A Meta-analysis." *The Gerontologist* 45: 90–106.

———. 2006. "Helping Caregivers of Persons with Dementia: Which Interventions Work and How Large are their Effects?" *International Psychogeriatrics* 18: 577–95.

REACH II Investigators (alphabetical order: Belle, S. H.; Burgio, L.; Burns, R.; Coon, D.; Czaja, S.; Gallagher-Thompson, D.; Gitlin, L.; Klinger, J.; Koepke, K. M.; Lee, C. C.; Martindale-Adams, J.; Nichols, L.; Schulz, R.; Stahl, S.; Stevens, A.; Winter, L.; and Zhang S.). 2006. "Enhancing the Quality of Life of Dementia Caregivers from Different Ethnic or Racial Groups: A Randomized, Controlled Trial." *Annals of Internal Medicine* 145: 727–38.

Schulz, R., and L. Martire. 2004. "Family Caregiving of Persons with Dementia: Prevalence, Health Effects, and Support Strategies." *American Journal of Geriatric Psychiatry* 12: 240–49.

Sung, K. 1995. "Measures and Dimensions of Filial Piety in Korea." *The Gerontologist* 35 (2): 240–47.

Taiwan Alzheimer's Disease Association. 2009. *Report on Prevalence of Dementia 2004.* www.tds.org.tw/html/front/bin/ptdetail.phtml?Part=022&Category=121256.

Tian, S. M. 2006. "On Demand and Realizing Pattern of Care for the Aged in China." *Social Sciences Journal of Colleges of Shanxi* 18 (7): 53–56.

Tsien, T. B. K. 2007. "Dementia Care and Services." *Hong Kong Nursing Journal* 43 (2): 15–18.

Wang, D. 2009. *Dementia Caregiving in Mainland China.* Manuscripts: Beijing Normal University.

Wimo, A., G. Ljunggren, and B. Winblad. 1997. "Costs of Dementia and Dementia Care: A Review." *International Journal of Geriatric Psychiatry* 12: 841–56.

Wimo, A., L. Jonsson, and B. Winblad. 2006. "An Estimate of the Worldwide Prevalence and Direct Costs of Dementia in 2003." *Dementia and Geriatric Cognitive Disorders* 21: 175–81.

Zhan, L. 2004. "Caring for Family Members with Alzheimer's Disease: Perspectives from Chinese American Caregivers." *Journal of Gerontological Nursing* 13: 19–29.

Zhang, Z. X., X. Chen, X. H. Liu, M-N. Tang, H. H. Zhao, Q. M. Qu, C-B. Wu, Z. Hong, and B. Zhou. 2004. "A Caregiver Survey in Beijing, Xian, Shanghai and Chengdu: Health Services Status for the Elderly with Dementia." *Acta Academiae Medicinae Sinicae* 26 (2): 116–21.

Zhang, Z. X., G. E. P. Zahner, G. C. Román, X-H. Liu, C-B. Wu, Z. Hong, X. Hong, M-N. Tang, B. Zhou, Q-M. Qu, X-J. Zhang, and H. Li. 2006. "Socio-demographic Variation of Dementia Subtypes in China: Methodology and Results of a Prevalence Study in Beijing, Chengdu, Shanghai, and Xian." *Neuroepidemiology* 27 (4): 177–87.

Zimmer, Z., M. B. Ofstedal, and M. C. Chang. 2001. "Impact of Cognitive Status and Decline on Service and Support Utilization among Older Adults in Taiwan." *Research on Aging* 23 (3): 267–303.

ELDERLY CARE IN SINGAPORE:
THE STATE AS LAST RESORT

Meng-Kin Lim

Singapore's population of 4.9 million people is relatively young: only 8 percent of residents were 65 years or older in 2009. But thanks to dramatic declines in mortality and fertility, the country is aging fast. In 2008 the infant mortality rate was 2.1 per 1,000 live births, average life expectancy at birth was 81 years, and the total fertility rate was 1.28 (MOH, 2009a). If the present trajectory holds, a staggering 25 percent of the population will be 65 years or older in 2030 (Department of Statistics 2001). The old-age dependency ratio, which in 1994 was one elderly dependent person to seven working adults, will be one to two in 2030 (Cheung 1996). This profound demographic change means the tiny island-state of seven hundred square kilometers will have to tackle a whole range of issues affecting the workforce, social security, housing, and health, to name a few.

In 2005 a tripartite committee comprising government, employers, and employees was formed to spearhead initiatives that would expand employment opportunities for older workers, including job redesign, wage restructuring, retraining, retention, and the shaping of positive perceptions toward older workers. The legal retirement age was raised from 55 to 62. Employers are encouraged to redeploy older workers while the latter are encouraged to scale down their expectations. A minister in the prime minister's office was appointed to handle the issues of the elderly, driving and coordinating policies that "give elders opportunities to stay active, healthy, and engaged" and overseeing their implementation across various government agencies. The government has also begun to invest heavily in elderly-friendly infrastructure and a continuum of community-based service-delivery systems and programs targeted at the healthy elderly, the frail elderly, and their caregivers. Health care for the elderly is clearly a priority issue. However, with the government resolutely opposed to state-funded national health insurance schemes, it remains to be seen whether health care for the growing ranks of the elderly can be sustainably financed.

While not unique in facing the problem of an aging population, Singapore—noted for its forward thinking and knack for anticipating change and adapting swiftly—should make for an interesting case study as it responds to the looming health-care crisis, holding lessons for other East Asian countries.

Paying for Health Care into Old Age

Singapore is in a strong position to embark on health-care reforms. It is the third-wealthiest country in the world, with a gross domestic product (GDP) purchasing power parity (PPP) per capita of US$50,299 (World Bank 2007), and it is ranked 6th out of 191 countries in overall health systems performance (WHO 2000). Singapore's democratically elected government has been in power since 1959, providing continuity and coherence in policymaking, in contrast to those countries that have seen frequent changes in government. Its most important advantage over other countries considering health-care reform, however, may be its lack of the "entitlement culture" that seems to plague the Western industrialized welfare states.

Figure 11.1 Singapore's Population Pyramid: 1957, 1980, and 2030

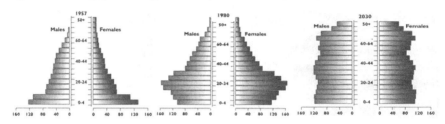

Source: Department of Statistics, Singapore 2001.

Figure 11.2 Percentage of Population 65 and Over, 1995–2030

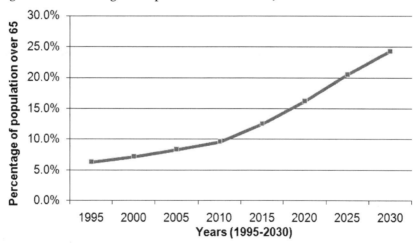

Source: Department of Statistics, Singapore 2001.

Since gaining independence from Britain in 1963 and from Malaysia in 1965, Singapore has eschewed egalitarian welfarism in favor of market mechanisms to allocate scarce health-care resources. Realizing that health-care costs would ineluctably rise as the population ages and technology advances, the government assiduously avoided policies that would transfer the financial burden to future generations, instead preferring to shift the cost of health care to private entities (Lim 2004). Compared to the Organisation for Economic Co-operation and Development (OECD) countries, which spent an average of 9 percent of their GDP on health care (OECD 2007), Singapore has successfully contained the level of health-care spending to between 3 and 4 percent of its GDP in the past four decades. In 2005 national health expenditure amounted to S$7.4 billion (US$5.2 billion, S$1 = US$0.7, 2009), a mere 3.7 percent of the GDP. Of this, the government expended only about S$1.8 billion (US$1.3 billion), or 0.9 percent, of the GDP (MOH 2009b).

Figure 11.3 Public versus Private Health Expenditure

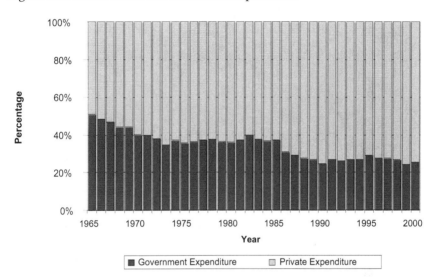

Source: Lim 2004.

So, if not the state or the next generation, who will pay for the health-care needs of Singapore's elderly? Five high-level ministerial committees have been convened since 1982 to address this question, along with those related to other anticipated needs of the elderly (see table 11.1), and the answer has always been the same: There is no magic bullet. Financial responsibility for Singapore's elderly lies with the individual, the family, and the community—in that order—and only lastly with the state. The landmark 1999 *Report of the Inter-Ministerial Committee on the Ageing Population* reaffirmed the family's responsibility to care for its elderly, with institutional care a measure of last resort.

At first glance, this hands-off approach to the care of elderly citizens may be misconstrued as inhuman or even suggestive of ingratitude, for at the leading edge of Singapore's silver-haired wave are the "baby boomers"—the generation

179

that trailblazed Singapore's rapid industrialization and fueled its economic miracle. Digging deeper, however, we find the government's firm guarantee, made in 1993, that no Singaporean will ever be denied needed health care because of lack of funds. This declaration undergirds Singapore's health-care system. In other words, universal health-care coverage exists, and it extends to the elderly. But how can this be possible under a "state as last resort" regime?

Table 11.1 Past High-level Inter-ministry Committees on the Problems of the Aged

1982–1984	Advisory Council on the Aged
1988–1989	National Advisory Council on the Family and the Aged
1989–1997	Inter-ministerial Committee on Health Care for the Elderly
1997–1999	Inter-ministerial Committee on the Ageing Population
2004–present	Committee on Aging Issues

Source: Author's review of related policy documents.

Cost-sharing and Targeted Subsidies

Health-care financing in Singapore is guided by the principle of cost-sharing: the government will heavily subsidize health-care costs, but the majority of the populace, who should be able to afford the subsidized levels, must copay. The core features of Singapore's unique "3M" health-care financing system have not changed since its inception: Singapore's hardworking citizens are required, during their productive years, to save for their own future health-care needs through *Medisave* and are urged to insure against major illnesses through *MediShield*; the poor and needy can receive health care through a state-funded *Medifund* scheme (Lim 1998).

- *Medisave* was introduced in 1984 as a compulsory health savings account for employees or self-employed persons who are Singaporean citizens or permanent residents. It is tax-exempt and interest-yielding, and represents 6.5 to 9 percent (depending on age) of wages earmarked for future hospitalization, day surgery, and certain outpatient expenses. As the Medisave account can be used to pay for the hospitalization and other approved medical bills of one's spouse, children, or parents, there is a small element of risk-pooling within the family. Upon the death of the account holder, any unspent balance is passed on to the beneficiaries. In 2008 the combined Medisave accounts of all Singaporeans amounted to S$42billion (US$29.9billion)—a significant sum considering it is about six times Singapore's annual national health-care expenditure. In 2008, eight out of ten Singaporeans admitted to hospitals used Medisave to pay their bills.

- *MediShield* is a voluntary low-cost insurance scheme designed to protect households from large and unexpected financial losses due to illness. It provides coverage for "catastrophic" illnesses such as heart surgery and liver transplantation, for which Medisave is likely to be inadequate. Premiums can be paid from Medisave. Singaporeans who want more benefits or amenities such as better hospital rooms may purchase enhanced "shield" plans offered by private insurers. The government requires these plans, at a minimum, to incorporate the basic Medishield plan, while supplemental rider plans provide the desired additional coverage. There are currently twenty-five such "integrated" shield plans offered by three private insurers catering to the varied health insurance needs of Singaporeans. In 2008, 84 percent of Singapore's population was covered under MediShield-type plans.
- *Medifund* is the state-funded safety net that takes care of the poor and needy. It was set up in 1993 as a state-funded safety net for Singaporeans who cannot afford medical expenses even after government subsidy, Medisave, and MediShield. The interest from a large government-sponsored endowment fund (which currently stands at $1.7 billion) is distributed to both public hospitals and nonprofit hospitals run by voluntary welfare organizations, to cover the costs of patients genuinely unable to pay their hospital bills.

Singapore's unique cost-sharing and risk-spreading formula has, to some extent, countered the "moral hazard" generally associated with fee-for-service, third-party reimbursement; hence, it has moderated rising health-care costs to some extent. By treating the majority of health-care users as copaying partners and offering special provisions to the minority who cannot afford to pay, Singapore cleverly avoids providing the rich with health-care handouts, as would be the case under a universal coverage system that ignores income status.

A further redistributional element is embedded in the graded system of public hospital wards. The latter are stratified according to the level of comfort and amenities, thus allowing preferential targeting of subsidies to the lower classes of wards (see table 11.2). Patients who opt for C-class wards enjoy a subsidy of up to 80 percent, whereas patients who choose A-class beds are not subsidized at all. The MOH estimates that more than 96 percent of B-class patients and almost 98 percent of C-class patients should be able to fully pay their bills from their Medisave account.

In January 2009, after discovering that many who could afford the better classes of wards had opted for the heavily subsidized C- and B2-class wards, sometimes crowding out lower-income patients, the government further introduced means testing to determine eligibility. It promised that the additional revenue derived from the reduced subsidy for the higher-income groups would go toward subsidizing the lower-income groups; that patients who could not afford the lower classes of wards despite the subsidies would get additional financial assistance through Medifund; and that persons aggrieved by means testing would have their cases reassessed on a case-by-case basis. Because the government has kept to its promise to be flexible at the margins and err on the side of generosity (e.g., by being sensitive to the circumstances of retirees and others who are not employed), implementation has not been contentious thus far.

Table 11.2 Government Subsidies According to Class of Ward

Class	Subsidy	Differences in Amenities
A	0%	1–2 beds, air-conditioned, attached bathroom, TV, phone, choice of doctor
B1	20%	4 beds, air-conditioned, attached bathroom, TV, phone, choice of doctor
B2+	50%	5 beds, air-conditioned, attached bathroom
B2	65%	6 beds, no air conditioning
C	80%	>6 beds, no air conditioning

Source: Author's review of related policy documents.

Supplemental Schemes and Affirmative Action

In addition, supplemental schemes are available to alleviate the financial burden of health-care costs on the elderly. A means-tested public assistance scheme (PAS) provides financial assistance to the destitute, frail, or disabled elderly. All Singaporeans above age 60 are already entitled to a 75 percent subsidy of the fees charged at government polyclinics. These are one-stop health centers, eighteen in all, which provide subsidized outpatient medical care as well as follow-up care for patients discharged from hospitals. They offer a wide range of services including immunization, health screening, health education, and laboratory and pharmacy services. Recipients under the PAS, however, are entitled to free medical services. Help from various charitable organizations is also available, and a primary care partnership scheme (PCPS) subsidizes treatment of chronic diseases by private general practitioners and dentists who take part in the government-spearheaded chronic disease management program, which will be discussed later in this chapter.

Established in 2002, ElderShield is another affordable, severe-disability scheme to provide insurance coverage to those who require long-term care. Singaporean citizens and permanent residents (PRs) with Medisave accounts are automatically covered under ElderShield at the age of 40, unless they opt out. With premiums payable from Medisave accounts, ElderShield provides a fixed payout calculated as sufficient to cover a substantial portion of the patients' out-of-pocket share of subsidized nursing-home care or home care, up to a maximum of S$400 per month for six years. The scheme was further enhanced in 2007 with the introduction of innovative, supplementary plans from private insurers, offering features such as higher monthly payouts, longer periods of coverage, and greater options. In 2008 ElderShield covered some 850,000 people out of the eligible 1.2 million (age 40 and above).

The state also has an ElderCare Fund, to which the government contributes significant amounts annually from its budgetary surplus. Set up in 2000 and targeted to reach S$2.5 billion in 2010, the fund is intended to cover anticipated increases in subsidies to voluntary welfare organizations that offer care to the elderly. In 2007 Medifund Silver was carved out from Medifund to provide even more targeted support for Singaporean patients aged 65 or over who are unable to pay their bills in public-sector hospitals and other Medifund-approved institutions providing intermediate and long-term care.

Affirmative action is built into the schemes as they evolve. Notably, the government periodically tops up (again, from budget surplus) the various schemes in such a way as to preferentially benefit the less well-off and the elderly. In 2001, for example, to encourage the uninsured elderly to open MediShield accounts, the government paid for basic MediShield premiums for two years for all Singaporeans aged 61 to 69, at a total cost of S$110 million. It also set aside S$19 million to help the elderly pay for their ElderShield premiums. Approximately 65 percent of the eligible elderly enrolled in the program, with the result that approximately 90 percent of Singaporeans between the ages of 61 and 69 now have health-care benefits.

By 2004, S$2.75 billion had gone into both the Medisave and MediShield top-up schemes for the elderly. In 2008, to help older Singaporeans pay for their increased MediShield premiums, the government paid up to S$450 per person into the Medisave accounts of all those aged 51 and above—a one-time exercise that cost the government S$220 million. The government also paid S$400 million into the ElderCare Fund in 2008 (bringing its size to S$1.5 billion) and added S$200 million to the Medifund (bringing its size to S$1.6 billion). And in 2009, despite the financial crisis and economic recession, the government topped up Medifund with $100 million, of which a portion is allocated to Medifund Silver.

Public-Private Providers and Market Orientaton

The government has acknowledged the need to develop new, comprehensive geriatric health-care services in hospitals, and to create social and community support for caregiving to elderly persons. But again, not all the solutions can come from the public sector. Increasing emphasis is being placed on public-private partnerships that build on the existing public-private mix of health-care providers. Many also believe that competitive pressures encourage all providers—public and private—to be efficient.

Primary health care is easily accessible through general practitioners in private clinics (80 percent) and government outpatient polyclinics (20 percent). In 2006, there were a total of 11,545 hospital beds in 29 hospitals and specialty centers in Singapore, giving a ratio of 2.6 beds per 1,000 people. Seven public hospitals (providing multidisciplinary, acute, inpatient services; specialist outpatient services; and 24-hour emergency services) and 6 national specialty centers (for cancer, heart, eye, skin, neuroscience, and dental care)—ranging in size from 185 to 2,064 beds—account for 72 percent of the beds. Sixteen private hospitals (between 20 and 505 beds) account for the rest. In addition, traditional Chinese practitioners in the private sector see an estimated 12 percent of daily outpatients. Patients have complete freedom to choose among providers.

Starting in 1985, all public-sector hospitals have been successfully restructured to give them autonomy, private-sector efficiency, financial discipline, and a strong market orientation (Phua 1991). Initially managed by a monolithic government company (the Health Corporation of Singapore), the restructured hospitals underwent further reorganization in 2000, splitting into two competing clusters—the National Healthcare Group and the Singapore Health Services— but they remain 100 percent owned by, and accountable to, the MOH.

The fact that all of Singapore's major private-sector health-care players are listed on the Singapore Exchange reflects the government's favorable disposition toward the commercialization of health-care services. All public-sector and most private-sector hospitals are Joint Commission International (JCI) accredited. Together, they attract some 500,000 foreign patients a year. The government has set a target of one million foreign patients by 2012, reckoning that it will generate S$3 billion in revenue and create 13,000 new jobs in the process.

Step-down and Long-term Care

Residential long-term care facilities that cater to those requiring skilled nursing or rehabilitation services following discharge from acute-care hospitals fall into three categories: community hospitals, chronic sick hospitals, and nursing homes for the elderly. *Community hospitals* are intermediate care facilities that cater to patients who are fit for discharge from acute-care hospitals but require inpatient convalescent and rehabilitative care. *Chronic sick hospitals* provide skilled nursing and medical care on a long-term basis to older persons with advanced, complicated medical conditions. *Nursing homes for the elderly* provide long-term skilled nursing care for older persons who do not have families or caregivers to look after them at home. All of these facilities are presently managed either privately or by voluntary welfare organizations and provide important "step-down" health-care services to the elderly.

There are now more than 9,200 nursing home beds; about 75 percent of them are in homes run by voluntary welfare organizations, and the rest are in privately run nursing homes. Although the government has, as a matter of principle, been discouraging families from sending their elderly to nursing homes except as a last resort, the MOH has recently announced that it intends to increase the number of beds to 14,000 over the next decade, with voluntary welfare organizations and the private sector leading the way.

Under a longstanding incentive policy, the government subsidizes 90 percent of the capital costs and 50 percent of the recurring operating costs of facilities run by voluntary welfare organizations. It also provides subsidies (75 percent, 50 percent, or 25 percent, depending on means testing) to needy persons at these facilities. In addition, since 2003 the MOH has extended subsidies to accredited private nursing homes for patients who qualify through means testing. Finally, it recently announced its intention to allow the use of Medisave for home-based and community-based services that help the elderly to remain in their own homes for as long as possible.

As long as step-down health services are left to the private and volunteer sector, however, long-term care for the elderly will remain fragmented. Thus, in an effort to streamline these services, the MOH recently grouped them around three acute-care hospitals, each with a geriatric department. Within each of the three geographical zones (west, central, and east) the geriatric department of a general hospital will provide professional leadership for the development of geriatric step-down care in each zone and to the community hospitals and nursing homes in the form of structured training and quality assurance programs and shared resources, including laboratory services. Selected nursing homes now also serve as "nodal points" that provide a full range of community-based services for the aged.

Palliative Care and End-of-life Issues

Despite its attention to other areas of health care, the government has long left palliative care in the hands of charitable and voluntary welfare organizations. Currently, 55 percent of Singaporeans who are terminally ill die in hospitals, whereas 28 percent die in their homes. In 2007 hospices cared for 1,200 patients, and an additional 3,200 patients were cared for through five home-based hospice services. In all, about S$5 million in state subsidies went to 4,400 patients, an amount the MOH has conceded is small, given the 17,000 deaths here every year. In 2008, there were only fifteen doctors working in palliative care in the whole country. The Singapore Hospice Council estimates that about 70 percent of people with terminal illnesses are dying without hospice palliative care in Singapore.

Acknowledging this situation to be unsatisfactory, the MOH has recently announced a slew of initiatives to "raise the quality of life of the dying, ease their pain, and preserve their dignity and support their care" (Lim 2008). Plans are afoot to train more doctors and nurses in palliative medicine, creating a national pool of palliative health-care professionals. Palliative care may even be recognized as a medical subspecialty. The MOH has also announced plans to add 25 hospice places to the 125 currently available at the 4 existing hospices run by voluntary groups, in the first instance.

The government has also recognized that nursing homes are presently ill-equipped to care for the dying. They frequently send their patients back to the hospital the moment their conditions deteriorate. A pilot project studying how to better integrate acute care, long-term care, and palliative care is underway in six nursing homes, supported by a nearby acute-care public hospital with staff trained in palliative care.

A set of guidelines on advance care planning is also being developed for health-care professionals, so that they can help patients and their families make informed decisions about their treatment plans. A public education effort will be mounted to encourage people to think about end-of-life care long before such choices are imminent.

Laws on Family Care and Advanced Medical Directives

Perhaps the most controversial policy implemented so far is the imposition of a legal obligation on children to maintain their parents. So much for filial piety! With the passage of the Maintenance of Parents Act (1996), Singapore became the world's first country to require grown-up children to care for their aging parents.

A less controversial measure is the Advanced Medical Directives Act of 1996, aimed at reducing unnecessary suffering of both the terminally ill elderly and their families. The directive states that people medically certified as brain-dead can be relieved of medical life support, if they had so willed it when alive and in possession of their mental faculties. However, fewer than 10,000 people have signed such a directive since the Act came into effect in 1997.

Chronic Disease Management

Thus far, the most promising health-care reform undertaken in Singapore is the nationwide disease-management program started in 2006. A concerted effort to change the way medicine is practiced, the program is predicated on the growing expert consensus that a holistic approach to chronic diseases can achieve better health outcomes than episodic care, while cutting costs. For example, by having diabetes patients work closely with their doctors and nurses to maintain good control of their blood sugar, serious and costly complications (such as blindness, kidney failure, or foot amputation) can be avoided.

In 2006 the MOH kicked off the program with four chronic diseases: diabetes mellitus, hypertension, hyperlipidemia, and stroke, for which there are established disease-management protocols. The aim was to steer patients with chronic diseases toward a model of "seamless" care by encouraging hospitals to routinely discharge them to the care of general practitioners (GPs) enrolled in the program. The GPs track the patients' progress and take part in hospital-run continuing medical education programs to keep them updated on the latest developments in chronic-disease management. The MOH provides the clinical protocols and mounts educational campaigns with the message that GPs are just as good as and less expensive than hospital-based specialists. This includes assuring the public that the GPs enrolled in the program are actively upgrading their professional skills. But it will ultimately be up to the GPs to show that patients with chronic illnesses that require monitoring get better and more responsive services if seen by a regular family physician instead of a hospital-based specialist. To provide the right financial incentives for shifting the care of such stable, chronic conditions to primary care doctors, the Medisave purse strings were loosened in 2007 to allow patients with the four chronic conditions to use up to S$300 a year from Medisave to copay for their treatment. Following one year of implementation, some 70,500 patients had withdrawn a total of S$15 million to pay for their outpatient treatment. Not only did patients welcome the financial relief of being able to use Medisave money to cover the costs of the consultations, but they also reported traveling shorter distances to see their GPs (instead of hospital specialists) and having an improved relationship with their doctors. Encouraged by this initial success, the government in 2008 added two more conditions—asthma and chronic obstructive pulmonary disease (COPD)—to the program. In 2009, schizophrenia and major depression were also added to the list.

Gearing Up for the "Silver Tsunami"

At the time of writing, the government had announced another set of new measures that will cost $500 million over the next five years. These measures are intended to prepare Singapore's health-care system for a "silver tsunami"—a reference to the fact that the number of Singaporeans over 65 will triple between now and 2030, rising from 300,000 to 900,000. New community hospitals will be built to boost capabilities in treating chronic diseases such as stroke, heart and kidney failure, and other age-related conditions such as dementia, while enhancing the capabilities for long-term care, including rehabilitation, home care, and palliative services after patients have been discharged from hospitals. To cope with the surging demand, the MOH will add more than 2,000 nursing-home beds over the next five years. Work on 5 new nursing homes will start within 2 years, including a 300-bed home for patients with psychiatric problems to be ready by 2012. The MOH will also release from its land bank two plots designated for the building of private nursing homes. It will also help two existing homes run by voluntary welfare organizations to relocate to new and larger facilities.

Subsidies to intermediate and long-term care facilities (including community hospitals, nursing homes, and hospices) will be increased to meet growing patient needs. Also announced are a second heart center and a second cancer center, two new general hospitals, and a third medical university (the two existing medical schools produce 310 doctors a year, not enough to meet current demand). All told, despite the current economic recession (or perhaps because of it), the public sector will add 4,500 new health-care jobs over the next two years.

It also appears that the 3Ms will be complemented by 3Es, for it was also announced that a new scheme, *Eldersave*, will be developed to supplement *ElderShield* and *Elderfund*. No details are available at the time of writing, but the basic idea would be to encourage younger people who are employed to set aside more of their savings—for example, more than what Medisave already requires—to provide for their health-care needs when they are old. Thus, present health-care configurations are by no means fixed or final. If anything, Singapore's health-care system is a perpetual work in progress.

Conclusion

Even as the silver tsunami draws nearer, Singaporean health care is not yet in crisis mode—there is still time to adapt and gear up. Like many other countries, the government is busy putting into place the right health-care policies and appropriate financial and organizational structures to make such care affordable, while ensuring health care for all. Singapore appears to be better placed than most to surmount the coming challenges. Singapore has a strong government willing to make hard-nosed decisions, a pragmatic population conditioned to cost-sharing and turning to the state for help only as a last resort, and a health-care system with built-in incentives that promote demand-side responsibility and discourage supply-side waste. These are some of the reasons for believing that Singapore's health-care system, which is constantly evolving and adapting, will not only survive, but also thrive when the silver tsunami makes landfall.

References

Cheung, P. 1996. "Ageing Population." In *Geriatric Medicine for Singapore*, edited by K. M. Chan, K. B. Yap, and S. F. Wong. Singapore: Singapore Gerontological Society, Amour Publishing.

Department of Statistics (Singapore). 2001. *Census of Population 2000: Advance Data Release.*

Lim, M. K. 1998. "Health Care Systems in Transition II. Singapore, Part I. An Overview of the Health Care System in Singapore." *Journal of Public Health* 20: 16–22.

———. 2004. "Shifting the Burden of Health Care Finance: A Case Study of Public-private Partnership in Singapore." *Health Policy* 69 (1): 83–92.

———. 2008. "Expanded State Role in the Care of the Dying." *Health Policy Monitor*, October. http://hpm.org/survey/sg/a12/3.

MOH (Ministry of Health). 2009a. *Health Facts Singapore.* www.moh.gov.sg/mohcorp/statistics.aspx?id=5524.

———. 2009b. *Healthcare Financing.* www.moh.gov.sg/mohcorp/hcfinancing.aspx?id=104.

OECD (Organisation for Economic Co-operation of Development). 2007. *OECD Health Data 2007.* www.oecd.org/dataoecd/53/10/38976580.pdf.

Phua, K. H. 1991. "Privatization and Restructuring of Health Services in Singapore." Institute of Policy Studies, Occasional Paper no. 5, Time Academic Press, Singapore.

WHO (World Health Organization). 2000. *The World Health Report 2000. Health Systems: Improving Performance.* Geneva.

World Bank. *List of GDP (PPP) per capita by country, 2007.* http://en.wikipedia.org/wiki/List_of_countries_by_GDP_%28PPP%29_per_capita.

INDEX

A

affirmative action, Singapore, 183
aging ("graying") of population
 behavioral and policy responses, 21–22
 China, 24–25, 25f, 38–39, 63
 costs and benefits, 5, 9–12, 27–31, 41, 141
 factors leading to, 4, 12, 25–26, 26f, 35, 40
 Hong Kong, 158–59
 India, 24–25, 25f
 Japan, 13, 24–25, 25f, 97–98, 102–3, 102f
 negative assumptions, 21
 regional variations, 24, 24f
 sex ratios and, 6–7
 Singapore, 177, 178f, 187–88
 sociobehavioral responses to, 37
 South Korea, 109, 123, 123f
 as uneven process, 4, 7–8, 28, 37
 worldwide trends, xi, 21–22, 22f
Alzheimer's Association, 161–62, 165–66
Alzheimer's disease, definition, 159. *See also* dementias
Anhui Province, China, migration from, 13–14, 63–64
Austria, elders in labor force, 49

B

baby booms, 8, 97
 United States, 8, 25
 Japan, 43, 44, 49, 50, 97
 Singapore, 179
Basic Elderly Pension Act, 2007, South Korea, 128
benefits, South Korean pension system, 122n1, 124–25, 124n1
birth rates, xi, 8, 43–44, 44f. *See also* demographic trends, overview

C

cai li (bride price), 82
"Care for Girls" campaign, China, 73

centenarians, 45
Central Social Insurance Council, Japan, 104
Chaohu, Anhui Province, China, migration from, 64
children. *See* family caregiving responsibilities
China. *See also* dementias; health-care system
 aging of population
  causes, xi–xii, 63
  impact on kinship networks, 40
  impact on labor force, 36–37, 37f
  inequalities associated with, 38–39
  trends, 12, 24–25, 25f, 36–39, 37f
 birth waves, socioeconomic impacts, 8
 dependency ratios, 4–5, 5f, 7f
 diabetes mellitus in
  costs of treatment, 141–42
  prevalence, 15–16, 140–41, 140t
  typical treatment path, 148–49
 economic inequalities, 38–39
 the elderly
  care for by family members, 64–68, 66f, 77–79, 91t, 157
  care for grandchildren, 67
  coresidence with children, 65
  factors impacting well-being of, 157–58
  gender-based labor divisions and, 68–70, 69t, 70f
  impacts of gender and migration on, 13–14
  income sources, 65–66
  marriage and remarriage rates, 85–89, 86t, 88t, 90t, 92
  rural, care/support options, 13–14
  urban *vs.* rural populations, 83–85, 84t, 85t
 elderly with dementia in
  cultural attitudes and, 160
  economic costs, 165–66
  home-based caregiving approaches, 164

191

ABOUT THE CONTRIBUTORS

Syed Aljunid is a professor of health economics and senior research fellow at the United Nations University–International Institute for Global Health. Previously he served as a consultant in public health medicine and head of the Department of Community Health, Faculty of Medicine, National University of Malaysia (UKM). He obtained his MD from the UKM, MS in public health from the National University of Singapore, and PhD in health economics and financing from the London School of Hygiene and Tropical Medicine. He has been a fellow of the Academy of Medicine Malaysia since 2000.

Aljunid's main research interest is in the strengthening of health-care systems in developing countries through research and development in health economics and financing. He is currently involved in supporting developing countries to develop and implement case-mix systems, a health management and information tool to enhance the quality and efficiency of health-care services. He was appointed as consultant and adviser to the Ministry of Health of Indonesia on the implementation of a case-mix system for public and teaching hospitals from September 2005 to December 2009. From September 2006, he served as a consultant for the Asian Development Bank in the implementation of a case-mix system for improving the quality and efficiency of health-care services covered by the National Health Insurance Scheme in Mongolia. Currently, he consults with the Philippine Health Insurance Corporation on the development and implementation of a case-mix system. Since 2006, he has directed the International Training Centre on Case-mix and Clinical Coding at the UKM to build human resources capacity in case-mix systems, with special focus on low- and middle-income countries.

Aljunid is the founder and president of the Malaysian Health Economics Association (MY-HEA), president of the Public Health Medicine Specialist Association of Malaysia, and executive board member of the Asia Pacific International Society of Pharmoeconomics and Outcomes Research. He has served as consultant to a number of international agencies, such as the World Health Organization, UN-AIDS, UNDP, UNICEF, GAVI, the Asian Development Bank, and the World Bank, for various international projects.

Le Thi Kim Anh earned her MD from the University of Medicine and Pharmacy, Ho Chi Minh City, Vietnam, and her master's in public health from the University of Queensland, Australia. She is currently a lecturer in the Faculty of Basic Science at the Hanoi School of Public Health, Vietnam.

Chu Viet Anh graduated as a public health practitioner from the Hanoi School of Public Health and currently works there as an assistant lecturer in the Department of Informatics and as a member of the Faculty of Basic Science.

In his current role, as Shorenstein Distinguished Fellow, **Michael Armacost** has been at the Walter H. Shorenstein Asia-Pacific Research Center (Shorenstein APARC) since 2002. In the interval between 1995 and 2002, Armacost served as president of Washington DC's Brookings Institution, the nation's oldest think tank and a leader in research on politics, government, international affairs, economics, and public policy. Previously, during his twenty-four-year government career, Armacost served, among other positions, as undersecretary of state for political affairs and as ambassador to Japan and the Philippines.

Armacost began his career in academia, as a professor of government at Pomona College. In 1969, he was awarded a White House Fellowship, and was assigned to the Secretary and Deputy Secretary of State. Following a stint on the State Department policy planning and coordination staff, he became a special assistant to the U.S. ambassador in Tokyo from 1972 to 1974, his first foreign diplomatic post. Thereafter, he held senior Asian affairs and international security posts in the State Department, Defense Department, and the National Security Council. From 1982 to 1984, he served as U.S. Ambassador to the Philippines, and was a key force in helping the country undergo a nonviolent transition to democracy. In 1989, President George Bush tapped him to become ambassador to Japan, considered one of the most important and sensitive U.S. diplomatic posts abroad.

Armacost is the author of three books, the most recent of which, *Friends or Rivals?* was published in 1996 and draws on his tenure as ambassador. He also coedited, with Daniel I. Okimoto, *The Future of America's Alliances in Northeast Asia*, published in 2004 by Shorenstein APARC. Armacost has served on numerous corporate and nonprofit boards, including those of TRW; AFLAC; Applied Materials; USEC, Inc.; Cargill, Inc.; Carleton College; and The Asia Foundation.

Alma Au is an associate professor in the Department of Applied Social Sciences of the Hong Kong Polytechnic University. For the previous twenty years, she worked as a clinical psychologist with the Hospital Authority in Hong Kong and the National Health Service in the United Kingdom. Funded by a number of external grants, she has completed research on patients with chronic illness including HIV, epilepsy, and dementia. She has published in various international journals and has received several awards for contributing to continuous quality improvement in the hospitals in which she has worked. Her current research and consultancy interests include developing assessment and treatment protocols for patients with neurocognitive difficulties as well as caregiver support and domestic violence.

K. L. Bairy completed his undergraduate medical education at the Medical College in Bellary, India, and went on to earn his MD and PhD in pharmacology from Kasturba Medical College, Manipal, India. He is now professor and head of pharmacology and director of the Manipal Centre for Clinical Research, Manipal University. Bairy has published more than one hundred research articles in national and international journals. His areas of research interest are psychopharmacology, diabetes mellitus, and reproductive toxicology.

David E. Bloom is Clarence James Gamble Professor of Economics and Demography at Harvard University, chair of the Department of Global Health and Population at the Harvard School of Public Health, and faculty director of Harvard University's Program on the Global Demography of Aging. He is a research associate at the National Bureau of Economic Research and fellow of the American Academy of Arts and Sciences. Bloom received a BS in industrial and labor relations from Cornell University in 1976, an MA in economics from Princeton University in 1978, and a PhD in economics and demography from Princeton University in 1981. He has worked extensively in the areas of health, labor, development economics, and demography. Longstanding themes include a focus on "healthier makes wealthier" and the "demographic dividend."

Amonthep Chawla is a research fellow at the Thailand Development Research Institute and a visiting lecturer at Thammasat University. His research on macroeconomics and population economics has been published in numerous working papers and journals, such as the *Asian Population Studies*, *Asia-Pacific Population Journal*, and the *NBER*. His recent research on the labor market has been implemented by the Ministry of Labor of Thailand. Chawla is an expert on national transfer accounts and has been actively involved as an instructor in a number of training workshops held in Asia, Africa, and the United States. He holds a PhD from the University of Hawaii.

Young Kyung Do earned MD and MPH degrees from Seoul National University, Korea, and a PhD from the University of North Carolina at Chapel Hill. After his postdoctoral fellowship at Stanford University in 2008–2009, he began his current position as assistant professor at the Duke–National University of Singapore Graduate Medical School Singapore.

Karen Eggleston joined the Walter H. Shorenstein Asia-Pacific Research Center in the summer of 2007 to lead the Center's Asia Health Policy Program. She is also a fellow at the Stanford Center for Health Policy. She holds a BA in Asian studies from Dartmouth College, an MA in economics and another in Asian studies from the University of Hawaii, and a PhD in public policy from Harvard University (completed in 1999). Eggleston studied in China for two years and was a Fulbright scholar in South Korea. In 2004, she was a consultant to the World Bank on health service delivery in China. Eggleston has been a research associate at the China Academy of Health Policy at Peking University, Beijing, since 2003, and a research associate at Xi'an Jiaotong University, Xi'an, since 2008.

Marcus W. Feldman is professor of biology and director of the Morrison Institute for Population and Resource Studies at Stanford University. Feldman leads a research group that uses applied mathematics and computer modeling to simulate and analyze the process of evolution, including the evolution of learning and the interaction of biological and cultural evolution and the transmission of learned behaviors in contemporary groups. He is a fellow of the American Academy of Arts and Sciences and is author or coauthor of 440 refereed papers and books. He has collaborated with professors and students at Xi'an Jiaotong University for more than twenty years, and has been director of the Center for Complexity Studies at Xi'an Jiaotong University in Xi'an, China, since 2005.

Dolores Gallagher-Thompson received her doctorate in clinical psychology with a concentration in adult development and aging from the University of Southern California in 1979. Since that time, she has been a funded researcher in the areas of late-life depression, stress and family caregiving, and ethnicity and dementia caregiving. Currently she is professor of research in the department of psychiatry and behavioral sciences, Stanford University School of Medicine, and director of the Stanford Geriatric Education Center in the division of Internal Medicine. She also serves in several volunteer positions with the Alzheimer's Association in northern California and is currently developing online intervention programs for caregivers of older persons with significant memory loss. She has published numerous books and peer-reviewed journal articles in her areas of expertise.

Jeremy Goldhaber-Fiebert is an assistant professor of medicine at Stanford University's School of Medicine, a core faculty member at the Center for Health Policy/Primary Care and Outcomes Research, and a faculty affiliate of the Stanford Center on Longevity. His research focuses on complex policy decisions in health and medicine: how to improve population health given the reality of budgetary and other resource constraints. He is keenly interested in applying a model-based, decision-analytic framework to these problems as they relate to a range of infectious and noncommunicable diseases in both developed and developing countries. To do so, he constructs, calibrates, and validates computer-based models of diseases in populations that allow him to consider the health, economic, and distributional implications of alternative policies.

Goldhaber-Fiebert graduated magna cum laude from Harvard College in 1997, with an AB in the history and literature of America. After working as a software engineer and consultant, he conducted a year-long public health research program in Costa Rica with his wife in 2001. Winner of the Lee B. Lusted Prize for Outstanding Student Research from the Society for Medical Decision Making in 2006, he completed his PhD in health policy, concentrating in decision science, at Harvard University in 2008.

Sanita Hirunrassamee received her PhD in pharmacy administration from Chulalongkorn University in 2008. Her major areas of interest are health outcomes, especially in chronic diseases, and financial mechanisms in health insurance systems. She is currently an assistant director of the hospital financial center at Phramongkutklao Medical School in Thailand. Her work focuses on the analysis of drug utilization and the impacts of national health insurance policies.

Yifan Huang received her BA in psychology from Beijing Normal University (BNU) in 2008. She is currently studying for a master's degree in the School of Psychology at BNU. She is majoring in cognitive aging, and will graduate in July 2011.

Naoki Ikegami is professor and chair of the department of health policy and management at the Keio University School of Medicine, from which he received his MD and PhD. He also received an MA in health services studies with distinction from Leeds University (United Kingdom). From 1990 to 1991, he was a visiting professor at the University of Pennsylvania's Wharton School and Medical School. His publications include (with John C. Campbell) *The Art of Balance in Health Policy: Maintaining Japan's Low-Cost Egalitarian System* (Cambridge University Press 1998) and (with John Hirdes and Iain Carpenter) "Measuring the Quality of Long-term care in Institutional and Community Settings" in *Measuring Up—Improving Health Care Performance in OECD Countries* (OECD 2002). His research interests include comparative health policy, long-term care, and reimbursement systems.

Xiaoyi Jin has been a professor in the Institute for Population and Development Studies at Xi'an Jiaotong University since 2007. She received her PhD from Xi'an Jiaotong University in 2003, and was a postdoctoral researcher at Stanford University in 2005–2006. Her research interests include marriage forms, the preference for sons, intergenerational relations, and gender imbalance and its social implications in China. Since 2004, she has been the main participant in two joint projects. The first deals with cultural transmission and diffusion during the process of rural-urban migration in China and is supported by the International Program of Santa Fe Institute and Advisory Committee of Stanford's Center for Demography and Economics of Health and Aging. The second project is titled "Female Deficit and Social Stability in China: Implications for International Security" and is supported by Stanford's Presidential Fund for Innovation in International Studies. Jin also serves as principal investigator of two National Social Science Funds of China. She has received awards from the State Education Committee of China, one as part of the Program for New Century Excellent Talents at the University Level and the other from the Scientific Research Foundation for Returned Overseas Chinese Scholars. Jin has published 45 papers (27 in Chinese and 18 in English) and 3 books in Chinese.

Soonman Kwon is professor and former chair of the department of health policy and management at the School of Public Health, Seoul National University, South Korea. He is the director of the Brain Korea Center for Aging and Health Policy, a center of excellence funded by the Ministry of Education and Human Resources. After he received his PhD from the Wharton School of the University of Pennsylvania, he was assistant professor of public policy at the University of Southern California from 1993 to 1996. Kwon has held visiting positions at the

Harvard School of Public Health (Takemi Fellow and Fulbright Scholar), London School of Economics and Political Science (Chevening Scholar), University of Trier in Germany (DAAD scholar), and Hosei University in Japan. In the spring semester of 2006, he was a visiting professor of political science at the University of Toronto and taught comparative health policy.

Kwon's major areas of interest are in health economics and financing, comparative health policy and welfare states, aging and long-term care, the political economy of health-care reform, and health systems in low-income countries. He serves on the editorial boards of leading international journals such as *Social Science and Medicine, Health Economics Policy and Law, Health Systems in Transition,* and *Health Sociology Review.*

Kwon has served on numerous health policy committees of the government of South Korea, and has occasionally worked as a short-term consultant to the World Health Organization, the World Bank, and the German Technical Cooperation on health financing and policy in China, Cambodia, Laos, Malaysia, Mongolia, Pakistan, the Philippines, Uganda, and Vietnam. He has also consulted with the South Korean government in evaluating its development aid programs in North Korea, Ecuador, Fiji, Mexico, and Peru.

Hong Li earned her MD and MS degrees from the Medical School of Zhejiang University, China. She is currently professor and director of the Endocrinology Department and Diabetes Center of Sir Run Run Shaw Hospital, in the Medical School of Zhejiang University, China.

Shuzhuo Li received his PhD in 1991 from Xi'an Jiaotong University, China. He is currently Changjiang Professor of Population Studies, director of the Institute for Population and Development Studies, School of Public Policy and Administration, Xi'an Jiaotong University, and consulting professor at the Morrison Institute for Population and Resource Studies, Stanford University. He is a leading consultant for the National Office of Care for Girls Campaign China; a member of the Advisory Committee for the National Population and Family Planning Commission of China; a member of the Social Sciences Committee of Ministry of Education of China; and a consultant to Shaanxi Provincial Government, China.

As a principal and a coprincipal investigator, he has received grants from Chinese government agencies and foundations, UN organizations (including UNFPA, UNICEF, UNIFEM and FAO), as well as the NIH, NIA, Ford Foundation, MacArthur Foundation, and Plan International (China). His research areas include population and social policies in transitional China, transmission and diffusion of childbearing culture, aging and old-age support, rural-urban migrants and social networks, gender and reproductive health, girl-child survival and intervention strategy and policy, gender imbalance and social development, children's birth registration, farmer's livelihood strategies, and environmental change.

Meng-Kin Lim is associate professor of health policy and management at the Yong Loo Lin School of Medicine, National University of Singapore (NUS) and also concurrently academic director of the Master of Business Administration (Healthcare Management) Program at the NUS Business School, and public health director of the Association of Pacific Rim Universities World Institute (APRU).

Lim obtained his medical degree (with distinction in social medicine and public health) from the University of Singapore in 1974. He also holds a diploma in aviation medicine, an MSc in occupational medicine, and an MPH in health policy and management.

He is an elected fellow of the Royal College of Physicians of Edinburgh, the Faculty of Occupational Medicine (United Kingdom), the Aerospace Medical Association (United States), and the Academy of Medicine (Singapore). He is an elected academician of the International Academy of Aviation and Space Medicine, and an elected member of the New York Academy of Sciences and the American College of Physician Executives. Previous appointments include chief of the Singapore Armed Forces Medical Corps (1986–1995), founding director of the Defence Medical Research Institute (1994–1997), and chief executive officer of the Health Corporation of Singapore (1997–1999).

Lim has published over eighty scientific articles in international, peer-reviewed journals, including the *New England Journal of Medicine*, *Health Affairs*, *Health Policy*, *Medical Care*, *Quality and Safety in Health Care*, the *Journal of Health Policy, Politics and Law*, *British Medical Journal*, and the *British Journal of Public Health Medicine*. He consults extensively for the World Bank, the World Health Organization, and the Asian Development Bank, as well as the ministries of health of Singapore, China, Vietnam, Thailand, Indonesia, Malaysia, Brunei, Hong Kong, Iran, Lebanon, Egypt, the West Bank and Gaza, Kuwait, and Bulgaria.

Qingqing Lou is a diabetes nurse specialist (RN, BSN, AAPN) at Sir Run Run Shaw Hospital in the Medical School of Zhejiang University in Hangzhou, China.

Rikiya Matsukura is a staff researcher at the Nihon University Population Research Institute. He is currently serving as a UN-appointed consultant for the five-year development plan put forward by the Laotian government. Since 2002 he has worked as a guest researcher and lecturer at the Statistical Research and Training Institute of the Ministry of Internal Affairs and Communications, Japan. He also spent a year (2005–2006) as a collaborative researcher at the Japanese Government's Institute of Statistical Mathematics. He has more than twenty years of experience in statistical research and his research interests include the development of statistical methods for complicated models and the application of these methodologies to social science.

Matsukura has published articles in journals such as *Population and Development Review*, *The Japanese Economy*, *Asian Population Studies*, *Demography*, and *Asia-Pacific Population Journal*.

Amrizal M. Nur is a health economics and senior medical lecturer in the Faculty of Medicine, National University of Malaysia (UKM), Kuala Lumpur. Previously he served as a consultant in case-mix systems and health economics at the United Nations University–International Institute for Global Health.

Nur obtained his MD from Universitas Andalas Padang (Indonesia), MS in public health from UKM, and PhD in health economics and case-mix systems, Faculty of Medicine, UKM. His main interest is in supporting the health-care systems of developing countries through research and development in health economics and the case-mix system. He is currently working in a number of developing countries to develop and implement the case-mix system, a health management and information tool to enhance the quality and efficiency of health-care services. He was appointed consultant and adviser to the Ministry of Health–Indonesia in the implementation of a case-mix system for the health financing program in public and teaching hospitals in the country from September 2005 to December 2009. From December 2009, he was appointed as a consultant in the implementation of case-mix systems by the Philippine Health Insurance Corporation in Philippine.

Currently, Nur is consulting with the Consortium Private Hospital Uruguay (FEMI)/Sanatorio Americano to develop the case-mix system in Uruguay. He coordinates the International Centre for Case-mix and Clinical Coding, established in 2006 at UKM to build human resources capacity in the case-mix system, with special focus on low- and middle-income countries. He is currently a member of the Malaysian Health Economics Association.

Naohiro Ogawa is professor of population economics at the Nihon University College of Economics and Advanced Research Institute for Sciences and Humanities, Tokyo. He also directs the Nihon University Population Research Institute. Over the past thirty years he has written extensively on population and development in Japan and other Asian countries. More specifically, his research has focused on issues such as the socioeconomic impacts of low fertility and rapid aging, modeling demographics and social-security-related variables, as well as policies related to fertility, employment, marriage, child care, retirement, and care for the elderly. His recent work includes measuring intergenerational transfers. He has published numerous academic papers in internationally recognized journals. In collaboration with other scholars he has also edited several journals and books, the most recent of which is *Population Aging, Intergenerational Transfers and the Macroeconomy* (Edward Elgar 2007).

Ogawa has served on numerous councils, committees, and advisory boards set up by the Japanese government, and on international organizations such as the Asian Population Association, the IUSSP, and the World Health Organization. He is currently an associate member of the Science Council of Japan.

Maria Porter is a postdoctoral research fellow in the University of Oxford's department of economics and Nuffield College, and a James Martin Research

Fellow at the Oxford Institute of Ageing. She received her PhD in economics from the University of Chicago in 2007. She is currently studying aging-related issues in China.

Sauwakon Ratanawijitrasin is associate professor on the Faculty of Social Sciences and Humanities, Mahidol University. She was a Fulbright scholar (1988–1993) and a Takemi Fellow in International Health at the Harvard School of Public Health (1995–1996). She received a BS in pharmacy, an MA in public administration, and a PhD in public administration (Rockefeller College of Public Affairs and Policy, SUNY). Her dissertation won the best dissertation award from the U.S. National Association of Schools of Public Affairs and Administration in 1993.

Ratanawijitrasin's teaching and research are in the areas of pharmaceutical and health systems, policy and management, health insurance and financing, drug utilization, and systems thinking. In addition to academic responsibilities, she also works on system development and management. She is secretary general of the Pharmaceutical System Research & Development Foundation, and vice president of the Pharmaceutical Association of Thailand. Previously, she served as deputy executive director of the Association of South-East Asian Nations (ASEAN) University Network, and associate dean of the College of Public Health at Chulalongkorn University. She has also served as adviser to the Thai Parliamentary Special Commission on National Health Insurance Bill and the World Health Organization, among other organizations.

Nilay D. Shah is associate professor of health services research at the Division of Health Care Policy and Research at the Mayo Clinic College of Medicine in Rochester, Minnesota. Shah's research is focused on studying and improving the health-care delivery system. Shah has an ongoing research agenda for evaluating alternative models of chronic disease care delivery, medication adherence in chronic disease, policy implications of shared decision-making, and disparities in care. Other areas of ongoing research include optimizing treatment decisions in diabetes, the decision analytic modeling of diagnostic strategies across a spectrum of diseases, and evaluating the evidence base for quality measurement. He also has extensive experience working with large databases such as the Medical Expenditure Panel Survey, National Ambulatory Medical Care Survey, and various payer- and provider-based administrative data. Shah also has extensive experience with and continues to work on various topics related to pharmaceutical policy. He earned a BS in pharmacy and MS in hospital pharmacy administration from the University of Wisconsin School of Pharmacy, and a PhD in population health sciences from the University of Wisconsin, Madison.

Saperi bin Sulong is an associate professor in health management and health economics on the Faculty of Medicine, National University of Malaysia (UKM).

He also heads the Health Information Department and the UKM Medical Centre and serves as deputy head of its International Centre for Case-mix and Clinical Coding.

Sulong obtained his MD from the UKM in 1986 and PhD in public health (health management and economics) from the same university in 2007. He started his housemanship at Hospital Sultanah Aminah, Johor Bahru, and later worked as a medical officer at Muar Hospital in various clinical disciplines. He worked as a general practitioner from 1991 to 1998 before serving as a research fellow for a study titled "Comparison of the Cost-Effectiveness of Treating Injury Patients between Tertiary and Secondary Hospitals in Malaysia," a joint collaborative project of the Department of Community Health, UKM; the Ministry of Health, Malaysia; and the London School of Hygiene and Tropical Medicine, University of London. He obtained his PhD through the same study and later joined the Department of Community Health as a lecturer and also as a deputy head of the case-mix unit at the UKM Hospital. He is also a consultant to the National Productivity Corporation (NPC) Malaysia and APHM for a hospital benchmarking project on the performance of private hospitals in Malaysia for the health tourism industry.

Sulong's main research interest is strengthening the health-care systems of developing countries through research and development in health-care management and financing. He has consulted on the case-mix system for the Ministry of Health, Indonesia; the Ministry of Health, Mongolia; the Philippines Health Insurance Corporation, Philippines; and the Santorio Americano Insurance Corporation, Uruguay.

Sulong has published and coauthored several articles in journals and presented at conferences on subjects related to health economics and public health.

Byongho Tchoe is head of the Health Care Research Center of South Korea's Health Insurance Review and Assessment, as well as a senior research fellow at the Korea Institute for Health and Social Affairs and a 2008–2009 visiting scholar at Stanford University. As president of the Korean Association of Health Economics and Policy and vice president of the Korean Association of Social Security, he has helped to formulate health and social policy in South Korea for twenty-five years. Tchoe holds an MA in public policy from Seoul National University and a PhD in economics from the University of Georgia.

Teresa B. K. Tsien was educated in the United States with a master's in public health (gerontology) and a master's in social work (social development). She is currently the codirector of the Institute of Active Ageing and senior clinical associate and program director of the Department of Applied Social Sciences at the Hong Kong Polytechnic University. She is also a part-time lecturer in clinical gerontology at the Chinese University of Hong Kong. Tsien specializes in aging studies and research, especially in dementia care and caregiver support. She is a member of the Social Welfare Advisory Committee, the Guardianship Board, and the Community Chest. She has been elected as a member of the election committee for the chief executive of Hong Kong, representing the social welfare sector, and is a board member of the Hong Kong Council of Social Service. She also serves as an adviser and a consultant to five nongovernmental agencies serving the elderly. Her latest publications on aging include the papers "Dementia Care and Services" and "Older Adults as Caregivers in Hong Kong."

Shripad Tuljapurkar (Tulja) is professor of biology and the Dean and Virginia Morrison Professor of Population Studies at Stanford University. Tulja directs demographic programs at Stanford's Center for the Demography, Economics, and Health of Aging, and the Stanford Center for Population Research in the Institute for Research in the Social Sciences. At Stanford, Tulja is an affiliated faculty member with the Morrison Institute for Population and Resource Studies, the Woods Institute for the Environment, and the Interdisciplinary Program on Environment and Resources. Tulja and Jamie Jones (department of anthropology, Stanford) organize and run the Stanford Workshops in Formal Demography and the Stanford Workshops in Biodemography. At the University of California, Berkeley, Tulja is a member of the Center for the Demography and Economics of Aging. Research in the Tuljapurkar lab at Stanford uses theory and data to ask and answer questions about populations, ranging from human demographic change and contemporary societies to prehistory and the biodemography of lifespans.

Marian Tzuang received her BSW from National Taiwan University and MSW from the University of California–Berkeley, with a concentration in gerontology. She is presently the program coordinator at the Stanford Geriatric Education Center (GEC) and also the project coordinator for a research program to develop a fotonovela for Hispanic/Latino family caregivers (funded by the Alzheimer's Association). Further, she is the editorial coordinator for the journals *Clinical Geronotologist* and the *Journal of Mental Health and Aging*. Prior to joining Stanford GEC, she worked as a legislative assistant in Taiwan, and has completed internships at On Lok Lifeways, Family Caregiver Alliance, and San Mateo County Adult Protective Services in the San Francisco Bay Area.

Sudha Vidyasagar completed her undergraduate education at Stanley Medical College in Chennai and went on to earn her MD in internal medicine from Kasturba Medical College, Manipal, India. She is now professor and head of the Department of Medicine at Kasturba Medical College, Manipal. She has been actively involved in maintaining a diabetes registry at Kasturba Hospital in Manipal, which is a tertiary-care teaching hospital with 1,500 beds. She is interested in patient education programs for diabetics, and has published a book for patients titled *Living with Diabetes*, which features detailed dietary advice for Indian diabetics. Her research includes metabolic syndrome and prevention of noncommunicable diseases.

Dahua Wang received her PhD in developmental psychology from Beijing Normal University (BNU) in 2003. She is currently an associate professor at BNU. Her research focuses on cognitive aging as well as the mental health of the elderly. Specifically, she is interested in understanding aging and mental health through the lens of Chinese cultural norms.

Jian Wang is a professor of health economics and a director of health-care management at the Center for Health Management and Policy, Shandong University. He holds an MPH in social medicine from Shandong University, an MA in health economics from the University of the Philippines, and a PhD in economics from the University of Newcastle, Australia. He has research expertise in health financing and the economic evaluation of chronic disease in China. Wang was a key local expert on the Technical Assistance for EU-China Social Security Reform Co-operation Project–Component 2: Social Security Systems/Administration Development. He has consulted for the World Bank, the European Union, DFID, and UNICEF in China and Myanmar. In addition, Wang is a board member of the Public Policy China Healthy 2020 Committee. He has published papers in *Diabetic Medicine*, the *Cochrane Database of Systematic Reviews*, *Health Policy Plan*, the *Journal of Asian Economics*, and the *International Journal of Healthcare Finance and Economics*. He was a semifinalist in the Global Development Awards and Medals Competition 2009 for the Japanese award for Outstanding Research on Development. He has been granted projects from the Ministry of Science and Technology, Ministry of Education, Ministry of Health, and National Population and Family Planning Commission of China, and the World Bank. Recently, he has been working with associate professor Knut Reidar Wangen on a project titled "To What Extent Do User Fees Affect Hepatitis B Vaccine Coverage Rates in China?" and funded by the Research Council of Norway.

Peng Chih Wang is an assistant professor in the Department of Clinical Psychology at Fu Jen Catholic University, Taipei, Taiwan. He received his PhD in clinical psychology from the Pacific Graduate School of Psychology in Palo Alto, California, and completed two years of postdoctoral fellow training at the Stanford University School of Medicine. His primary research interests include dementia caregiver stress management, caregiver sleep disturbance, chronic illness management, and suicide among older adults.

Xiaoyong Wang, MD, is a senior researcher and clinician at the Provincial Hospital affiliated with Shandong University in Jinan, Shandong Province, China, and does research related to the delivery of care to patients with diabetes.

Qiong Zhang is a candidate for a PhD in quantitative economics at the School of Economics and Management of Tsinghua University. Between 2009 and 2010, she was a visiting researcher at the Walter H. Shorenstein Asia-Pacific Research Center in the Freeman Spogli Institute for International Studies at Stanford University. Zhang earned her BA in finance from Peking University in 2005. Her research focuses on health reform in China, demographic transition, and economic growth and transition.

Dongmei Zuo is a PhD candidate in the Management School of Xi'an Jiaotong University, China. She also works as a lecturer in the Institute for Population and Development Studies, School of Public Policy and Administration, Xi'an Jiaotong University, China. She is principal investigator of the research project "Dynamic Age Patterns of Intergenerational Exchanges among Older Persons in Rural China: Life Course Perspective," which is funded by the National Natural Science Foundation of China. In addition, she serves as a research assistant for a joint project (with the University of Southern California) titled "Longitudinal Study of Older in Anhui Province, China (LSOPAP)," which is supported by the National Institutes of Health, United States. Her research interests include social gerontology, intergenerational relationship, life courses, and social public policy.

RECENT PUBLICATIONS OF THE WALTER H. SHORENSTEIN ASIA-PACIFIC RESEARCH CENTER

Books (distributed by the Brookings Institution Press)

Rafiq Dossani, Daniel C. Sneider, and Vikram Sood. *Does South Asia Exist? Prospects for Regional Integration.* Stanford, CA: Walter H. Shorenstein Asia-Pacific Research Center, 2010.

Jean C. Oi, Scott Rozelle, and Xueguang Zhou. *Growing Pains: Tensions and Opportunity in China's Transition.* Stanford, CA: Walter H. Shorenstein Asia-Pacific Research Center, 2010.

Karen Eggleston, ed. *Prescribing Cultures and Pharmaceutical Policy in the Asia-Pacific.* Stanford, CA: Walter H. Shorenstein Asia-Pacific Research Center, 2009.

Donald A. L. Macintyre, Daniel C. Sneider, and Gi-Wook Shin, eds. *First Drafts of Korea: The U.S. Media and Perceptions of the Last Cold War Frontier.* Stanford, CA: Walter H. Shorenstein Asia-Pacific Research Center, 2009.

Steven Reed, Kenneth Mori McElwain, and Kay Shimizu, eds. *Political Change in Japan: Electoral Behavior, Party Realignment, and the Koizumi Reforms.* Stanford, CA: Walter H. Shorenstein Asia-Pacific Research Center, 2009.

Donald K. Emmerson. *Hard Choices: Security, Democracy, and Regionalism in Southeast Asia.* Stanford, CA: Walter H. Shorenstein Asia-Pacific Research Center, 2008.

Henry S. Rowen, Marguerite Gong Hancock, and William F. Miller, eds. *Greater China's Quest for Innovation.* Stanford, CA: Walter H. Shorenstein Asia-Pacific Research Center, 2008.

Gi-Wook Shin and Daniel C. Sneider, eds. *Cross Currents: Regionalism and Nationalism in Northeast Asia.* Stanford, CA: Walter H. Shorenstein Asia-Pacific Research Center, 2007.

Stella R. Quah, ed. *Crisis Preparedness: Asia and the Global Governance of Epidemics.* Stanford, CA: Walter H. Shorenstein Asia-Pacific Research Center, 2007.

Philip W. Yun and Gi-Wook Shin, eds. *North Korea: 2005 and Beyond*. Stanford, CA: Walter H. Shorenstein Asia-Pacific Research Center, 2006.

Jongryn Mo and Daniel I. Okimoto, eds. *From Crisis to Opportunity: Financial Globalization and East Asian Capitalism*. Stanford, CA: Walter H. Shorenstein Asia-Pacific Research Center, 2006.

Michael H. Armacost and Daniel I. Okimoto, eds. *The Future of America's Alliances in Northeast Asia*. Stanford, CA: Walter H. Shorenstein Asia-Pacific Research Center, 2004.

Henry S. Rowen and Sangmok Suh, eds. *To the Brink of Peace: New Challenges in Inter-Korean Economic Cooperation and Integration*. Stanford, CA: Walter H. Shorenstein Asia-Pacific Research Center, 2001.

Studies of the Walter H. Shorenstein Asia-Pacific Research Center
(published with Stanford University Press)

Yongshun Cai. *Collective Resistance in China: Why Popular Protests Succeed or Fail*. Stanford, CA: Stanford University Press, 2010.

Gi-Wook Shin. *One Alliance, Two Lenses: U.S.-Korea Relations in a New Era*. Stanford, CA: Stanford University Press, 2010.

Jean Oi and Nara Dillon, eds. *At the Crossroads of Empires: Middlemen, Social Networks, and State-building in Republican Shanghai*. Stanford, CA: Stanford University Press, 2007.

Henry S. Rowen, Marguerite Gong Hancock, and William F. Miller, eds. *Making IT: The Rise of Asia in High Tech*. Stanford, CA: Stanford University Press, 2006.

Gi-Wook Shin. *Ethnic Nationalism in Korea: Genealogy, Politics, and Legacy*. Stanford, CA: Stanford University Press, 2006.

Andrew Walder, Joseph Esherick, and Paul Pickowicz, eds. *The Chinese Cultural Revolution as History*. Stanford, CA: Stanford University Press, 2006.

Rafiq Dossani and Henry S. Rowen, eds. *Prospects for Peace in South Asia*. Stanford, CA: Stanford University Press, 2005.